HAYDN STUDIES

The advances in Haydn scholarship made in the past forty years or so, and in particular in very recent times, would have been unthinkable to earlier generations, who honoured the composer more in word than in deed. *Haydn Studies* deals with many new aspects of a composer who is perennially fresh, concentrating principally on matters of reception, style and aesthetics and presenting many striking new readings of the composer's work. Haydn has never played a major role in accounts of cultural history and has never achieved the emblematic status accorded to composers such as Beethoven, Debussy and Stravinsky, in spite of his radical creative agenda: this volume attempts therefore to broaden the base of our understanding of the composer.

W. DEAN SUTCLIFFE is a Fellow of St Catharine's College, Cambridge. He is author of *Haydn: String Quartets, Op. 50* in the series Cambridge Music Handbooks.

Haydn Studies

EDITED BY W. DEAN SUTCLIFFE

CAMBRIDGE
UNIVERSITY PRESS

PUBLISHED BY THE PRESS SYNDICATE OF THE UNIVERSITY OF CAMBRIDGE
The Pitt Building, Trumpington Street, Cambridge CB2 1RP, United Kingdom

CAMBRIDGE UNIVERSITY PRESS
The Edinburgh Building, Cambridge CB2 2RU, United Kingdom http://www.cup.com.ac.uk
40 West 20th Street, New York, NY 10011–4211, USA http://www.cup.org
10 Stamford Road, Oakleigh, Melbourne 3166, Australia

First published 1998

Printed in the United Kingdom at the University Press, Cambridge

Typeset in Adobe Minion 10.25/14 pt, in QuarkXPress™ [SE]

A catalogue record for this book is available from the British Library

Library of Congress cataloguing in publication data

Haydn studies / edited by W. Dean Sutcliffe.
    p.   cm.
Includes index.
ISBN 0 521 58052 8 (hardback)
1. Haydn, Joseph, 1732–1809 – Criticism and interpretation.
I. Sutcliffe, W. Dean.
ML410.H4H44   1998
780'.92–dc21   97–41722 CIP MN

ISBN 0 521 58052 8 hardback

Contents

Preface

The advances in Haydn scholarship that have been made in the past forty years or so would have been unthinkable to earlier generations, who honoured the composer rather more in word than in deed. The composer has once more become what he became in his lifetime, a big player on the musical stage – especially in the last ten to twenty years – and the industry surrounding his works shows no signs of a slump. Because of the late start suffered by Haydn in musicological terms, a sense of evangelizing zeal still surrounds much of the scholarly and performing activity on his behalf, informed by a confidence that the composer is 'on the up'. However, for all the advances made in our knowledge of Haydn, the balance of this progress has been rather uneven. Not surprisingly, most attention has been devoted to all the musicological problems surrounding such a vast and widely dispersed creative output – matters of authenticity, chronology, documentation, performance practice, and the establishment of reliable and scholarly editions. On the other hand, in hermeneutic terms, the Haydn industry is still young, perhaps in obedience to the old unwritten law of musical research that demanded a full tally of 'facts' before proper aesthetic interpretation could begin. This may be somewhat unfair, since work that answers this need has begun to appear in more than isolation, but there is no doubt that the general thrust of Haydn research has been highly positivistic. When some of this work has crossed the line into aesthetics, the results have often been disappointing, strikingly below the level of thought evident elsewhere. The result is that our perception of Haydn as a creative figure is quite undeveloped compared with the historical and aesthetic resonance that has accrued to all other comparably great composers. Certainly no major composer can have inspired less fanciful prose.

Accordingly, the chapters that make up this volume deal principally with matters of reception, style and aesthetics. Every contribution represents a quite fresh approach to an existing area of research or opens up new territory – in the very spirit of the composer himself. The first chapter treats a topic that has but rarely been touched on, and yet the image of Haydn today still has much to do with that created for him by the nineteenth century. Certainly compared with the extensive literature on the reception of Mozart and Beethoven during the Romantic era, Haydn has been scantily dealt with, this in itself proof of how tenacious the nineteenth century's imagery and priorities have been. It is just this imagery, as articulated by Leon Botstein, that has dictated the lack of fanciful prose. For all the comparatively bullish state of the Haydn industry – the marked increase in high-level scholarly thought about the composer and the growing exposure of many of his works in performance and recording – there is no doubt that the composer is a long way from being embraced by the wider musical public at the level which is his due. For this wider musical public the image of Haydn continues to be somewhat mundane and flat. There is another unwritten law, one more particular to Haydn, that seems to stipulate that one doesn't claim too much for the composer. Haydn is too rarely understood as the revolutionary he was; many 'insiders' know him to be an incomparably original composer and thinker about (or in) music, but this is far from being the public perception. This state of affairs, whose roots lie again in the ideology of nineteenth-century musical thought, was articulated not so long ago by Geoffrey Wheatcroft, when he described Haydn, without too much licence, as the composer 'who[m] concert promoters have always regarded as box office death, even if true musicians have a passion for him almost beyond any other composer'.[1]

Personal experience bears out the force of Wheatcroft's remarks. Among these 'true musicians', a large proportion of the Haydn devotees I have encountered have been composers. The mere mention of the composer's name has often been enough to prompt the most enthusiastic of testimonials. And yet, consistent with the previous unwritten law, this Haydn worship has always had an underground character – something passed on by word of mouth rather than practised in public. This testifies to some lingering nineteenth-century associations. Haydn must seem too slight a figure to place at the pinnacle of musical art; the traditional imagery would not allow him to be profound enough in thought or comprehensive enough

---

[1] Geoffrey Wheatcroft, 'Profile (Schiff's Unfashionable Talent)', *Daily Telegraph*, 7 September 1988, p. 14.

in range to occupy such a position. And so he remains something of a secret addiction.

Those who have declared their allegiance in one form or other have been of the most diverse creative proclivities, going well beyond those who might be thought to share common artistic concerns. Take the seemingly surprising example of John Williams, the maestro of film composers; for Williams, Haydn 'occupies pride of place' in his 'pantheon' of composing gods.[2] Two composers have been enlisted here to express themselves publicly on the subject. In Chapter 9 George Edwards investigates a neglected field – Haydn's recapitulations – and evokes the sheer technical command and resource that fascinates so many composers in particular. Chapter 10, by Robin Holloway, explores the significance and stature of the composer in the broadest terms. As has already been outlined, Haydn has never played a major role in accounts of cultural history, has never achieved the emblematic status accorded to such composers as Beethoven, Debussy and Stravinsky, although his creative agenda can be said to have been finally just as radical. This chapter sets the seal on the attempt of this book to broaden the base of our understanding of the composer.

Another legacy of the nineteenth century (which must be starting to assume demonic proportions for the reader) has been the strong emphasis on instrumental music as the core of the Viennese Classical style. The sacred music of the Classical era has altogether received little consideration, swept aside by the 'rise' of the sonata, symphony and other 'abstract' instrumental forms; the fact that religious vocal works preoccupied Haydn extensively during the last part of his career sits uncomfortably with the tendency to give most weight to his instrumental music. In Chapter 2 James Webster reconsiders some of the sacred vocal music, with particular attention to rhetoric, and offers a new governing idea, that of 'salvation', in the attempt to give Haydn's work in the field a stronger aesthetic profile. Chapter 3 continues the treatment of neglected vocal genres. Although literature on Haydn operas has increased modestly of late, what has been largely missing thus far is any attempt to provide readings of individual operas as artistic wholes. Jessica Waldoff undertakes this for *La vera*

---

[2] Edward Seckerson, 'Interview (He knows the score)', *The Independent* (weekend supplement), 25 May 1996, p. 3.

costanza. Ultimately, it can only be by focusing on particular works that any progress can be made in putting Haydn's operatic achievement on a firm footing. In the attempt to achieve this by giving Haydn a part to play in the intellectual history of the eighteenth century, the chapter shares an emphasis with many other essays in this volume, one that has not been apparent in the treatment of Haydn until rather recently.

Chapter 4 also represents an attempt to ground Haydn firmly in the intellectual history of his time, not just as a passive representative but as an active agent in creating a new understanding of the art of music. The 'aesthetic optimism' with which Daniel Chua concludes his discussion might be reinforced by recollecting Haydn's celebrated letter to the music lovers of Bergen, on the occasion of their performance of *The Creation*: 'There are so few happy and contented peoples here below; grief and sorrow are always their lot; perhaps your labours will once be a source from which the careworn, or the man burdened with affairs, can derive a few moments' rest and refreshment'.[3] Chua's optimism, though, is rather different from that normally associated with the figure of Papa Haydn. Received critical opinion has in fact only allowed for one time of aesthetic pessimism in the composer's career: in Chapter 5 Mark Evan Bonds argues for a reassessment of this *Sturm und Drang* period, primarily on technical rather than intellectual grounds. From this treatment it might almost appear that the technical features of the *Sturm und Drang* were appropriated or invented precisely so that they could function as obstacles, placed by the composer in his way so as to force a rethinking of technical habits and thereby in effect entailing a 'cours complet de la composition'. But this technical self-consciousness, as Robin Holloway reminds us, is one of Haydn's defining characteristics. In the following chapter Michael Spitzer deals with the notion of *Sturm und Drang* from a different standpoint and then argues for the continuity of the composer's approach between this and the 'lighter' *galant* style that followed. James Webster then reviews the symphonies written in these years of 'entertainment', in which Haydn was supposedly devoting his greatest artistic efforts to opera. If the *Sturm und Drang* label has given rise to many misunderstandings, so has the notion of a lighter style associated with the

---

[3] H. C. Robbins Landon, *Haydn: Chronicle and Works V: Haydn: The Late Years 1801–1809* (London: Thames and Hudson, 1977), p. 233.

later 1770s and beyond. The problematic image of 'entertainment' encapsulates our difficulties in dealing with some of the basic premises of Viennese Classicism, both in Haydn's and others' hands. No one can fail to notice the accessibility of the prevalent idiom, its sociability of tone, the amiability of much of its diction. While historically Mozart has been able to be rescued from any sense of superficiality that might be associated with such attributes, Haydn (as Leon Botstein explains) has not always been so fortunate. Our still largely Romantic sense of the role and function of music has tended to make the comic, amiable and social suspect in their own right, unless they are 'deepened' in some demonstrable way. We readily assume that profundity is to be equated with the overtly serious in tone or the melancholy; it is harder for us to accept that what may be modest or inviting or sociable is just as valid a tone of artistic voice as that which presents itself more earnestly.[4] Melancholia turns us inward to reflect on ourselves as individuals; comedy involves laughter which is generally shared, reminding us of our similarities with others and our position in a social community. Rather than being perceived as intrinsically inadequate, the language of comedy and amiability that Haydn did so much to imprint on his time should be heard for the novelty it was, historically speaking, and for the strength of its conviction.

The social implications of a comedic language and the immense power it can generate were recently brought home to me in the context of an undergraduate exam in Cambridge. As part of a first-year aural paper, the students had to listen to the finale of Haydn's Symphony No. 90 in C major, three times in all, and write an essay on what they heard. This is one of those movements where the composer offers the listener numerous false endings, the confusion augmented by the fact that the real final ending is less emphatic than an earlier false one, and the whole made infinitely more teasing by the repeat indicated for the second half of the movement. Anticipating the usual knowing titters from the assembled undergraduates, I found that what ensued was much more striking than that. The first few false endings, followed by fermatas, witnessed a rustling of pens on

---

[4] For an excellent discussion of these issues in depth see Wye J. Allanbrook, 'Mozart's Tunes and the Comedy of Closure', in James M. Morris, ed., *On Mozart* (Cambridge: Cambridge University Press, in association with the Woodrow Wilson Center Press, 1994), pp. 169–86.

papers, only for the listeners to find themselves conned, their musical instincts overturned. Each subsequent false ending saw a growing reluctance to begin the writing of the essay; when the movement finally did come to a close, it was followed by a long and delicious period of inactivity and silence. Clearly no student was going to make the first move and be embarrassed all over again. The atmosphere was electric with uncertainty. Eventually through the agony the comic premise could be glimpsed once more, as one could compare a personal response with that of one's neighbours and enjoy the shared confusion and surprise. If the students felt inadequate in the light of this performance, then so did I. What I thought had been grasped from a reading of the score fell well short of the artistic reality – an intensely imaginative dramatization of the listening experience. This was one of the most inspiring encounters I have had with Haydn. It is to be hoped that the arguments presented in this volume can do some justice to the power and importance of this great artist.

Editor's note

The piano sonatas and trios are referred to according to the numbering of the Universal Edition (edited by Christa Landon) and the Doblinger edition (edited by H. C. Robbins Landon) respectively.

As a volume entitled 'Haydn Studies' is already in existence (the Proceedings of the International Haydn Conference held in Washington, D.C., in 1975, edited by Jens Peter Larsen, Howard Serwer and James Webster, and published by Norton in 1981), it is suggested that any references to the current volume should take the form of 'Cambridge Haydn Studies'.

1 The consequences of presumed innocence: the nineteenth-century reception of Joseph Haydn[1]

LEON BOTSTEIN

1 The Haydn paradox: from engaged affection to distant respect

The mystery that plagues the contemporary conception and reception of Haydn and his music has a long and remarkably unbroken history. Perhaps Haydn experienced the misfortune (an ironic one when one considers the frequency of premature deaths among his great contemporaries or near contemporaries) of living too long. Years before his death in 1809 he was considered so old that the French and English had already presumed him dead in 1805.[2] Many wrote condolence letters and a Requiem Mass was planned in Paris. Haydn's music was both familiar and venerated. Raphael Georg Kiesewetter (1773–1850), writing in Vienna in 1846, reflected the perspective of the beginning of the nineteenth century in his *Geschichte der europaeisch-abendlaendischen oder unsrer heutigen Musik*. Haydn had 'elevated all of instrumental music to a never before anticipated level of perfection'. Haydn had a 'perfect knowledge of instrumental effects' and with Mozart (for whom Haydn was the 'example and ideal') created a 'new school which may be called the German or ... the "Viennese" school'. Theirs was the 'golden age' of music. Most significantly, Haydn's instrumental works represented the standard of what was 'true beauty' in music.[3]

Lurking beneath Kiesewetter's praise of Haydn (and his discreet expressions of doubt about the novelties of Haydn's successors, including

---

[1] This essay is an expanded and revised form of my essay entitled 'The Demise of Philosophical Listening', in Elaine Sisman, ed., *Haydn and his World* (Princeton: Princeton University Press, 1997), pp. 255–88. I am deeply indebted to the invaluable criticism and assistance of Elaine Sisman and Irene Zedlacher, and to the encouragement of Dean Sutcliffe and the writings of James Webster.

[2] Karl and Irene Geiringer, *Haydn: A Creative Life in Music* (Berkeley: University of California Press, 1982), pp. 182–3.

[3] 2nd edn (Leipzig: Breitkopf & Härtel, 1846), pp. 96, 98.

Beethoven), particularly in the notion of 'true beauty', was a not atypical late eighteenth-century engagement, on the part of connoisseurs of music, with the philosophical quest for a true, valid and therefore objective aesthetic experience and criterion of aesthetic apperception. The *locus classicus* of this concern is Immanuel Kant's *Critique of Judgement*, first published in 1790. Kant defined taste as the 'faculty for judging an object in reference to the imagination's *free conformity to law*'.[4] For Kant, the 'peculiar feature of a judgement of taste' was 'a subjective agreement of the imagination and understanding – without such an objective agreement as there is when the representation is referred to a definite concept of an object'. This notion of an 'agreement', or, as Paul Guyer has termed it, a 'harmony between imagination and understanding', had particular relevance for the perception and judgement of music in the eighteenth century. Kant expressed explicit caveats about music as an art form in terms of music's weaknesses *vis-à-vis* the 'culture' and 'expansion of the faculties' that 'concur in judgement'. Yet it is precisely instrumental music, absent from any claims to representation, narration and description, as in many Haydn quartets, trios, sonatas and symphonies, that provides the ideal case for the 'agreement' between imagination and judgement. Music becomes the perfect vehicle for the cultivation and display of taste. In turn, taste, that special merger of imagination and understanding, in the case of music lends 'rightful authority' to the person who possesses it over mere fashion and general opinion.

Kant argued that instrumental music can 'communicate universally', in part because of the necessity of music having a mathematical form. Music functions under rules that are essentially mathematical in their character, in view of the absence of aesthetical ideas in music that 'are concepts or determinate thoughts'. Music becomes an ideal example of aesthetic formalism. The mathematical character of music itself is not the cause of the enjoyment of music but is its 'indispensable condition', since it permits the unique 'animation of the mind' along with emotions and pleasures that harmonize understanding and imagination.[5]

---

4 Trans. J. H. Bernard (New York: Hafner, 1951), p. 77.
5 *Ibid.*, pp. 173–4. I am indebted to Paul Guyer's excellent discussion of these issues in his *Kant and the Claims of Taste* (Cambridge, Mass.: Harvard University Press, 1979), pp. 79–96.

As will become apparent later on, this elegant and clear construct of what it meant genuinely to respond to, appreciate and judge music was not unique to Kant. Rather, Kant's formulation brought an elaborate and extensive eighteenth-century philosophical tradition of speculation on the character and impact of music to its conclusion. That tradition ran parallel with an eighteenth-century aristocratic sensibility that connoisseurship of music was a genuine display of distinction. With the passing of Kiesewetter's (and also Beethoven's) generation during the first three decades of the nineteenth century – a generation comprised of individuals born around 1770 who came to maturity before the end of the century – this decidedly refined notion of musical connoisseurship and taste, which involved a high order of rational mental functioning as well as a powerful imagination and capacity for discernment, had become anachronistic.

This is evident not only in the writings of philosophers but among writers on music. Friedrich Rochlitz (1769–1842), who belonged to Kiesewetter's generation, in his 1824 book directed at the lay public, *Für Freunde der Tonkunst*, took special pains to praise Haydn as the most original and the richest composer, even when compared with Beethoven, precisely on the grounds of Haydn's command of the formal game of altering rhythmic patterns, accents and combinations in instrumental music. Citing the quartets, Rochlitz underscored Haydn's appeal precisely to the intellect, the understanding and therefore to the joys of the imagination triggered by the spontaneous recognition of the inventiveness and ingenuity contained in the structural and formal procedures of music.[6] With the decline in the prestige of the many varying forms of philosophical listening, the expectation that the pleasure of music involved some sort of objective harmonizing of rational thinking and the capacity for personal subjective musings disappeared. As a consequence, Haydn's place in history and the repertory changed. A genuine respect for him remained, but Rochlitz's and Kiesewetter's form of affection and regard, particularly Kiesewetter's idea that Haydn's instrumental works were 'true beauty' concretely realized, vanished.

---

[6] Friedrich Rochlitz, 'Der Componist und der Gelehrte: Ein Gespräch', in *Für Freunde der Tonkunst*, IV, 3rd edn (Leipzig: Carl Cnobloch, 1868), pp. 254–6.

Compare, for example, Adolph Kullak's treatise *Die Aesthetik des Klavierspiels,* first published in 1860 and then, from 1876 on, reprinted in four editions well into the twentieth century. This book was arguably the most widely read and influential book on piano teaching and playing of the nineteenth century – the dominant enterprises of the musical profession and public of the age. Kullak repeats the view that came to pervade the nineteenth-century opinion of Haydn in the years after the death of Beethoven. According to Kullak, Mozart, and subsequently Beethoven, followed a 'path opened by Haydn'. But they achieved greater perfection. By that Kullak meant that Mozart and Beethoven realized a 'spiritual importance' inherent in music. Haydn failed to take the next logical step from his own remarkable innovations, which was a 'psychological' one. This would have led him to strive for a profundity that his music never achieved. Haydn's music lacked the 'inner seriousness', the 'dark and demonic' and the 'interior depth of mood' characteristic of Mozart and Beethoven.

Haydn's music was therefore 'untouched by the hardships of mature life'. His music was childlike, natural, full of joy, naïve, happy. Haydn's ideal of beauty had once been innovative in that it mirrored a new sense of freedom. It emerged out of Haydn's rejection of past constraints, including religious dogma, and a 'crystallized canon of old ideas'. Yet despite its novelty and natural 'freshness', Haydn failed to realize the immanent power of his own formal innovations and remained tied to a superficial notion of symmetry, proportion and evident harmony. The ambitions and virtues held in high regard by Kiesewetter had been transformed into evident limitations. Haydn's greatness, although uncontested, lay primarily in breaking the new ground on which Mozart and Beethoven could develop.[7]

As the nineteenth century progressed, despite the myriad of conflicts and quarrels about music and its character, Kullak's version of Haydn's place in music history and his conception of the virtues and shortcomings of Haydn's music not only became unexceptional, but it remained at once strikingly stable and uncontroversial. Perhaps the most dramatic and influential statement of the standard view of Haydn (from which Kullak doubtlessly drew) was contained in Franz Brendel's *Geschichte der Musik in*

---

[7] See Martin Gellrich's introduction to Kullak, *Die Aesthetik des Klavierspiels* (Regensburg: Con Brio, 1876; rpt 1994) and the text, p. 21; also the 4th edn, ed. Walter Niemann (Leipzig: C. F. Kahnt Nachfolger, 1905), pp. 21–2.

Italien, Deutschland und Frankreich, first published in 1852. Brendel was nearly forty years younger than Kiesewetter and was a contemporary of Schumann and Mendelssohn. He became the editor in 1845 of Schumann's influential *Neue Zeitschrift für Musik*. Brendel (a decade older than Kullak) began with the premise that Haydn was 'Mozart's predecessor'. Haydn opened up the 'modern age' and his work was 'the soil' from which Mozart came. Haydn was an example of how historical necessity worked through an individual. He emancipated musical art from tradition and authority. Instrumental music, which Haydn developed, marked the first incarnation of the freedom of the spirit through music in modernity.

Haydn, however, was a man of order and convention whose interior genius was limited by his exterior self-presentation and modesty. The outer forms of his being remained decisive in his creative work. Therefore his forms were left without 'being filled with a corresponding content'. His world view, when compared with that of Mozart and Beethoven, was the least developed and least diverse. His capacity to imagine love – the crucial source of musical inspiration – and the feminine was inferior to that of Mozart and Beethoven. Haydn's essential practicality limited his expressive capacity. He revealed a 'teasing retreat' from conflict in life. He was therefore the master of the joke and adept at conveying moods. Mozart commanded irony, and Beethoven, owing to the immense pain of his life, was the composer of profound humour.

If Beethoven could be compared to Schiller and Jean Paul and Mozart to Goethe, Haydn was closest to Wieland. Haydn mirrored purity, nature, innocence, childhood. In the end, he was capable of engaging love only as an abstract cosmic and universal idea, as the force uniting the opposing elements that create chaos. Mozart individualized love and rendered it a subjective experience. Unlike Beethoven, Haydn did not penetrate any of the contradictions of the world, least of all in love; contradictions are, at most, merely alluded to on the surface of his works.[8]

Little within this picture has changed since Brendel's time. In contemporary concert life, we notice many versions of annual 'Mostly Mozart' festivals and weekend-long 'Beethoven Experiences'. Two popular Hollywood films have been made on the lives of Mozart and Beethoven.

[8] Brendel, *Geschichte der Musik in Italien, Deutschland und Frankreich*, 2nd edn (Leipzig: Matthes, 1855), I, pp. 300–5, and II, pp. 28–51.

There is no 'Mostly Haydn' series being planned and no film under contract. Of the massive output of music Haydn left behind, only a small fraction appears regularly on modern concert programmes. When a Haydn work is programmed, it is rarely as the main event.

The Haydn 'problem' bequeathed by the last century to our own was perhaps best expressed during the first decade of the twentieth century in two anecdotes recounted by the legendary conductor Felix Weingartner. He described his encounter with Joseph Joachim when, in 1907, as part of the preparation for the upcoming centennial Haydn activities, they were both invited to sit on the advisory committee of the Breitkopf & Härtel complete Haydn edition. Weingartner had had little prior contact with Joachim, who was suspicious of Weingartner's Wagnerian and Lisztian sympathies. None the less, at the meetings Joachim (then a man of over seventy, who would die later that year) more than once took Weingartner's hand and asked, 'Truly, was not Haydn indeed a *great* man?'

That Joachim's affectionate question might well have been apt in the climate of a century ago can be gleaned from Weingartner's second anecdote. When the centennial Haydn celebrations took place in Vienna in 1909, he, as Mahler's successor at the Imperial Opera, was asked to programme something that could be part of the Haydn anniversary. Weingartner expressed his dismay that the Festival Committee failed to grasp the brilliance of his idea that a new production of Mozart's *Magic Flute* would be the ideal tribute. Not accepting the fact that Haydn was 'everything but a dramatic composer', they insisted on a Haydn opera. Weingartner's approach mirrored the nineteenth-century notion that Haydn's imposing significance and achievement were most evident in his role as the indispensable intermediary step to Mozart and Beethoven.[9]

2   The nineteenth-century consensus

The history of the critical and cultural reception of music remains inextricably bound to shifting conceptions within history of what, in the final analysis, constitutes the work of music. Indeed, continuities and major

---

[9] Felix Weingartner, *Lebenserinnerungen* (Zürich: Orel Füssli, 1929), II, pp. 70 and 202.

shifts in reigning attitudes about music alter the course of compositional ambitions; they also force a reconstruction of the narrative of music history.[10]

The starting-point for Haydn as a composer was the eighteenth-century strategy best articulated by Kant that might properly be termed 'philosophical listening'. However, the later part of the century, during Haydn's most celebrated and productive periods, witnessed the articulation of the early Romantic emphasis on music as an aesthetic experience in real time tied to the imagination and the nearly inarticulate inner self – a concept best described in the late eighteenth-century writings of such early Romantics as Jean Paul and Wackenroder. After Haydn's death, by the mid-nineteenth century – the era of Brendel and Kullak – a move beyond the early Romantic notions was well under way. Although 'music as experience' retained its prestige with particular composers and sectors of the public, later in the century the emphasis shifted to an allegiance to music as text, to the printed score, which became analogous to a book that might be sampled, read, studied and returned to at will. The character of this approach to music demanded of the listener and amateur a novel but commanding self-conscious awareness of history, tradition and precedent. An attitude towards music as a mirror of the historical moment, representative of the generation of Eduard Hanslick and Johannes Brahms, was not uppermost in the early Romantic enthusiasm for music.

Despite such shifts in fundamental expectations and norms of reception over the nineteenth century, the critical response to Haydn's music – whether understood as a performed event or as a text to be studied and re-read – did not change. The significant disputes during the nineteenth century involving musical taste and culture altered the view of Bach, Mozart and Beethoven, but not the understanding of Haydn. In the case of no other major composer was there so little evolution, so much consistency, so little genuine shift in aesthetic judgement and response.

---

[10] See Hans Robert Jauss, *Toward an Aesthetic of Reception* (Minneapolis: University of Minnesota Press, 1982); *Die Theorie der Rezeption: Rückschau auf ihre unerkannte Vorgeschichte* (Constance: Universitätsverlag Konstanz, 1987); and Lydia Goehr, *The Imaginary Museum of Musical Works* (Oxford: Oxford University Press, 1992), for the most recent and frequently cited introduction to the historical and philosophical issues.

Consider, for example, the contrast between the changes in the reception of Mozart's music and the stasis in attitudes towards Haydn. In the 1881 revision of his classic 1854 tract on music's inherent autonomy, *On the Beautiful in Music*, Eduard Hanslick used the change in Mozart reception, and thus in the representation of Viennese Classicism itself, as a way of strengthening the anti-Wagnerian argument that emotion could not serve as the essential content of music. Whereas a few generations earlier Mozart's symphonies had been seen as vehicles of 'vehement passion, bitter struggle and piercing agony' that contrasted with the 'tranquillity and wholesomeness of Haydn', the two composers had now become amalgamated as part of an 'Olympian Classicism'.[11] Mozart, once favoured by the early nineteenth-century Romantics, had become more like Haydn. By the end of the nineteenth century, this distanced image of Mozart was abandoned again, as witnessed by the Mozart revival of the *fin de siècle*.[12] But Haydn stayed in the same place.

Throughout the nineteenth century, no one sensed a need to challenge the predominant view of Haydn's music. The perception of Haydn as innocent, naïve, cheerful, healthy, supremely well-crafted but essentially entertaining and emotionally distant, if not irrelevant, displayed a tena-

11 *Vom Musikalisch-Schoenen: Historisch-kritische Ausgabe*, ed. Dietmar Strauss (Mainz: Schott, 1990), pp. 31–3. The fact that Mozart's music permitted a variety of subjective responses that varied over time was evidence, according to Hanslick, that music was objective: that there was no inherent emotional meaning to the work of music itself. Implicit in this argument was Hanslick's criticism of modern Wagnerian emotionalists, who, as they relentlessly pursued contemporary musical fashion, either lost or never possessed the capacity to grasp the visceral intensity that Mozart might properly inspire. Hanslick may have been aware that during the mid-nineteenth century, particularly in France, Mozart's symphonic music was considered inferior to Haydn's and certainly subordinate in importance to Mozart's operas. Despite this Parisian preference for Haydn, Berlioz had little use for him, and could barely sit through a performance of one of his symphonies. See Katharine Ellis, *Music Criticism in Nineteenth-Century France: La Revue et Gazette musicale de Paris 1834–1880* (Cambridge: Cambridge University Press, 1995), pp. 84–93.
12 See Gernot Gruber, *Mozart and Posterity*, trans. R. S. Furness (Boston: Northeastern University Press, 1994); also Heinrich Schenker, 'Ein Wort zur Mozartrenaissance' (reprinted from the *Neue Revue*, 1897), in *Heinrich Schenker als Essayist und Kritiker*, ed. Hellmut Federhofer (Hildesheim: Olms, 1990), pp. 252–6.

cious constancy after its first appearance in the age of early Romanticism. E. T. A. Hoffmann had set the stage with his claim that 'Haydn's compositions are dominated by a feeling of childlike optimism ... a world of love, of bliss, of eternal youth ... no suffering, no pain; only sweet, melancholy longing for the beloved vision'. In this sense Haydn becomes the basis upon which 'Mozart leads us deep into the realm of spirits'. And, of course, Beethoven 'sets in motion the machinery of awe, of fear, of terror, of pain and awakens the infinite yearning which is the essence of Romanticism'.[13] This interpretation was reinforced by Carpani's epistolary Haydn biography of 1812,[14] and from the evident restraint and caveats in Stendhal's version of Carpani a decade later.[15] These two writers compared Haydn to a master genre or landscape painter – to Claude Lorrain, the great seventeenth-century painter – whose canvases, despite their virtues, did not provide the beholder with an evident subjective viewpoint or the self-conscious opportunity to invent a passionate, interior response. By 1812 Haydn already seemed distanced and historical to a new generation. The isolated individual placed within the landscape and the outer world, the figure to be found or implied in the paintings of Caspar David Friedrich, was absent from a conception of landscape painting associated with Haydn. While Beethoven would be routinely linked with Friedrich, Haydn would be compared instead with Tintoretto (as he was by Schumann)[16] or (stylistically) with David; he would not be compared with Delacroix. One explanation for this was offered by Adolf Bernhard Marx, who pointed to Haydn's relative monothematicism, as opposed to the greater dialectical tension of

13   Cited from the essays on Beethoven's Fifth Symphony and Beethoven's instrumental music, in *E. T. Hoffmann's Musical Writings*, ed. David Charlton, trans. Martyn Clarke (Cambridge: Cambridge University Press, 1989), pp. 97–8 and 237–8.

14   *Le Haydine, ovvero lettere su la via e le opere del celebre maestro Giuseppe Haydn* (Milan: C. Buccinelli, 1812).

15   See the excellent introduction and edition by Richard N. Coe of Stendhal, *Lives of Haydn, Mozart and Metastasio* (London: Calder and Boyars, 1972). For a good but brief context for Stendhal see Robert Alter and Carol Cosman, *A Lion for Love: A Critical Biography of Stendhal* (Cambridge, Mass.: Harvard University Press, 1986).

16   Robert Schumann, *Tagebücher*, ed. Georg Eisman, I, 1827–1838 (Leipzig: VEB Deutscher Verlag für Musik, 1971), p. 281, took this comparison from Carpani, in Stendhal, *Lives of Haydn, Mozart and Metastasio*, p. 141.

contrasting themes in the sonata forms of Mozart and Beethoven later favoured by Romanticism.[17]

Critical comparisons of Haydn to a distant but honoured precursor such as Lorrain or Tintoretto allowed nineteenth-century composers and commentators to lavish praise on Haydn's technical command and his role in the development of instrumental music, particularly the sonata, quartet and symphony. Yet Haydn was condemned to a form of aesthetic and cultural irrelevance. Where the Bach revival led to a revaluation of Bach as a figure at once historical and contemporary, Haydn served throughout the nineteenth century as a merely historical one. He was the acknowledged master, the father of autonomous instrumental musical discourse. Meanwhile, his music was said to be bereft of profound emotional inspiration or narrative significance.

The search for meaning in Haydn did not get very far beyond formalism. Schopenhauer may have been inspired by Haydn's music to discover the possibilities of self-referential meaning, autonomy and significance in music, but he overlooked Haydn's overt attempts to convey extra-musical meaning. Johann Friedrich Herbart rejected altogether the significance of the text in *The Creation* and *The Seasons*, declaring, 'fortunately, [Haydn's] music needs no text; it is mere curiosity that impels us to know what he has tried to illustrate. His music is simply music, and it needs no meaning to make it beautiful.' An admirable but bloodless notion of formal perfection was conceded, but that was all.[18]

Haydn conceivably could have provided a rallying point for midcentury proponents of so-called absolute music, the ideal of purely musical meaning. Indeed, to them Haydn's consummate craftsmanship was preferable to fashion and philistinism. In comments made in 1839, Schumann hailed 'Altvater' Haydn as welcome relief from 'this chronically diseased era of music', in which one only rarely could be 'inwardly satisfied'. Haydn, whose music offered satisfaction because of its conservative integrity, provided relief from a painful awareness of inadequacy by being 'clear as sun-

---

[17] *Die Lehre von der musikalischen Komposition*, 5th edn (Leipzig: Breitkopf & Härtel, 1879), III, pp. 595–6. Thanks to Scott Burnham for the reference.

[18] Cited in Peter le Huray and James Day, eds., *Music and Aesthetics in the Eighteenth and Early Nineteenth Centuries* (Cambridge: Cambridge University Press, 1981), p. 454.

light . . . bereft of any sense of ennui with life, and inspiring nothing except for joy, love of life, and a childlike happiness about everything'. Still, Haydn's virtues did not connect to the sensibilities that led Schumann to embrace Thomas Moore's 'Lalla Rookh' as an inspiration for his *Das Paradies und die Peri*.[19] In 1841 Schumann displayed his more usual weariness with the old master, complaining that 'Haydn's music has always been played here often and one can no longer experience anything new with him. He is like an intimate friend of the family [*Hausfreund*] whom one meets always with respect and gladly. But a deeper relevance for today's world he does not possess.'[20]

Schumann's heirs – Hanslick and other anti-Wagnerians – struck the same note. Writing in November 1856, just two years after the completion of his magnum opus, Hanslick noted in a review of quartet concerts:

> One began as usual with Haydn, the father of the quartet, a praiseworthy custom, so long as one does not neglect the sons in relation to the father. The representation of the old master with two works in a cycle of six evenings is entirely sufficient. In the first place, on account of nearly one hundred years of unrivalled attention, Haydn's quartets are so deeply rooted in our blood, not only on the part of amateurs but Haydn's successors as composers, that we feel, in the case of every one of these clear and cheerful musical works, that we are encountering an old friend. Furthermore, it was part of the historical character of the Haydn era that his quartets represented much more the common elements of a genre than a differentiated, sharply defined individuality. It is revealing that one always refers to 'a Haydn quartet' whereas one is precise with regard to the specific work one is talking about in the case of Beethoven. It is important for the hearer of Beethoven which of the series of Beethoven quartets he wishes to hear, because they are all distinctly individual, which is not the case with Haydn. The reasons do not lie exclusively with the fundamentally different personalities of the two masters. The manner of composition was entirely different in their respective times. Anyone who wrote more than one hundred symphonies and came close to that in terms of quartets, could not possibly invest in each of these works a distinct richness of individuality.

[19] Robert Schumann, *Gesammelte Schriften*, ed. Martin Kreisig (Leipzig: Breitkopf & Härtel, 1914), I, p. 450. It is possible that Schumann, like others, sought to downplay Haydn as a model, particularly for this work, which can be heard as deriving from Haydn's achievements in the late oratorios.   [20] *Ibid.*, II, p. 54.

Insofar as Beethoven wrote ten times less, he was able to put into a work ten times more.[21]

Familiarity, the saying goes, breeds contempt. Hanslick's views never changed. In 1891 he commented with some irony on Haydn's choral madrigal 'The Storm' that, since the world had experienced a wholly new set of storms in the hundred years since the work's composition, Haydn's representation of calm was more boring than comforting. In 1896 Hanslick seemed more intrigued by the revival of Gassmann than in hearing Haydn again.

The 'opposition' during the nineteenth century, the so-called New German School and the Wagnerians who dominated the end of the century, paid Haydn slightly different, but hardly more appreciative, compliments. Franz Liszt seems to have given no attention to Haydn at all, except for a passing interest in *The Creation* and by using a Haydn sonata to demonstrate how he could make a modern piano sound like a spinet.[22] In 1850 Hans von Bülow, during his early Wagnerian phase, spoke again of Haydn's 'childlike immediacy'. In 1856 Bülow followed Schumann's use of Haydn, defending him against the fake connoisseurship of the general public, which, seeing music as an aspect of affirmative cheerfulness, liked hearing Haydn too much and for the wrong reasons. In an essay on Wagner's *Faust* Overture in 1858, Bülow spelled out the right reasons for praising Haydn: his 'populist simplicity' and 'richness of motifs of high nobility'. Years later, in correspondence from the 1880s about concert programming, Bülow reiterated the familiar view of Haydn as rulemaker and precursor. His choice of a Haydn symphony on a programme that also featured the 'Jupiter' Symphony and the 'Eroica' was contingent on how it related to the Mozart and prepared the audience for the Beethoven.[23]

---

[21] *Sämtliche Schriften: Historisch-kritische Ausgabe*, ed. Dietmar Strauss, I/3, *Aufsätze und Rezensionen 1855–1856* (Vienna: Böhlau, 1995), pp. 306–7.

[22] Haydn is totally absent from August Goellerich's diary of Liszt's piano master classes. See the English-language edition of Wilhelm Jerger's text in Richard Louis Zimdars, *The Piano Master Classes of Franz Liszt 1884–1886* (Bloomington: Indiana University Press, 1996); and Alan Walker, *Franz Liszt*, III, *The Final Years 1861–1886* (New York: Knopf, 1996), p. 287.

[23] *Briefe*, VII, 1886–1894, ed. Marie von Bülow (Leipzig: Breitkopf & Härtel, 1908), pp. 126, 129 and 420–1; and *Ausgewählte Schriften 1850–1892* (Leipzig: Breitkopf & Härtel, 1911), p. 208.

For Richard Wagner, Haydn was the composer who stressed the dance and the populist roots of art music, another commonplace and oft-repeated idea (which competed with the notion of the childlike) in nine-teenth-century historical narratives. Beethoven was the logical historical outgrowth, the composer who 'opened up the boundless faculties of instru-mental music for expressing elemental storm and stress';[24] on the other hand, Haydn's craftsmanship lay in hiding 'contrapuntal ingenuity' in the 'rhythmic dance melody', so that 'the character of the dance peculiar to a dance ordained by the laws of freest Phantasy ... the actual breath of Joyous human life' was illuminated. None the less, Beethoven was to Haydn 'as the born adult to the man in second childhood'. In Haydn's instrumental music, the demonic essence of music is 'playing with its fetters, with the childishness of a greybeard born'.[25]

For all the ink that has been spilled on the aesthetic controversies of the mid-nineteenth century regarding programme music and 'absolute' music, both camps viewed Haydn in much the same way. This commonality offers an opportunity to challenge the idea that the overt split in nine-teenth-century aesthetic approaches was as stark as their proponents and subsequent defenders wanted posterity to think. Underlying the divide were shared notions of what constituted music of significance for the con-temporary listener.

One might have thought that the respect Herbart and Hanslick paid to the purity of Haydn's music would have inspired a certain allegiance to Haydn's oeuvre on the part of the most committed anti-Wagnerians. Yet all that Clara Schumann and Joachim (in his youth) could seem to hear in Haydn was a foreshadowing of Beethoven, particularly in Haydn's Adagios, or an exotic cheerful folksiness in his closing rondos.[26] Clara

---

[24] 'The Art Work of the Future', in *Prose Works*, ed. William Ashton Ellis (New York: Broude, 1892/1966), I, pp. 120–1. For reasons of historical consistency I am using the standard Wagner translation.

[25] 'Beethoven', in *Prose Works*, V, p. 82.

[26] Joseph Joachim, *Briefe*, I, 1842–1857 (Berlin: Julius Bard, 1911), pp. 288, 295, 308; III, 1869–1907, p. 342. Also Johannes Brahms and Joseph Joachim, *Briefwechsel*, I (Berlin: Deutsche Brahms-Gesellschaft, 1908; Tutzing: Hans Schneider, 1974), p. 221; *Clara Schumann–Johannes Brahms. Briefe aus den Jahren 1853–1896*, ed. Berthold Litzmann (Leipzig: Breitkopf & Härtel, 1927), I, pp. 118–19.

Schumann's concert repertory contained only two sonatas for violin and piano and nothing more.[27] Brahms presents a more complex case. In his extensive library, amidst the manuscript and first-edition treasures, there is very little Haydn to be found, in contrast to the extensive collection of works by Beethoven, Mozart and Schubert. He did copy out a few works by Haydn, and he also varied the St Antoni Chorale, which he believed to be by Haydn. The Serenade, Op. 11, opens with a striking resemblance to Haydn's London Symphony, No. 104, and it has been argued that Haydn was crucial to Brahms's compositional struggle in the 1850s as he searched for models and sources that might differentiate himself from Schumann.[28] None the less, for both pro- and anti-Wagnerians, the underlying expectation remained the same: music was supposed to be capable of inspiring and commanding the interior of one's soul, and Haydn's music failed to do so, whereas Bach's and Mozart's, not to speak of Beethoven's, did.

One slight reason may have been the extent to which Haydn's music was a crucial component of serious musical education, given that what we learn in school often emerges tainted by the brush of official approval. Familiarity with Haydn was an indispensable part of nineteenth-century self-cultivation (*Bildung*), and his work retained a visible place in concert life throughout the century. *The Seasons* and *The Creation* remained staples of the amateur choral tradition in German-speaking Europe.[29] A limited but none the less varied array of Haydn's symphonies – twenty-one, to be precise – was part of the Vienna Philharmonic repertory between 1860 and 1910.[30] A somewhat more generous selection, including excerpts from

[27] Claudia de Vries, *Die Pianistin Clara Wieck-Schumann* (Mainz: Schott, 1996), p. 366.

[28] Brahms made a copy of the slow movement of an early Haydn symphony, No. 16 in B flat major (1762), in about 1870 and copied it out for Joachim a year later. He also copied out a vocal pastorella attributed to Haydn, possibly in 1863, and chose the St Antoni Chorale as the theme of his orchestral variations, Op. 56b. See Margit L. McCorkle, *Johannes Brahms: Thematisch-Bibliographisches Werkverzeichnis* (Munich: Henle, 1984), Anhang VI Nr. 4, Nos. 63, 67, 68, p. 723.

[29] See, for example, notices of performances throughout German-speaking Europe in the Viennese *Neue Musikalische Presse* from the mid-1890s on, and in the *Neue Musik-Zeitung* published in Stuttgart and Leipzig from the same period.

[30] See Richard von Perger, *Fünfzig Jahre Wiener Philharmoniker* (Vienna: Carl Frome, 1910).

operas and choral works, marked the Leipzig Gewandhaus repertory during the same period. But even in Leipzig, Haydn stood behind Beethoven and Mozart. Owing in part to the influence of English taste, Haydn retained a stable place in the repertory of American symphony orchestras until the last quarter of the nineteenth century, when performances of his music experienced some decline.

Friedrich Nietzsche wrote that 'to the extent that the temperament of genius [*Genialität*] can coexist with a thoroughly good man, Haydn possessed it. He goes to the very edge of the line which morality prescribes for the intellect; he just makes music that has "no past".'[31] Nietzsche, in his post-Wagnerian phase, put the collective nineteenth-century view in its most profound form. Haydn's achievement was as the figure in history who was universally credited with developing Classical forms and instrumental music, the artist whose normative achievement retrospectively transcended the historical. His music sounded as if it had no precursors and, in the sense of Nietzsche, successfully defied the nasty nineteenth-century habit of historicization.

At the same time, a residual sense of blandness and excessive respectability remained; insofar as conventional middle-class morality could ever be associated with the aesthetic realm, Haydn managed it. Nietzsche's formulation was his own gloss on the widely accepted link between innocence–childhood–purity and Haydn. His use of the word 'Genialität' is conscious, as is his use of 'Moralität'. As Nietzsche knew, both words overtly suggest parallel English terms, which carry different meanings explicitly relevant to Haydn's London years. The German use of geniality suggests both greatness and creativity, as well as the English meaning of an unobjectionable cheerfulness. Haydn as a 'personality' in the nineteenth-century sense was nowhere to be found: he had transcended the mundane and the purely human by writing himself out of his own music. He invented music as a formal, abstract enterprise without, however, developing its capacity to be profound and therefore transcend conventional morality.

Neither Wagnerians nor anti-Wagnerians seemed to need to delve beyond this position. Hearing Haydn as the composer without a past meant

---

[31] *Menschliches, Allzumenschliches*, Zweiter Band, in *Werke*, III, ed. Karl Schlechta (Munich: Hanser, 1954), pp. 934–5.

15

there was no historical persona to approach, and no need to 'undo' the way in which his music had been heard from the beginning of the century on, as had been the case with Bach, Mozart and Beethoven. In the mid-1880s, when Nietzsche penned his aphorism, Haydn had 'no past', in part because the reception of his music had never evolved.

Perhaps Haydn's most crucial formal contribution was that he had realized, as the historian Emil Naumann put it, 'the great natural law of organic development' in musical language and form in ways independent of non-musical narrative patterns. His music seemed as normative as it was unobjectionable; it was cheerful, wholesome, eminently healthy.[32] It prepared the way for other composers who would engage and capture the imagination. Ludwig Nohl, writing in 1866, allowed that Haydn, as the developer of the sonata, had set the stage for Mozart and Beethoven to invest the form with 'truly ennobled and grandiose pictures of humanity and life', thereby lifting it out of the realm of 'mere wordless play of sounds'. Nohl used practically the same language as Nietzsche would later use in describing Haydn's inspiration as 'genial' and his work as a 'source of pleasure and edification'.[33] In an era beset by controversy, hostility and a nearly obsessive reflection on originality, historical precedent and the nature and character of music, such ritual praise was damning indeed. Bach, Handel, Mozart and Beethoven were reheard, rethought, and actively fought over – but not Haydn.

This late nineteenth-century consensus regarding Haydn seemed so all-pervasive that it motivated Hermann Kretzschmar to weigh in with a long dissenting view, stressing the composer's profundity and emotional depth. In the introduction to his discussion of the Haydn symphonies in his classic guide to the concert repertory, *Führer durch den Konzertsaal*, he wrote: 'An astonishingly large number of music lovers and musicians, including names possessed of the most celebrated reputations, believe that they can honor "Papa" Haydn with a mixture of condescension by considering him "genial" and "childlike"'. To understand Haydn, Kretzschmar believed, one had to concentrate on how he transformed the mundane and rendered his material majestic and mythic. In Kretzschmar's view, Haydn

---

[32] *Deutsche Tondichter von Sebastian Bach bis auf die Gegenwart* (Berlin: Oppenheim, 1882), p. 147.
[33] *Musikalisches Skizzenbuch* (Munich: Merhoff, 1866), pp. 150–1.

should be compared to Aeschylus and Sophocles.[34] Like the great Greek tragedians, he transformed the simple into the profound.

Kretzschmar's association of Haydn with Aeschylus and Sophocles was a rare perception. Though nineteenth-century music critics were obsessed with the relationship between formal procedures and narration and representation, the 'master' of form, Haydn, was excluded from the discussion. Mozart, Beethoven and Schubert were seen as using Haydn's strategies, and in the process achieving a narrative-through-music that appeared compelling. Meanwhile, the narrative in Haydn's music – either subjective (in the listener) or objective (in the music itself) – had no import. This view persisted despite the acceptance of programmatic titles for many symphonies.

Advocates of programme music in the nineteenth century cited Beethoven's *Pastoral* Symphony as a model and recognized an emotional content in Mozart. Yet Haydn's efforts at tone-painting and the profound philosophical content of many of his instrumental works produced no resonance. Richard Strauss had only a marginal interest in Haydn, though Mozart always rivalled Wagner as a source of inspiration for him. And even a Haydn defender such as Leopold Schmidt, the Berlin critic and enthusiastic Straussian, unconsciously ended up reinforcing the picture of Haydn's music as somehow sterile and distant. In his highly successful popular 1898 Haydn biography, Schmidt argued that Haydn should properly be seen more as a 'youthful revolutionary' than as 'an old man in a wig'. By this he meant that the example of Haydn's command of musical form might well have a larger influence on future generations than it seemed to exert on contemporary composers. Picking up on a similar theme struck fifty years earlier by Schumann, Schmidt lamented the contemporary circumstance in which music is 'freed from old traditions', yet strives in confused ways to 'unclear objectives'. As he put it, 'the pressure for originality, which is not based on historical evolution or transcendent creative talent, too quickly takes on the symptoms of the sickly. It is therefore desirable that so pure and fundamentally healthy an artistic spirit as Haydn's should function for a long time as a productive inspiration.' For Schmidt, Haydn understood that the point of all music was the spreading of joy: 'The naturalness of his

---

[34] Vol. I (Leipzig: Breitkopf & Härtel, 1919), p. 113.

LEON BOTSTEIN

musical inspiration and realization should remain a model for us'.[35] Once
again Haydn was held up as the antidote to philistinism and excess (of the
kind audible in Mahler). Schmidt's language linking Haydn to medicinal
and moral purity is totally unlike the prose applied traditionally to
Beethoven or Mozart. As with Nietzsche and Wagner, Schmidt's emphasis
on health reveals the weakness of Haydn's position in the *fin de siècle*.

The many handbooks written for the musical public during the nineteenth century further confirm this impression. In the *New Musical Lexicon
of Music* of 1857 Adolf Bernhard Marx and the editors once again stressed
the affirmative qualities of Haydn. Though Marx also talked about Haydn's
'natural inwardness and profundity', he explicitly delimited, as did
Hoffmann, Haydn's attribution of emotional and intellectual meaning,
pointing out that even when Haydn deals with the sorrowful and the grim,
he does so as a 'loving father', for whom balance and moderation are never
lost.[36] Two lexica from the 1880s, one by August Reissman, the multi-
volumed *Mendel Lexicon*, and the supplemental *Lexicon* to the Cologne
Neue Musikzeitung, repeat these ideas, adding only that Haydn's historical
role was primary as the father of instrumental music and the 'true creator of
the sonata form'.[37] As Reissman put it, Haydn did not so much invent any
new forms as bring 'order', by creating 'regulated organization' that resulted
in the mature forms of instrumental music.

The situation in America was much the same. In his 1874 lectures
entitled *History of Music* Frederic Louis Ritter, the influential Belgian-born
American composer and conductor, began his treatment of Haydn by
acknowledging the original eighteenth-century view that in Haydn, instruments 'sing like the inspired organs of an ideal sphere'. But he quickly

[35] *Joseph Haydn* (Berlin: 'Harmonie' Verlagsgesellschaft für Literatur und Kunst,
1898), p. 116. Schmidt's biography appeared in Heinrich Reimann's popular
series *Berühmte Musiker: Lebens- und Charakterbilder nebst Einführung in die
Werke der Meister*.

[36] See *Die Musik des neunzehnten Jahrhunderts und ihre Pflege: Methode der Musik*
(Leipzig: Breitkopf & Härtel, 1873), p. 178.

[37] The lexica are August Reissman and Hermann Mendel, eds., *Musikalisches
Conversations-Lexicon* (Berlin: Oppenheim, 1880); Eduard Bernsdorf, ed.,
Neues Universal Lexicon der Tonkunst (Dresden: Schaefer, 1857); P. J. Tonger,
Conversations-Lexicon der Tonkunst, Beilage der Neuen Musikzeitung (Cologne:
Hassel, n. d.).

18

descended into the nineteenth-century pattern. Haydn is credited with creating the modern symphony and string quartet, but the dominant impression his music makes is of a 'whole emotional world' of 'childlike naïveté, unrestrained joy, good-natured humor'. Haydn was capable of 'a healthy humor . . . touching pathos and unreserved joy, all the more tender and naïve feelings' but his music was 'seldom darkened by deep passion'.[38]

The impediment that nineteenth-century attitudes posed for an ambitious re-evaluation of Haydn was not entirely lost on the scholars who gathered in Vienna in 1909 to celebrate the Haydn centenary. The stultifying insistence on the formal and foundational merits of his work to the exclusion of any larger meaning or significance, however, was countered in a disappointing manner. Feverish nationalisms and political rivalries were raging on the Continent in the years just before World War I. One might have wished for a serious reinterpretation that would have asserted a new relevance for Haydn in such a context. Instead, the 1909 conclave made a virtue out of the seeming absence of controversy regarding Haydn's music and its historical position. Alexander Mackenzie exclaimed that he was proud to honour the memory of Haydn as the father of all 'cosmopolitan musicians. . . . The childlike simplicity of Haydn's music still delights us all', he noted, as he called for a 'closer union and more perfect harmony between musicians of all countries'.[39] Guido Adler's opening speech to the congress celebrated Haydn's connection with populism, his roots in folk music and his unique place in connecting Viennese Classicism to the immanent and essential universalism of music.

As the twentieth century progressed, nineteenth-century notions of

---

[38] *History of Music: In the Form of Lectures*, 2nd series (Boston: Oliver Ditson, 1874), pp. 172 and 181.

[39] See Guido Adler, ed., *Haydn-Zentenarfeier. Bericht III. Kongress der Internationalen Musikgesellschaft Wien 25–29 Mai* (Vienna: Artaria, 1909), pp. 41, 45, 52–3. This view is strikingly reminiscent of Joachim's letter to his nephew Harold in 1898, in which he remarked, in response to Henry Hadow's view of Haydn, that he 'lifts the material into a higher sphere and has the German gift to assimilate so that it becomes a universal, ideal thought, intelligible to all nations'. To Joachim's credit, he argued that the slow movements of Haydn were equal in their depth and religiosity to those of Bach and Beethoven, but in making this claim he knew that his view was distinctly a minority one. Joachim, *Briefe*, III, pp. 481–2.

Haydn continued to be influential, despite the post-World War I context of neoclassicism.[40] How can one interpret, for example, the fact that in Arnold Schoenberg's 1911 *Theory of Harmony* there is barely a mention of Haydn and, in contrast to Mozart, not a single Haydn musical example is used?[41] An intense new musicological interest, sparked by the first modern complete edition of Haydn's works,[42] sought to untangle a dense growth of authenticity problems and at the same time dust off works by Haydn not performed since the eighteenth century. Writing in 1951, John H. Mueller noted that this effort at a revival in the early twentieth century could be explained in part because Haydn's symphonies spoke 'directly to the twentieth-century era', because they 'are possessed of the utmost lucidity and elegance . . . and an integrity absolutely unmarred by any affectation, exaggeration, or bombast' and offer 'scintillating relief from the congested orchestration of the late Romantics'.[43] In fact, Mueller was only partially correct: the twentieth century has seen not one Haydn revival, but at least three. The first, early in the twentieth century, occurred precisely in reaction against late Romanticism, but was overshadowed by an even greater resurgence of interest in Mozart. The second, after the Second World War, was sparked by another attempt at a new edition and the first modern performances of many works, often organized by H. C. Robbins Landon. And during the third, in the twenty-odd years since the Haydn festival-conference in Washington in 1975 (followed by the Haydn Year 1982, his 250th birthday), the musicological era met the early performance era in ways that sought to reclaim Haydn as a composer of passion and intensity to match Haydn the composer of elegance and refinement. But there is a long way to go: Haydn still fails to speak as directly to us as he might, because Mozart

40 Scott Messing, *Neo-Classicism in Music: From the Genesis of the Concept through the Schoenberg/Stravinsky Polemic* (Ann Arbor: UMI Research Press, 1988), p. 62.
41 Schoenberg's pedagogical writings later in his career give somewhat more space to Haydn, but Mozart and Beethoven overwhelm Haydn as representatives of Classical procedures in composition. See *Fundamentals of Musical Composition*, ed. Gerald Strang and Leonard Stein (New York: St Martin's Press, 1970).
42 This edition, by Mandyczewski and others (Leipzig), was begun belatedly in 1907 (compared to the series of *Gesamtausgaben* of Bach, Mozart, Beethoven and others begun decades earlier, in some cases already in the 1850s) and broke off in the 1930s after the publication of only a small portion of Haydn's works.
43 *The American Symphony Orchestra: A Social History of Musical Taste* (Bloomington: Indiana University Press, 1951), p. 212.

and Beethoven continue to dominate our conception of him. The notion of Haydn as precursor lingers.

Why, then, did the nineteenth century consistently define Haydn's compositional mastery in terms of simplicity, humour, cheerfulness, geniality, folksiness, order, all implying an absence of passion and a lack of emotional, narrative and psychic relevance?

3   Four aspects of paradoxical innocence: Haydn's deification into irrelevance

The explanation for the respectful but bland deification of Haydn in the nineteenth century – as a composer of more crucial historical significance than continuing aesthetic and cultural valence – possesses four dimensions of increasing complexity. First is what might be called the 'touchstone' approach: the use of Haydn as a stable and neutral measure of cultural criticism. Second are the rituals of nineteenth-century biography that made Haydn both an unfortunate victim of the *ancien régime* and a populist figure, and therefore easier to set to the side. Third is the larger subject of nineteenth-century attitudes toward the aesthetics of the eighteenth century, which reveals the diminishment of one of its great achievements and pleasures, that which might be called philosophical listening. Finally comes the transformation of late eighteenth-century views on music-making and musical communication, in which we see a new ideology of connoisseurship that reflected the need to create a normative and hierarchical Classicism in response to the enormous increase in the size of music's audience. These dimensions of Haydn reception will be taken up in turn.

Haydn as touchstone

Haydn served as a constant instrument of cultural self-criticism for nineteenth-century figures from Schumann to Schmidt. Unlike Bach, Handel, Mozart and Beethoven, however, Haydn was not appropriated as a source of inspiration and emulation. Precisely because he was not an object of contemporaneity, he and his music could function as a clear-cut contrast. As we have seen, Haydn was effectively and reflexively used as a symbol of cultural criticism because, as Hanslick pointed out, he was considered a neutral and nearly unobjectionable part of standard musical education. One passed through Haydn on the way to musical maturity just the way music history passed through Haydn on the way to Mozart and Beethoven. Taking the wrong turn – a descent into philistinism – meant failing to learn the lessons of history.

The comparative neutrality of Haydn within the nineteenth-century construct of the Classical canon, his availability as a symbol of cultural criticism and contrast, is perhaps best highlighted by one of the recurring peculiarities of nineteenth-century Haydn scholarship: the emphasis placed on the change in Haydn's music after his encounter with Mozart. Gustav Hoecker and Leopold Schmidt were unequivocal in their view that the most lasting part of Haydn's repertory, particularly the later symphonies and oratorios, reflected Mozartian influence. This was one way in which Haydn's place in the repertory continued to be justified.[44] Another way to earn Haydn a place of honour was to argue for his relation to Beethoven. In this way, Haydn's role as touchstone revealed him to be an influence that was already completely absorbed.

Biographical assumptions

The issue of greatest concern to nineteenth-century biographers was that Haydn had not been a free artist but the servant of the aristocracy. This point may be painfully obvious, but unfortunately it is poorly understood. Nineteenth-century biographies of Mozart focused on his rebellion against the Archbishop of Salzburg, as well as on his conflict with his father and the presumed snubbing of Mozart by the Viennese aristocracy. These biographical episodes gave Mozart the aspect of a neglected Romantic genius whose frustrations lent his music an interior depth and secret melancholy. Such depths seemed absent from the consistently public and overt meanings of Haydn. There seemed to be an inner Mozart, but commentators either refused or failed to find significant subtexts in Haydn, a man who wore the Esterházy livery with apparent willingness. As Wagner put it, Haydn's greatest achievements were his late works, written independently of Esterházy but under foreign patronage, whereas Mozart never 'arrived at

---

[44] See Gustav Hoecker, *Das Grosse Dreigestirn: Haydn, Mozart, Beethoven* (Glogau: Flemming, *c.* 1898), p. 130.

comfort: his loveliest works were written between the elation of one hour and the anguish of the next'.[45]

It turns out that Haydn's private life and the dynamics between personal happiness and the writing of music were far more interesting and complicated than any nineteenth-century biographer was willing to emphasize. Although both Haydn and Mozart married on the rebound, so to speak – that is, to the sisters of the women with whom they really were in love – the commonplaces of Haydn's life story, as seen by the nineteenth century, make no allowance for the image of Haydn the artist as abandoned, lonely, troubled or psychically complex (even if Carpani, for one, was explicit on the matter of Haydn's unhappy marriage). His poignant comment of 1790 to his friend Marianne von Genzinger on the restrictions to which he had to submit – 'it is indeed sad always to be a slave' – was not assimilated into a more complicated picture of Haydn's psyche.[46] The absence of a powerful nineteenth-century biographer of the stature of Otto Jahn (Mozart) or Alexander Wheelock Thayer (Beethoven) further reinforced the popular stereotypes about Haydn and helped set him apart. Carl Ferdinand Pohl's death in 1887 meant that the two volumes of his important biography of Haydn (1875–82) brought Haydn up only to the end of the Eszterháza years in 1790; the third volume, dealing with the most popular and well-known works, had to wait until Hugo Botstiber completed the book in 1927.

But issues of Haydn's employment and the quantity of music he wrote remained uppermost in nineteenth-century attitudes. There seemed to be something socially deferential and perhaps even superficial about Haydn's music. Obeisance to formalities and manners, to the public aspect of music as entertainment for aristocrats, was first derided by the generation of composers who came of age after the fall of Napoleon. Berlioz was typical in assuming that Haydn's music was composed as the occasion demanded, not as the composer might have wished, and that its inner spirit was not the result of any subjective search for self-expression. The historian and aesthetician Heinrich Köstlin, in his 1874 history of music, delighted in

[45] 'Beethoven', *Prose Works*, V, p. 88.

[46] Letter of 27 June 1790, in H. C. Robbins Landon, *Haydn: Chronicle and Works II: Haydn at Eszterháza, 1766–1790* (London: Thames and Hudson, 1978), p. 745.

recounting that Haydn, in order to write music, first had to dress in a socially acceptable manner and become '*salonfähig*' (fit for the salon).[47] Haydn's status suffered from nineteenth-century aesthetic reactions to the French Revolution, especially the effort to transform the sensibility for music into a middle-class achievement reflective of individuality rather than a mark of aristocratic cultivation and manners. On the other hand, late Haydn appealed to subsequent generations of listeners, and not only because the music appeared to conform to an evolutionary scheme of increasing differentiation and complexity – the late Haydn was also the Haydn emancipated, if not from his wig, at least from the Esterházy livery. Nevertheless, the embrace of this late music by the English could not compete with the Romantic image of Mozart as misunderstood by the Viennese court and aristocracy. Likewise, despite the facts, Beethoven's eccentricities and apparent overt challenges to social conventions fitted the Romantic prejudices, as did the myth of Schubert's extreme poverty and obscurity.

By the mid-nineteenth century, the Wagnerian prejudice against success in one's own time, particularly with a philistine, self-satisfied public, also militated against a reconsideration of Haydn. The obvious contrast, of course, was Beethoven, who was seen as the ambiguous, striving, emotionally expressive Romantic artist cast adrift by society, in constant conflict with the philistines around him. His stature grew in the later nineteenth century with the notion that his late music, unlike Haydn's, had experienced opposition and bewilderment in its time, only to be accepted by later generations. The nineteenth century could take credit for truly understanding Beethoven. As for Haydn, given his success in his own time, his music could not be considered incomprehensible or opaque and thus progressive.

One element in Haydn's biography held unusual attraction for nineteenth-century attitudes, however: his origins. This was his status, unique within the Classical pantheon, as a simple 'man of the people', a quality seen as being exemplified by *The Seasons*. In the 1930s Ernst Kris and Otto Kurz developed a path-breaking theory on the origins and function of the different types of artists' biographies. Taking their interpretative lead, we

---

[47] *Geschichte der Musik im Umriss* (Leipzig: Breitkopf & Härtel, 1910), pp. 416–18.

can see that the accepted version of Haydn's life story fits a familiar biographical pattern for artists that dates back to Classical antiquity. Haydn's story is that of the extraordinary talent fortuitously discovered, despite his humble origins: here was a simple peasant genius who, after an early rescue from his village by a perceptive relative (leading to the choir school at St Stephen's in Vienna), just happened to live in the same building in Vienna as the famous Italian composer-conductor Nicola Porpora. Porpora recognized the greatness of the young man and gave him his first opportunity. Like the great painters of the Renaissance discovered by chance, Haydn overcame the obstacles created by the poverty and obscurity of his birth.[48]

This story held tremendous appeal for a nineteenth century nostalgic for simpler times, before industrialization and urbanization. Mozart, Beethoven and C. P. E. Bach all had fathers who were musicians themselves, so they fell into the less attractive and certainly more mundane pattern of the musician as artisan who is trained in the father's workshop. The fact that Haydn's ancestors were of no social significance and had no connection to anything artistic added an aura to his achievement. He was therefore credited with a unique capacity to speak to ordinary people. His use of the dance and the simple tune lent him a lasting connection to an illiterate, uneducated populace; he remained, rhetorically, a symbol of inspiration for the lower classes. Félix Clément, the music historian and composer writing in the 1860s, identified, among other virtues, Haydn's remarkable discipline and capacity for and devotion to work as part of his idealized image: an example that contrasted sharply with the self-indulgent modern pseudo-artistic personality.[49]

This helps to explain recurrent references by nineteenth-century critics to the folk roots of Haydn's music and his use of apparently

---

[48] See *Die Legende vom Künstler: Ein geschichtlicher Versuch* (Vienna: Krystallverlag, 1934; Frankfurt: Suhrkamp, 1995). The tradition of biography for the great visual artists was well developed, owing to the work of Vasari. In response to the growing audience for music, it was only in the nineteenth century that a comparable popular and general formula for composers came into being. It is ironic that Haydn had a partial unexpected benefit from the new industry of musician biographies that took its cue from the visual arts.

[49] *Les Musiciens célèbres depuis le seizième siècle jusqu'à nos jours*, 2nd edn (Paris: Librairie Hachette, 1873), p. 121.

Hungarian, Croatian and Austro-German folk material.[50] The dance rhythms and vitality of his music were readily associated with glorified memories of a fast-vanishing village and rural culture. Haydn's many dances for courtly consumption had no place in this account, but his acknowledged capacity for wit was incorporated into the general line of argument. By the 1820s the urban, middle-class artist and his audience had begun to romanticize the rural world as a place of cheerfulness, happiness, innocence and vitality: precisely the terms associated with Haydn's music. The misreading of Rousseau and the distinction between nature and civilization assisted in the nineteenth-century reception of Haydn as, ironically, the least artificial and the most natural of all composers.

The Seasons helped to make this point for the nineteenth century. In a great work of music, Haydn managed to ennoble the simple people, the ordinary landscape and daily life. This populist affinity, which was not evident in The Creation, made The Seasons a potent symbol.[51] Since naturalness, however attractive, was no longer accessible to artists trapped in the lonely spaces of the nineteenth-century urban European world, Haydn became a bittersweet vehicle of nostalgia and a remembrance of things long past.[52] This point was underscored by the sustained popularity of The Seasons in the programmes of choral societies.

The demise of philosophical music

Partly because of this 'simple peasant' myth, it has been assumed that Haydn, unlike Beethoven or most subsequent composers, was poorly educated and had very little interest in matters literary or philosophical.[53]

---

[50] Laurence Berman, *The Musical Image: A Theory of Content* (Westport, Conn.: Greenwood, 1993), pp. 182–5.

[51] See H. C. Robbins Landon, *Haydn: Chronicle and Works V: Haydn: The Late Years: 1801–1809* (London: Thames and Hudson, 1977).

[52] It is not surprising, therefore, that in this context that runs from E. T. A. Hoffman to Hanslick, there is a curious absence of sympathy for Haydn's religious music. It seemed too mundane and earthbound; see Charlton, *E. T. A. Hoffmann's Musical Writings*, pp. 370–1.

[53] See László Somfai, *Joseph Haydn: His Life in Contemporary Pictures* (New York: Taplinger, 1969); and, in contrast, James Webster, *Haydn's 'Farewell' Symphony and the Idea of Classical Style: Through-Composition and Cyclic Integration in his Instrumental Music* (Cambridge: Cambridge University Press, 1991).

Mozart's letters reveal an individual with a profound and reflective intelligence. Beethoven's intellectual ambitions were never doubted and were confirmed by his library. Though Haydn's music, particularly his operas, amply satisfies a search for a connection between music and ideas, his ambiguous legacy as an opera composer and the absence of a compelling written record of the order of the Mozart letters have helped to obscure his view of music and musical meaning.

However, as recent scholars have made clear, Haydn was engaged with the relationship between aesthetics and ethics, and the intersection between art and morality, even beyond his statement that he had often 'tried to portray moral characters in his symphonies'.[54] The conception of a piece of instrumental music as making a philosophical argument recognizable and significant from the point of view of the listener was not part of the Romantic complex of listening habits, but it was integral to Haydn's work from the 1760s and 1770s on and particularly to his late instrumental music, the work most familiar in the nineteenth century.

Haydn's achievement lay in the creation of music that fulfils, perhaps as closely as any, an eighteenth-century theoretical view of what music should be as an art form, especially in contrast to painting. Insofar as music was not about any form of imitation or, as Adam Smith put it, the 'reflective disposition of another person', it was abstract – in effect, the closest equivalent to pure thought and self-reflection. Smith argued that instrumental music was 'a complete and regular system', that it filled up 'completely the whole capacity of the mind so as to leave no part of its attention vacant for thinking of anything else.... The mind in reality enjoys ... a very high intellectual pleasure, not unlike that which it derives from the contemplation of a great system in any other science.'[55]

---

[54] Haydn's remark to his biographer Griesinger, from the latter's *Biographische Notizen über Joseph Haydn* (Leipzig: Breitkopf & Härtel, 1810), in Vernon Gotwals, trans., *Haydn: Two Contemporary Portraits* (Madison: University of Wisconsin Press, 1968), p. 62. See David P. Schroeder, *Haydn and the Enlightenment: The Late Symphonies and their Audience* (Oxford: Clarendon Press, 1990); Elaine R. Sisman, 'Haydn's Theater Symphonies', *Journal of the American Musicological Society* 43 (1990), 292–352; and Webster, *Haydn's 'Farewell' Symphony*.

[55] *Essays on Philosophical Subjects*, ed. W. P. D. Wightman and J. C. Bryce (Oxford: Oxford University Press), pp. 171–3.

The sense of total engagement that results in a welcome and satisfactory emotional and aesthetic conclusion aptly characterizes the response to Haydn's music in London.[56] It fits Edmund Burke's notion of the sublime as 'astonishment', with gradations including awe and terror. The power of the sublime was that it 'entirely filled the mind' with its object. By virtue of its temporality, its creation of tension through sound, and the impact of vibrations on the body, music created the possibility of 'a succession of great parts', a vehicle that could instil emotionally a sense of vastness and greatness and thus create the 'artificial infinite'. Music can 'anticipate our reasonings, and hurries us on by an irresistible force'.[57] This is a virtual description of the role of expectation and memory in listening to Haydn's late symphonies. Haydn's music satisfied the expectation put forward by Christian Gottfried Körner, who applied to music his friend Schiller's idea of an aesthetic education. Körner argued that to achieve a sense of beauty through music, the ear had to be trained. If music was to achieve its goals as an instrument of beauty and ultimately ethical ennoblement, the listener needed to have an understanding capable of discriminating form within the sounds of instrumental music. This required explicit instruction. Precisely because music 'forgoes the advantages of the other arts' and in effect 'gives us nothing to think about', whatever meaning we are able to find in it is of a high order, since it is created freely by us, the listeners. Music, when given form, shapes its own visceral emotional power into self-sufficiency, permitting the composer and listener to invest music with order, clarity and wide-ranging meaning.[58]

Music as an art was the taming of the acknowledged emotional power of hearing and sound. The eighteenth century placed a premium not only on form but on the symbolic achievement of resolution within the musical

---

56 See Simon McVeigh, *Concert Life in London from Mozart to Haydn* (Cambridge: Cambridge University Press, 1993), pp. 92–156.

57 *On the Sublime and Beautiful* (London: private print, 1812; facsimile print, Charlottesville: Ibis Publishing, n. d.), pp. 202, 234–5. It should be noted that the use of Adam Smith and Edmund Burke in this discussion is explicitly justified by the fact that Haydn read Smith and Burke; copies of the relevant works by both authors were in his library. See Sisman, *Haydn and his World*, pp. 420–1 of the Appendix.

58 'Über Charakterdarstellung in der Musik', in *Aesthetische Schriften*, ed. Joseph P. Bauke (Marbach: Deutsche Schillergesellschaft, 1964), pp. 24–8, 45–8.

experience. Resolution meant the reconciling of the disparate and conflicting elements of an emotional experience, as mirrored by contrasts in the music. The sublime and the beautiful could be achieved through a formal structure that was designed around music's 'regaining the home tonic', as Körner put it. In his later symphonies, Haydn revealed what David P. Schroeder has described as the capacity not only to 'persuade' but to engage the listener in a unique and powerful emotional narrative that finally becomes a philosophical and cognitive experience.[59]

The much-talked-about link in eighteenth-century philosophy between truth and beauty rested in part on the capacity of the perceiver to recognize and respond to intrinsic structural parallels between truth and beauty. As Zelter wrote to Goethe in 1826, Haydn's works 'are the ideal language of truth ... they might be exceeded but never surpassed. His genius is nothing less than the expression of a soul born free, clear, and innocent.'[60] If the discovery of clear, consistent and complete laws lay beneath the differentiated and imperfect appearance of nature as understood by Newton and Locke, then the perception of beauty in music composed, as well as music perceived by the listener, required the working-out and recognition of the musical argument. That argument, in turn, had to reflect laws analogous to those of the mind and the physical universe. The praise lavished on Locke and Newton for revealing the laws of nature and human understanding framed the objective for instrumental music. A Haydn symphony therefore became a philosophical argument whose command of the sense of beauty and the sublime, the rational and the emotional, mirrored back to the listener through total engagement in the moment of hearing (associationist connections with the extra-musical included, as in Haydn's 'The Storm') the fundamental coincidence of truthfulness and rationality in the world and in the mind.

For the eighteenth-century connoisseur, hearing a Haydn symphony was a way not *into* subjectivity, but a way to *transcend* subjectivity. Music's abstract language permitted the experience of the sublime and the beautiful that issued from the recognition of moral truth inherent in all parts of

---

[59] See *Haydn and the Enlightenment*. See also the essay by Mark Evan Bonds, 'The Symphony as Pindaric Ode', in Sisman, *Haydn and his World*, pp. 131–53.

[60] *Briefwechsel zwischen Goethe und Zelter*, II, 1799–1827, ed. Max Hecker (Frankfurt: Insel, 1987), p. 473.

the universe. The English audience that heard Haydn's symphonies in the late eighteenth century had known how to appreciate his quite religiously based ambition to realize in music a medium for philosophical and moral contemplation. As Burke and Smith recognized, such an ambition demanded music's access to both the sensual and the intellectual, the emotional and the rational, the sublime and the beautiful. It is a tribute to the symmetry of history that Kant's synthesis of these issues in *The Critique of Judgement* first appeared and was read widely in the same decade during which Haydn wrote his greatest works.

The nineteenth century, in contrast, had lost fundamental sympathy for this rational philosophical project. As a result, it found the music of Haydn cold, lacking in the human qualities most often linked to the perception of subjectivity. Mozart and Beethoven, never identified in the same way as part of the eighteenth-century rage for music as a philosophical system, did not suffer the same fate. As the nineteenth century evolved, it took its cue from Herder's perception that the indeterminate and darker nature of music deprived it of its immediate function as a symbolic system of morality. For the Romantics, the boundlessness of music was connected to a non-rational act of imagination conceived as the subjective transformation of experience; they posited an ontology and ultimately a cultural conception of music radically different from the assumptions under which Haydn worked. The underlying culture now rejected the idea of music as a complete philosophical system; and so the genuine pleasure afforded by the philosophical contemplation of music, at which Haydn excelled, became a lost habit. Both the music of Haydn and the idea of reason behind it suffered in the nineteenth-century dichotomy between emotion and reason, the rational and irrational, and the collapse of the eighteenth-century philosophical psychology of rationality and enlightenment.

The ideology of connoisseurship and the need for a normative Classicism

If nineteenth-century music critics were keenly aware of Haydn's presumed status as a servant composing on demand at the behest of the aristocracy, they were equally conscious of the transformation of the audience and the public role of music in their own time. Because they assumed that the sensibility towards music resided within the perceiver as well as the creator, they considered the consciousness of the listener crucial. As the century developed, the evolution of a refined musical consciousness was soon linked to the ideal of *Bildung*, or self-cultivation, as once exemplified exclusively by the cultivated aristocrat.[61] Although the aristocrat as employer was easily vilified, the aristocrat as connoisseur became idealized. *Bildung* emerged as an ambivalent category of middle-class self-assertion, ambition and insecurity.

The formation of the Society of the Friends of Music in Vienna during the Napoleonic era represented an unusual alliance between the high aristocracy and an elite middle class. In Vienna the Society became the basis of an ever-expanding world of participants in musical life who took on roles as amateurs, patrons and listeners. The explosion of the choral movement in the 1840s and 1850s mirrored the further growth of public musical life in German-speaking Europe. Musical culture on the Continent, especially in Paris and Vienna during the 1830s and 1840s, generally approximated to the scale of public musical life that Haydn encountered in London in the early 1790s. Before 1848, during the period of restoration, this new musical public constituted a mix of an old aristocracy and an urban middle class. Within the new non-aristocratic public, music benefited from its heritage as a form of aristocratic entertainment. Arno Mayer has argued that the values of the old regime were never entirely displaced during the nineteenth century, despite the radical political and economic changes (and Marxist ideas about cultural formation).[62] Music constitutes a powerful case in point. Self-cultivation, as an ideal of middle-class education, involved approximating and appropriating the connoisseurship that was historically associated with Nicolaus Esterházy. The discerning listener assumed through culture the pose and manner of the eighteenth-century aristocrat.

This nineteenth-century ideology of connoisseurship depended on the creation of a normative Classical past, one historically linked to an era of aristocratic privilege in which music was a narrowly distributed and highly

---

61 See Kevin Barry, *Language, Music and the Sign: A Study in Aesthetics, Poetics and Poetic Practice from Collins to Coleridge* (Cambridge: Cambridge University Press, 1987), pp. 1–27.
62 *The Persistence of the Old Regime: Europe to the Great War* (London: Croom Helm, 1981).

refined social instrument and ritual. At the same time, a set of new expectations was placed on the music of the present. These new expectations, which we usually identify as characteristic of Romanticism, defined new music as emerging from Beethoven, the composer who extended the normative procedures of a Classicism associated with a closed circle of aristocrats into a language accessible to the educated individual, irrespective of social origins.

From the beginning of the Romantic era, an uneasy tension existed between the demand that music be understood as an independent, abstract form of communication and the thought that music possessed a deep relationship to some psychological geography of human expressiveness and inner reflection. Music-making and listening became analogous to the experience of reading alone. Precisely because of this analogy to reading, music had to connect with the subjective imagination in a way that reflected itself in so-called non-musical meanings, either of narration or representation.

This was true of instrumental music as much as vocal. Beethoven was clearly a composer of drama and rhetoric, in which the gestures of instrumental music in relation to extra-musical meaning seemed profound but unstable.[63] The widely held Wagnerian perception that Mozart's genius lay in his operas and vocal music led to the idea that his instrumental music also had a vocal and therefore human cast to it. Because of this, its line and structure were susceptible to Romantic listening: one could hear in Mozart an interior narrative. In Haydn, on the other hand, there seemed to be only the playfulness of sound. That Haydn was a composer of drama and rhetoric was a view that lay in the past – and future.

The perception of the absence of extra-musical profundity in Haydn's instrumental music, despite its acknowledged exemplary virtuosity in techniques of musical elaboration, transformation and variation, has remained almost second-nature throughout the history of Haydn reception. Here biography and social history intersect. Being cheerful and telling jokes that result from the virtuosic manipulation of self-consciously simple

---

[63] See George Barth, *The Pianist as Orator* (Ithaca: Cornell University Press, 1992); and Mark Evan Bonds, *Wordless Rhetoric: Musical Form and the Metaphor of the Oration* (Cambridge, Mass.: Harvard University Press, 1991).

building-blocks did not satisfy the expectation of inner boundlessness. However, it did seem to fit the desire for entertainment associated with a discredited historical elite – and to satisfy a later generation's sense of its sophisticated musical and aesthetic judgement. Understanding Haydn was considered a mark of cultivation, a prior condition to being able to discern truth in one's own time. Since Beethoven had to be saved from philistine reductionism, it was critical that he be evaluated not just in emotional terms, but through a recognition of his greatness in purely musical terms – that is, in relation to the procedures established by Haydn. Just as Haydn was understood as a necessary precursor to Beethovenian Romanticism, the individual in the cultivation of his own taste had to recapitulate the encounter with Haydn, and therefore the formal language of music that lay beneath any attempt at expressiveness. Thus elevated into the model of pure formalism, Haydn could not help but fail to capture the imagination of the new kind of listener.

Meanwhile, Haydn's great oratorios remained beloved as works in which amateurs could participate. Despite the greatness of the music contained in them, the extra-musical aspects of The Creation and The Seasons seemed mere surface phenomena that did not disturb the formal integrity of the compositional method. The same was alleged with respect to the symphonies with descriptive titles. The moments of illustration in which Haydn indulged were no longer controversial, but obvious; and whatever deeper extra-musical intent Haydn wished to convey was no longer interesting or audible.[64] Joachim singled out Haydn's Adagios because they sounded the most like Mozart and Beethoven. Slow movements in Haydn seemed most susceptible to the highly prized habits of subjective appropriation. The outer movements of the sonatas, quartets and symphonies appeared as cheerful formal exercises that established the essential normative rules of future musical games and communication. Haydn had become the law-giver of Classicism.

The cultural conservatives of the 1840s and 1850s failed to realize that, in rescuing the formal part of the eighteenth-century musical tradi-

---

[64] See the telling analysis of Haydn's programme music (in which only the Seven Last Words of Christ is taken seriously) in Friedrich Niecks, Programme Music in the Last Four Centuries (London: Novello, 1906), pp. 73–8.

tion, they were abandoning the philosophical ambitions from which it had sprung. In order to rethink Haydn, the stubborn veneer of nineteenth-century habits of reception, which have extended well into this century, must be dissolved and scraped away. When we try to understand Haydn from the perspective of the eighteenth century rather than the nineteenth, we rapidly realize that Haydn's music carried for its listeners and contemporaries gravity, philosophical depth, passion and complex beauty. His formal achievements, celebrated as such by nineteenth-century criticism, engendered in his own lifetime precisely that emotionally intense response later generations considered somehow missing.[65] And this means, of course, that formal achievements – as Haydn himself did not fail to point out – were never only what Haydn was about.

[65] Compare the enthusiastic and perceptive reaction by the painter Philipp Otto Runge (1777–1810) to the symbolism of the *The Seasons*, quoted in Le Huray and Day, *Music and Aesthetics in the Eighteenth and Early Nineteenth Centuries*, p. 522.

2 Haydn's sacred vocal music and the aesthetics of salvation

JAMES WEBSTER

Now and then Haydn said that instead of so many quartets, sonatas and symphonies, he should have written more vocal music, for he could have become one of the leading opera composers.

1

Thus Haydn's biographer Georg August Griesinger transmitted the ageing composer's assessment of his œuvre – the only one of its kind that has come down to us.[1] Although this sentiment appears in the middle of Griesinger's only sustained discussion of Haydn's ideas about his art, it has rarely been taken seriously. The reason is obvious enough: it radically conflicts with the traditional modern focus on the composer's instrumental output – 'the father of the symphony', the first great exponent of the string quartet, the master of wit and irony, the hero of 'Classical style' – a focus that is maintained even in the most interesting recent new approaches to Haydn's music. Among his vocal works, only *The Creation* and *The Seasons*, a few Masses and the occasional 'canzonet' from the London years have enjoyed much resonance in modern musical life or scholarship; the rest – like his 'early' or 'immature' instrumental music – has been systematically marginalized.[2]

[1] Georg August Griesinger, *Biographische Notizen über Joseph Haydn* (Leipzig: Breitkopf & Härtel, 1810), p. 118 (trans. Vernon Gotwals, *Joseph Haydn: Eighteenth-Century Gentleman and Genius* [Madison: University of Madison Press, 1963], p. 63). Although for the convenience of readers I cite the location of a standard English version when quoting from primary sources (for example Gotwals, *Joseph Haydn*; Landon, *Chronicle and Works* [London: Thames and Hudson, 1976–80]), all translations are my own.

[2] On these views of Haydn's career and the processes of marginalization entailed see James Webster, *Haydn's 'Farewell' Symphony and the Idea of Classical Style: Through-Composition and Cyclic Integration in his Instrumental Music* (Cambridge: Cambridge University Press, 1991), pp. 335–57.

35

Yet vocal music constitutes fully half of Haydn's œuvre. Admittedly, during the 1780s and the first half of the 1790s he composed relatively little vocal music (and hardly any sacred music) and his most familiar instrumental works originated precisely during these years. But this emphasis was atypical. Both his first and his last completed compositions were Mass settings and he cultivated vocal music extensively during every other phase of his long career. He was an excellent tenor in the chamber (if not the theatre); he sang for the Prince of Wales, and wrote to his publisher Artaria regarding a set of lieder that 'after they are completed I will sing them myself, in the best houses. A master must see to his rights by his presence and by correct performance [*wahrer Vortrag*].'[3] Griesinger noted that '[Haydn] also criticized the fact that now so many musicians compose who have never learned how to sing. "Singing must almost be reckoned one of the lost arts; instead of song, people allow the instruments to dominate".'[4] Nor can Haydn's (rueful?) wish that he had composed even more vocal music be explained away by appealing to his loss of strength in old age or by his (to us) unexpected emphasis on opera.[5] The proof, as it were, is that during his last period in Vienna, when he had become a culture-hero and could do virtually whatever he wanted, he composed primarily vocal works, most of them sacred.

He believed strongly in the artistic quality of his vocal music, including his lieder, operas and other genres that modern reception has little valued. In 1781 he claimed to Artaria that

> my lieder, through their variety, naturalness and beautiful and grateful melodies, will perhaps surpass all others. . . . Now something from Paris. Mr le Gros, director of the *concert spirituel*, wrote me all sorts of nice things about my *Stabat mater*, which was given there four times to the greatest applause. . . . They were surprised that I was so extraordinarily successful in vocal music; but *I* wasn't surprised at all, for they haven't heard anything

[3] 20 July 1781; *Joseph Haydn: Gesammelte Briefe und Aufzeichnungen. Unter Benützung der Quellensammlung von H. C. Robbins Landon*, ed. Dénes Bartha (Kassel: Bärenreiter, 1965), p. 101 (Landon, *Chronicle and Works II: Haydn at Eszterháza, 1766–1790* [London: Thames and Hudson, 1978], p. 449).

[4] Griesinger, *Biographische Notizen*, pp. 114–15 (Gotwals, *Joseph Haydn*, p. 61).

[5] Admittedly, the critical reception of Haydn's operas remains contested; see Jessica Waldoff's 'Sentiment and sensibility in *La vera costanza*' in this volume.

yet. If they could only hear my little opera [*Operetta*] *L'isola disabitata*[6] and my most recent opera *La fedeltà premiata*! I assure [you] that nothing comparable has yet been heard in Paris, and perhaps not even in Vienna; it is only my bad luck that I'm stuck in the country.[7]

In his autobiographical sketch of 1776 Haydn summarized his output as follows:

> Among others, the following of my works have received the greatest approval:
> The operas *Le pescatrici, L'incontro improvviso* . . . *L'infedeltà delusa*; the oratorio *Il ritorno di Tobia*, performed in Vienna; the *Stabat mater*, about which I received . . . a letter from the great composer Hasse with undeserved words of praise. . . .[8]
> In the chamber style [*camer Styl*] I have had the good fortune to please almost all nations except Berlin, as is proved by public newspapers and letters I have received; I am only puzzled that the . . . Berliners' reviews of my pieces know no mean. . . . I know why: because they aren't capable of producing certain of my pieces.[9]

The primacy of vocal works in Haydn's mind is clear. He begins with a proud listing of individual, large-scale compositions for both theatre and church, in some cases adding circumstantial details; only later does he turn to the third venue, the chamber (which in this context connotes all instrumental music). Here, however, he does not cite so much as a single work (or even a genre), but indulges in a long polemic against 'Berlin' critics of his music.

A characteristic assessment not tied to Haydn's own person is found in Ernst Ludwig Gerber's 1790 account of the composer's career. He begins

---

6   This work of 1779 is a small-scale *opera seria* on a libretto by Metastasio, in which Haydn set all the recitatives as *accompagnati*.

7   27 May 1781; *Briefe*, pp. 96–7 (Landon, *Chronicle and Works II*, pp. 446–7).

8   Compare Haydn's letter of March 1768 (*Briefe*, pp. 56–7; Landon, *Chronicle and Works II*, p. 144).

9   *Briefe*, p. 77 (Landon, *Chronicle and Works II*, pp. 398–9). Haydn emphasizes his vocal works by listing them in quasi-outline form; this is rendered here in ordinary prose. For an interpretation of this document as exemplifying eighteenth-century principles of rhetoric, see Elaine R. Sisman, *Haydn and the Classical Variation* (Cambridge, Mass.: Harvard University Press, 1993), pp. 24–5.

by describing the 'sensation' aroused by Haydn's early string quartets, but continues: 'Meanwhile Haydn's great genius drove him from one stage of perfection to the next, until, around the year 1780, he attained the highest level of excellence and fame *through his church and theatre works*'.[10] Of the string quartets, Op. 33, from the very next year, of which modern historiography has made so much, there is no mention.

But to Haydn, vocal music was a matter not only of personal and professional pride, but of aesthetics. Scholars have only recently recognized that Haydn could have possessed anything like a coherent aesthetics. Although he did not philosophize and was indeed no intellectual in the strict sense, he was well read, broadly interested in people and customs, and circulated freely in what may be termed enlightened-conservative Habsburg culture.[11] He certainly held conscious principles regarding music.[12] The purpose of a composition was to move the listener. In order to achieve this, it should have 'a fluent melody ... no superfluous ornaments, nothing overdone, no deafening accompaniments', a viable basic 'idea', and coherent 'development and sustaining of that idea'; if the latter is lacking, 'nothing remains in the heart'. These precepts assume engaged listeners, who certainly approach a composition with many (pre-)conceptions, but are prepared actively to follow what we may call its argument, in a rhetorical sense. In addition, in letters Haydn often mentioned other desiderata of good music, including originality, 'fire', 'delicacy' or 'subtlety' (*Delikatesse*) and variety of effect, usually conveyed by the expression 'light and shade' (*chiaroscuro*).

---

[10] Ernst Ludwig Gerber, *Lexikon der Tonkünstler*, I (Leipzig, 1790), col. 611 (emphasis added). Gerber's much longer biography in the *Neues Lexikon der Tonkünstler* (1810) does mention Op. 33, but with no sense of it having been a historical or stylistic watershed.

[11] Georg Feder, 'Joseph Haydn als Mensch und Musiker', in Gerda Mraz, ed., *Joseph Haydn und seine Zeit* (Eisenstadt, 1972; = *Jahrbuch für österreichische Kulturgeschichte*, II), pp. 46–8; Maria Hörwarthner, 'Joseph Haydns Bibliothek – Versuch einer literarhistorischen Rekonstruktion', in Herbert Zeman, ed., *Joseph Haydn und die Literatur seiner Zeit* (Eisenstadt, 1976; = *Jahrbuch für österreichische Kulturgeschichte*, VI), pp. 157–207.

[12] Webster, *Haydn's 'Farewell' Symphony*, pp. 227–36. The quotations of Haydn's own words in this paragraph are from Griesinger, *Biographische Notizen*, pp. 113–17 (Gotwals, *Joseph Haydn*, pp. 60–2).

Regarding sacred vocal music, Haydn not only asserted its moral efficacy, as in his much-quoted letter about *The Creation* to a provincial schoolmaster,[13] but was even reported to have harboured programmatic feelings of a personal nature about certain numbers from the late oratorios. His former pupil Sigismund von Neukomm wrote that

> in response to my enthusiastic admiration of the great bass aria 'Behold, O weak and foolish man, Behold the picture of thy life' (from 'Winter', *The Seasons*), Haydn said, 'This aria refers to *me*!' And in this wonderful masterpiece he really did speak entirely from his inmost soul [*aus seinem innersten Innern*], so much so that he became seriously ill while composing it, and one must assume that this was the decisive point when the Lord, Who giveth and Who taketh away, closed Haydn's glorious career, and allowed him to see 'his life's image and his open grave'.[14]

These utterances (to which many more could be added) document the centrality of vocal music to Haydn's musical thinking and self-image. They also document his seriousness and moral earnestness – aspects of his art that have been undervalued, owing to our focus on the wit and formal inventiveness of his instrumental music. In fact, notwithstanding those qualities, his instrumental music is also fundamentally serious, especially in a 'rhetorical' sense;[15] from this point of view there was no fundamental split in his aesthetics or musical persona between the two realms. (As is well known, he stated that he had often portrayed 'moral characters' in his symphonies.[16]) Hence there is every reason to take his vocal music 'seriously' as well, especially since – and this is after all the point – it is fully the equal of his instrumental music in originality and constructive power, and since the sacred works, at least, were arguably greater in cultural significance and resonance during his lifetime.

[13] *Briefe*, p. 373 (Landon, *Chronicle and Works V: Haydn: The Late Years: 1801–1809* [London: Thames and Hudson, 1977], pp. 70–1); compare Webster, *Haydn's 'Farewell' Symphony*, p. 229.

[14] Horst Seeger, 'Zur musikhistorischen Bedeutung der Haydn-Biographie von Albert Christoph Dies (1810)', *Beiträge zur Musikwissenschaft* 1/3 (1959), 30 (the final, quoted phrase is from the text of the same aria).

[15] Hartmut Krones, 'Rhetorik und rhetorische Symbolik in der Musik um 1800: Vom Weiterleben eines Prinzips', *Musiktheorie* 3 (1988), 117–40; Mark Evan Bonds, *Wordless Rhetoric: Musical Form and the Metaphor of the Oration* (Cambridge, Mass.: Harvard University Press, 1991), chapter 2; Sisman, *Haydn and the Classical Variation*.

[16] Griesinger, *Biographische Notizen*, p. 117 (Gotwals, *Joseph Haydn*, p. 62).

2

Haydn's church music comprises two groups of works: Mass Ordinary settings (Hoboken XXII; most now published in *Joseph Haydn Werke*, series XXIII) and what scholars amusingly refer to as his 'smaller' or 'other' liturgical works (Hoboken XXIII); both are listed in Table 2.1. The Masses cluster in the decade from the mid-1760s to the mid-1770s (Nos. 2, 4–6 and perhaps 7) and the final Vienna years (Nos. 9–14). Both periods of intense cultivation seem to have been instigated in part by external factors. In 1766, following the death of his predecessor Gregor Joseph Werner, Haydn acceded to the post of Kapellmeister (his initial position, as Vice-kapellmeister, entailed responsibility only for the *Camer musique*). Nor did he begin modestly; the *Missa Cellensis* (1766) and the *Stabat mater* (1767) are elaborate works on the largest scale. Then, after the long hiatus resulting from Joseph II's prohibition of elaborate church music and the lack of opportunities in London, all but one of the six late Masses were composed in satisfaction of his (otherwise limited) duties as Esterházy Kapellmeister, for performance on the name-day of the Princess.

The last six Masses, although not conceived or disseminated as an 'opus', exhibit an overall generic consistency (not to be confused with uniformity). The earlier ones, by contrast, are notably heterogeneous, reflecting their presumed composition for different institutions.[17] Particularly striking is the variety among the five Masses of 1766–75: the huge, festive-traditional *Missa Cellensis* in C, with trumpets and drums; the *Missa Sunt bona mixta malis*, in D minor and *stile antico*;[18] the darkly passionate, mid-length 'Great Organ Mass' in E flat major, coloured by exuberant passages for solo organ (presumably performed by Haydn himself) and by English horns (compare Symphony No. 22, 'The Philosopher', in the same key); the *Missa Sancti Nicolai* in G major, also of middle length, combining a sweetly pastoral air with intensity; and the 'Little Organ Mass' in B flat major, a *missa brevis* of quiet, almost pietistic fervour. Even the 1782

---

17 On Mass types in Haydn's milieu, see Bruce C. MacIntyre, *The Viennese Concerted Mass of the Early Classic Period* (Ann Arbor: UMI Research Press, 1986).

18 The same conjunction of style and key appears in the psalm 'Non nobis Domine', Hob. XXIIIa:1; compare the Kyrie and Benedictus of the 'Nelson Mass', also in D minor.

'Mariazellermesse', which shares with the *Missa Cellensis* the key of C, scoring with trumpets and drums and association with the pilgrimage church of Mariazell, contrasts with it through greater compactness and an emphasis on sonata style.

Regarding the 'other' works, their variety of function, style and scale makes them difficult to conceptualize as a genre.[19] Hoboken divides his Group XXIII into four subgroups roughly according to liturgical function: (a) 'Graduals, offertories and motets'; that is, settings for the Proper (the genuine works seem all to be offertories) – (b) Marian antiphons; (c) '*Te Deum* settings and other choruses' – that is, hymns and the like; (d) the mis-leadingly titled 'Arias' (Haydn's own title was 'Cantilena', and the group includes one duet) – that is, pastorellas, composed in 'folk' style on vernacu-lar texts, primarily for use during Advent. The majority are distributed rather evenly over the first half of Haydn's career, up to *c.* 1775, with only three chronologically isolated works thereafter; this pattern doubtless reflects their varied destinations and purposes (most of which are still unknown). They vary widely in style and scale, from the dark, massive *Stabat mater* and the more intimate but equally stern 1771 *Salve regina*, both in G minor, to the tender devotion of the 'Lauda Sion' hymn-settings and the English psalms; from the festive jubilation of the choral *Te Deum* settings with trumpets and drums in C to the pastorellas for solo voice(s) and strings, redolent of Austrian peasant crèches. Even particular sub-genres may exhibit marked contrasts: the four 'Lauda Sion' hymns from the

---

[19] These works have not yet appeared in *Joseph Haydn Werke* (hereafter JHW), except for the *Stabat mater* (XXII/1). For a detailed survey of the sources see Irmgard Becker-Glauch, 'Neue Forschungen zu Haydns Kirchenmusik', *Haydn-Studien* 2 (1969–70), 167–241; see also Landon, *Chronicle and Works I: Haydn: The Early Years, 1732–1765* (London: Thames and Hudson, 1980), pp. 147–79, 275–9, 494–514 (with extensive musical examples); *Chronicle and Works II*, 234–51 *passim*; Marianne Helms, 'Joseph Haydns "Kleinere Geistliche Werke"', *Haydn-Studien*, forthcoming. Oratorios, cantatas (such as *Applausus*) and other works on religious texts (lieder, part-songs, canons, etc) are omitted from Table 2.1, as are liturgical *contrafacta*; for the latter, see Becker-Glauch, 'Neue Forschungen', 177–92, 233–5. For work-lists that include the *contrafacta* and variously liberal selections of doubtful and spurious works (not always acknowledged as such), see Hoboken, *Joseph Haydn: Thematisch-bibliographisches Werkverzeichnis* (Mainz: Schott, 1957–71); Becker-Glauch, 'Neue Forschungen', 237–41; *The New Grove Dictionary of Music and Musicians* (London: Macmillan, 1980), VIII, pp. 361–3.

Table 2.1 Haydn's sacred vocal music[a]

Date	Masses[b] — Hob. XXII; title; key	Others[c] — Hob. XXIII; title; key	Type; liturgical association; vocal forces (when not chorus)
'1749'	1 *Missa Brevis*; F		
		c5 'Lauda Sion'; C, C, C, C	Hymns; Corpus Christi procession
c. 1750?		b1 *Salve regina*; E	Marian antiphon; Vespers Soprano solo + chorus
1756		c1 *Te Deum*; C	Hymn of thanksgiving
1762–3?		a2 'Animae Deo gratae'; C[d]	Motet; Proper (offertory) Soprano solo + chorus
1760s?		a3 'Ens aeternum'; G	Motet; Proper (offertory)
1766 (–1773?)	5 *Missa Cellensis in honorem B. V. M.*; C ('Missa Sanctae Ceciliae')		
1767		XXbis *Stabat mater*; g	Sequence/hymn (Holy Week) SATB solo + chorus
late 1760s?		c4 *Quatuor Responsoria de Venerabili* ('Lauda Sion'); B flat, d, A, E flat	Responsories; Corpus Christi procession
c. 1767–9	2 *Missa Sunt bona mixta malis*; d[e]		
c. 1768–9	4 *Missa in honorem B. V. M.*; E flat ('Great Organ Mass')		
c. 1768–9		c3 'Alleluia'; G	[Proper (offertory)][f]
c. 1768–70		d3 'Herst Nachbä'; D[g]	Pastorella ('Cantilena') Soprano solo
1771		b2 *Salve regina*; g	Marian antiphon; Vespers SATB solo + obl. organ
1772	6 *Missa Sancti Nicolai*; G		

Date	Work		Description
early 1770s?		d1 'Ein' Magd, ein' Dienerin'; A	Aria ('Cantilena pro Adventu') Soprano solo
c. 1775?		d2 'Mutter Gottes'; G	Duet ('Cantilena pro Adventu') Soprano and alto solo
c. 1775–8	7 *Missa brevis Sᵗ Joannis de Deo*; B flat ('Little Organ Mass')		
1782	8 *Missa Cellensis*; C ('Mariazellermesse')		
1780s?		a1 'Non nobis, Domine'; d	Psalm; Proper (offertory)
rev. 1790s?			
1794–5		ʰ Six English Psalms	'New' psalter
1796	9 *Missa Sᵗ Bernardi von Offida*; B flat ('Heiligmesse')		
1796	10 *Missa in tempore belli*; C		
1798	11 *Missa in Angustiis*; d ('[Lord] Nelson Mass')		
1799	12 'Theresienmesse'; B flat		
(1798–)1800		c2 *Te Deum*; C	Hymn of thanksgiving
1801	13 'Creation Mass'; B flat		
1802	14 'Harmoniemesse'; B flat		

Notes

ᵃWith the exceptions noted below, only genuine, extant works (excluding *contrafacta*) are listed; compare the main text, note 19.

ᵇAuthentic titles are *italicized*; where none is given, Haydn wrote only 'Missa', or no authentic title survives. Common nicknames are given in quotation-marks. The *Missa Rorate Coeli Desuper* (Hob. XXII:3), whose authorship is highly uncertain, is omitted (for score and critical assessment see *JHW* XXIII/1a).

ᶜBased on Becker-Glauch, 'Neue Forschungen'; *The New Grove*; and Helms, 'Joseph Haydns "Kleinere Geistliche Werke"' (see n. 19).

ᵈHaydn's authorship probable, but not proved.

ᵉOnly the Kyrie and a fragment of the Gloria are extant.

ᶠIn the sources, this work follows a *contrafactum* from the cantata *Applausus* that was intended as an offertory. (That is, by liturgical function it would belong in Hoboken's Group XXIIIa.)

ᵍIn Hoboken with the spurious *contrafactum* text 'Jesu redemptor omnium'.

ʰHoboken, II, p. 181 (Group XXIII, 'Nachtrag').

1750s are all in C major, vivace and $^3_4$, while those from the late 1760s are in a tonally interesting set of four different keys and alternate andante $^3_4$ with largo *alla breve*; the *Salve regina* of 1756 in E major, with much 'Italianate' writing for the solo soprano, contrasts with that in G minor.[20]

*

In the remainder of this study I will examine four compositions, two from around 1770 and two from the late Vienna years: the *Missa Cellensis*, the *Salve regina* in G minor, the 1800 *Te Deum* and the 'Harmoniemesse'. In this context I can offer a systematic overview only of the *Salve regina* (in §3); the other discussions (in §4) are limited to individual movements or passages. Throughout, I will focus on two topics: Haydn's interpretation of his texts and his through-compositional aesthetics of salvation.

Haydn's sacred vocal works are multifariously and imaginatively responsive to their texts.[21] All of them treat many textual phrases or concepts in terms of what has been called 'musical imagery' (*musikalische Bildlichkeit*).[22] Although this concept includes 'word-painting' in the narrow sense of singing birds, croaking frogs, and so forth (already much criticized in Haydn's day), it goes beyond this to encompass various rhetorical traditions and even musical conceptualizations of textual images and ideas. The latter include musical analogies to non-acoustical phenomena (for example, long notes on 'aeternum' or 'Ewigkeit', an effect praised by Haydn's brother Michael),[23] musical topics (march, hunt, the various

---

[20] On the E major *Salve regina* see Carl Maria Brand, *Die Messen von Joseph Haydn* (Würzburg: Triltsch, 1941), pp. 16–29; Landon, *Chronicle and Works I*, pp. 158–66. A brief comparison is found in Walter Pass, 'Melodic Construction in Haydn's Two *Salve Regina* Settings', in Jens Peter Larsen, Howard Serwer and James Webster, eds., *Haydn Studies: Proceedings of the International Haydn Conference, Washington, D. C., 1975* (New York: Norton, 1981), pp. 371–4.

[21] For a sketch of a general theory of 'textuality' in Haydn's late oratorios (much of which would apply here as well), see James Webster, 'The *Creation*, Haydn's Late Vocal Music, and the Musical Sublime', in Elaine R. Sisman, ed., *Haydn and his World* (Princeton: Princeton University Press, 1997), p. 69.

[22] Anke Riedel-Martiny, 'Das Verhältnis von Text und Musik in Haydns Oratorien', *Haydn-Studien* 1 (1965–7), 205–40, especially 224ff.; Gernot Gruber, 'Musikalische Rhetorik und barocke Bildlichkeit in Kompositionen des jungen Haydn', in Vera Schwarz, ed., *Der junge Haydn* (Graz: Akademische Druck- und Verlagsanstalt, 1972), pp. 168–91.

[23] 'Here and there you will be surprised; and what my brother brings off regarding "Ewigkeit" in his choruses is nothing short of extraordinary.' Quoted in Albert

dances and so forth),[24] 'semantic' associations (for example, the flute with the pastoral) and so-called 'key-characteristics'.[25] In addition, through a complex dialectical process, Haydn's music also appropriates and realizes many of these textual aspects in a 'deeper' sense; we will encounter examples of this below.

As far as musical structure and procedure are concerned, the importance of through-composition in Haydn's music can now be taken for granted.[26] However, in sacred vocal music the aesthetics of through-composition takes on even greater significance. Notwithstanding the inevitable distinction between Haydn the man and the artistic persona 'in' his music, the organization of these works is not a matter of coherence or cyclic integration alone. Despite the wit and irony of his instrumental music, despite his hard-nosed business practices, Haydn was a devout believer; to cite merely the most obvious sign, he almost always inscribed his autographs 'In nomine Domini' at the head and appended 'Laus Deo' at the end. In his sacred vocal music the most important conceptual image (as opposed to the word-painterly type) is that of salvation. When he projects such an image by through-compositional means, at or near the end of a work, it becomes a goal, in a personal, religious sense: a new state of being, a musical realization of the desire for a state of grace.

3

The text of the *Salve regina* in G minor is one of the four so-called Marian antiphons.[27] Haydn often seems to have depended on the Blessed Virgin Mary as a source of comfort and hope; he inscribed both the *Missa*

Christoph Dies, *Biographische Nachrichten von Joseph Haydn* (1810), ed. Horst Seeger, 2nd edn (Berlin: Henschelverlag, 1962), p. 179.

[24] Leonard Ratner, *Classic Music: Expression, Form, and Style* (New York: Schirmer, 1980), parts I–II; Wye J. Allanbrook, *Rhythmic Gesture in Music: 'Le nozze di Figaro' and 'Don Giovanni'* (Chicago: University of Chicago Press, 1983), introduction and part I.

[25] Rita Steblin, *A History of Key Characteristics in the Eighteenth and Early Nineteenth Centuries* (Ann Arbor: UMI Research Press, 1983).

[26] See Webster, *Haydn's 'Farewell' Symphony*.

[27] The work has not yet appeared in *JHW*; Landon's edition in the Doblinger series (Vienna, 1964) is based on the autograph. An adequate recording based on historical principles is Martin Haselböck and the Wiener Akademie (Novalis 150–095–2).

Cellensis and the 'Great Organ Mass' 'in honorem Beatissimae Virginis Mariae' (or 'B. V. M.'), and, according to a plausible anecdote, he composed either the *Stabat mater* (another Marian text) or the *Salve regina* as a thanksgiving offering after having recovered from a severe illness.[28] Haydn's setting calls for four solo voices ('a quattro voci ma soli'), obbligato organ and strings. The organ part (which he presumably performed himself) plays not only an expressive-figurative role but a structural one as well, owing to its ritornello-like introductions and confirmatory cadential passages.

Adagio

1	**Salve** regina, mater misericordiae:	Hail, Queen, mother of mercy,
2	Vita, <u>dulcedo</u>, et spes nostra, salve.	Our life, sweetness, and hope, hail!
3	Ad te <u>clamamus</u>, <u>exules</u>, filii Hevae.	To thee we cry, exiles, children of Eve.
4	Ad te <u>suspiramus</u>, <u>gementes et flentes</u>	To thee we sigh, groaning and weeping
5	In hac <u>lacrimarum valle</u>.	In this vale of tears.

Allegro

6	Eia ergo, advocata nostra,	Therefore, Thou our advocate,
7	Illus tuos <u>misericordes</u> oculos ad nos converte.	Thy compassionate eyes turn upon upon us.

Largo – Allegretto

8	Et **Jesum**, benedictum fructum ventris tui,	And Jesus, blessed fruit of thy womb,
9	**Nobis** post hoc exilium **ostende**.	Show to us after this exile.
10	**O** clemens: <u>o</u> pia: <u>o</u> dulcis virgo Maria.[29]	O merciful, o kind, o sweet virgin Mary!

Bold face   becomes an element of the musical form
<u>Underlinings</u>   musical imagery

[28] James Webster, 'Haydns Salve Regina in g-Moll (1771) und die Entwicklung zum durchkomponierten Zyklus', *Haydn-Studien* 6 (1986–94), 247, n. 7, and the references given there; this study contains a much fuller version of the material presented here. Example 2.1 of the present essay is adapted from the corresponding example in the article cited above and is used here by kind permission of G. Henle Verlag; I thank Dr Martin Bente for his assistance.

[29] The Latin is given according to John Harper, *The Forms and Orders of Western Liturgy from the Tenth to The Eighteenth Century* (Oxford: Oxford University Press, 1991), pp. 274–5 (where, however, my line 10 is divided in two, after 'pia'). Haydn's orthography varies in many details.

The text falls into two primary sections of five lines each. First the believers greet Mary (lines 1–2) and portray their miserable condition (3–5). Then they pray that She take pity on them (lines 6–7) and that She grant them a sign of Jesus, their saviour (8–9). They close, however, with a renewed, threefold invocation of the Virgin.

Haydn does not merely 'set' this text; he interprets it. Although the work is cast in three movements, it is in many respects through-composed (see Ex. 2.1). The broadly constructed opening Adagio sets each of its five lines of text as an independent paragraph on a different theme (line 4 even divides into two distinct subsections). The work begins with a long organ solo (see Ex. 2.2); following a half-cadence prepared by an augmented-sixth chord on E♭ (bars 4–5), it moves through three successive deceptive cadences, also on E♭ (bars 7, 9, 11), until the voices unexpectedly cry out 'Salve!' on an augmented-sixth chord, yet again on E♭.[30] This striking event creates a structural role for the submediant. There has still been no full cadence (bar 15 is not a cadence but a beginning-over); even though one is eventually heard in the middle of the first vocal paragraph (bar 24), it is in turn trumped by the voices' renewed outburst on 'Salve!' and half-cadence in bars 33–5. The entire opening is governed more by the augmented sixths on E♭ and their resolutions to the dominant than by the tonic. On the second text-line, 'Vita, dulcedo', the music turns to the relative major and develops with ever greater expressiveness until a twofold structural cadence in B flat major (voices, bar 52; organ, bar 54).

Up to this point we have a typical exposition for a large-scale vocal movement: introduction; first paragraph in the tonic; second paragraph in the related key (see the horizontal brackets above the staff in Ex. 2.1).[31] But the continuation utterly fails to conform to the expectation of an overall

[30] This effect is unique in Haydn's earlier church music; later it became more common (see below).

[31] On vocal expositions see Mary Hunter, 'Haydn's Aria Forms: A Study of the Arias in the Italian Operas Written at Eszterháza, 1766–1783', Ph.D. diss., Cornell University (1982), chapter 5; James Webster, 'The Analysis of Mozart's Arias', in Cliff Eisen, ed., *Mozart Studies* (Oxford: Clarendon Press, 1991), pp. 117–18.

Example 2.1 *Salve regina* in G minor, harmonic structure

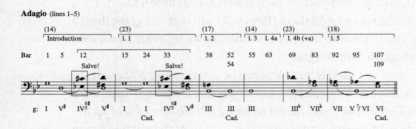

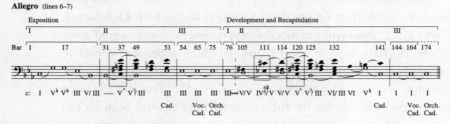

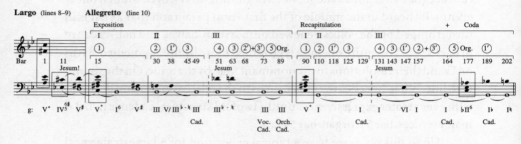

Example 2.2 *Salve regina* in G minor, Adagio, bars 1–16

Example 2.3 *Salve regina* in G minor, Adagio, bars 96–109

binary or sonata form. Each text-line receives a separate paragraph and the various motifs and topics seem to have little to do with each other; instead, as if no other source of coherence were available, Haydn increasingly focuses on word-painting. This leads to a climax on line 5 (see Ex. 2.3): the voices imitatively tumble down into the 'vale of tears', eventually sinking into the lowest register under increasingly dark and mysterious harmonies, until, literally at the last moment, and via an apparently non-

50

Example 2.3 (*cont.*)

functional progression, the Adagio modulates into E flat major and closes there.

This ending is highly rhetorical, and not merely because of its striking word-painting. In the eighteenth century the key of E flat was a familiar symbol of death and the underworld.[32] More unusually, the entire movement has closed outside the tonic, in this dark, troubled submediant. The form, the succession of ideas, the tonal plan: all aspects of this music – including Haydn's sinners – have lost their way. Such a mystery cannot be explained away even by this ending's strong link to the opening paragraph, with its continual cadences on to and dissonant vocal entries over E♭. Haydn's *Salve regina* is through-composed: whatever may eventually prove to be its coherence cannot take place on the level of individual movements, but only over the course of the entire work.

The middle Allegro in $\frac{3}{8}$ is a binary movement in C minor; each of its two parts comprises three paragraphs (see Ex. 2.1, second system). The first part is another clear exposition, while the second part conflates

---

[32] Wolfgang Osthoff, 'Mozarts Cavatinen und ihre Tradition', in Wilhelm Stauder *et al.*, eds., *Festschrift Helmuth Osthoff zum 70. Geburtstag* (Tutzing: Hans Schneider, 1969), pp. 139–77; Stefan Kunze, *Mozarts Opern* (Stuttgart: Reclam, 1984), pp. 297–9.

Example 2.4 *Salve regina* in G minor, Largo, bars 1–22

development and recapitulation: the first two paragraphs discuss the same topics as before, but in expanded and modulatory fashion, while the tonic enters at the end of the second paragraph and is maintained throughout the third. The texture alternates between solo song, contrapuntal elaboration and expressive homophony. Especially noteworthy is the diminished-seventh chord on C for the words 'misericordes oculos' (highlighted in Ex. 2.1). It first appears (bars 37–48) in an overall context of E flat major;

Example 2.4 (*cont.*)

Haydn sits on it for twelve full bars, in such an exposed manner (*pp*) that we grasp its component notes F♯ and (yet again) E♭ as a reminder of the still under-articulated overall tonic, G minor. However, it resolves 'normally' to a cadential 6–4 over B♭, the local dominant. In the parallel passage (bars 120–4) the local tonic actually is G minor; nevertheless, Haydn demonstratively refuses to allow it to cadence there, instead leading it (again!) to E flat, and on to the cadence and closing paragraph in C minor.

The final movement opens with a tenor recitative on lines 8–9, in which the supplicants ask to be shown a sign of Jesus (see Ex. 2.4). It begins on the same diminished seventh as before (in a different inversion); however, instead of resolving normally, it descends chromatically into remote regions. Eventually D♭ (bar 7) turns into the dominant of the dominant (C♯, bar 9), the tenor cadences; the organ, now obbligato, cadences deceptively on a vaguely familiar motif, echoed by the violins – and suddenly all four singers call out the crucial words 'Jesum ostende nobis', on the same motif and the same augmented-sixth chord on E♭ as at their initial entry in the Adagio. This moment makes audible what has been latent all along: the entire work is shaped as a single, through-composed utterance. An important aspect of this crucial passage is that Haydn takes these three key words, already sung by the tenor, out of their immediate context and rearranges them; he further emphasizes them by

Example 2.5 *Salve regina* in G minor, Allegretto, bars 171–202

inserting them (in still another permutation) into the Allegretto (bars 51ff., 131ff.).

The recitative leads without break into the finale proper, again in (moderately) fast triple metre; it is a sonata without development (see Ex. 2.1, bottom system). It begins *in medias res*, on the same diminished seventh (now back on C, as in the Allegro); although this now resolves regularly to a first-inversion G minor triad, there is still no stable root-position tonic. The threefold cry 'O clemens, o pia, o dulcis' continually generates threefold

Example 2.5 (*cont.*)

musical phrases, whether for all four singers in homophony (bars 15ff.; theme 1) or as a heartfelt syncopated cry for the soprano alone, answered by the others (bars 38ff.; theme 1'). Following the cadence of the second paragraph in the recapitulation (bar 129) – the first perfect cadence in G minor since bar 24 of the Adagio – the third paragraph brings numerous extensions, including one last deceptive cadence on Eb, with a new version of the syncopated cry 1', now for all four voices in imitation (bar 147). What in the exposition was a straight clinching cadential passage for the organ (bars 73–89) is also interrupted, by a massive vocal entry on the Neapolitan sixth (bars 177ff.; see Ex. 2.5); Eb is still a critical pitch. The singers hush to *pianissimo* and even fade out *a cappella*, the orchestra bursts in and the structural cadence in G minor follows directly (bars 188–9). Yet the tenor immediately raises his voice with the syncopated cry 1', for the first and only time on the tonic (rather than a dominant); we hear a hint of Bᵇ; and over a tonic pedal and semi-plagal cadence the *Salve regina* unexpectedly closes on the only tonic major chord in the entire work.

This cadence is everything other than a conventional 'Picardy third'. Haydn's sinners have been singing in heartfelt prayer, one that until now has received no answer. Closure in G minor, long postponed, is finally achieved; yet in that very moment, as if by an act of grace, their cries are transformed into an image of salvation.

55

4

The *Missa Cellensis* would be one of Haydn's most astonishing productions in any context, but it is doubly impressive when one considers that it is his first large-scale sacred vocal work.[33] (This would be true even if, as some scholars have argued, Haydn composed only the Kyrie, Gloria and perhaps Credo movements in 1766 and did not complete the Mass until *c.* 1772–3[34]). It is a huge Mass of the 'solenne' type (often mis-called 'cantata mass'), not uncommon in Haydn's milieu; each of the five main sections is subdivided into numerous complete and independent movements, in the manner of Bach's Mass in B minor.[35] Its overall stylistic orientation has generally been described in terms of a mixture of 'Baroque' or 'conservative' features and 'modern' or 'fashionable' ones.[36] It would take a volume to depict its glories; in this discussion I shall focus on the Credo.

Although Haydn's Credo conforms to the common three-movement, fast–slow–fast plan of the period (MacIntyre, p. 320), it is in many respects

---

[33] The work has recently appeared in *JHW* (XXIII/1a); a good recording in historical style is Simon Preston conducting the Academy of Ancient Music and the Christ Church Cathedral Choir of Oxford (L'oiseau-lyre 417–125–2). It was destined originally either for the pilgrimage church at Mariazell in Steiermark (whence 'Cellensis': 'for Zelle') or for a Viennese church associated with it; see Otto Biba, 'Die kirchenmusikalischen Werke Haydns', in Gerda Mraz *et al.*, eds., *Joseph Haydn in seiner Zeit: Eisenstadt, 20. Mai–26. Oktober 1982* (Eisenstadt: Amt der Burgenländischen Landesregierung, 1982), p. 143. The familiar nickname 'Missa Sanctae Ceciliae' is inauthentic; it derives from the supposition that Haydn composed the Mass for a certain Viennese order that honoured the patron saint of music with very long Masses of this type; see Biba, 'Die kirchenmusikalischen Werke', pp. 142–4; Leopold M. Kantner, 'Das Messenschaffen Joseph Haydns und seiner italienischen Zeitgenossen: Ein Vergleich', in Georg Feder *et al.*, eds., *Joseph Haydn: Tradition und Rezeption* (Regensburg: Bosse, 1985), pp. 149–51.

[34] See James Dack, 'The Dating of Haydn's *Missa Cellensis in Honorem Beatissimae Virginis*: An Interim Discussion', *Haydn Yearbook* 13 (1982), 97–112; *JHW* XXIII/1, viii-ix. The argument is intriguing but not compelling; for the time being the question must remain open (an opinion shared by MacIntyre, whom I thank for an informative communication on the topic).

[35] Landon, *Chronicle and Works II*, pp. 229–30; MacIntyre, *The Viennese Concerted Mass*, pp. 110–17, esp. [112]. Further citations to MacIntyre's survey are given parenthetically in the text.

[36] For example, Brand, *Die Messen von Joseph Haydn*, pp. 63–99; Landon, *Chronicle and Works II*, pp. 230–1; Daniel Heartz, *Haydn, Mozart and the Viennese School 1740–1780* (New York: Norton, 1995), pp. 299, 303–4.

through-composed. The music takes inspiration from the text throughout; many of the illustrative motifs seem so effective precisely because of their obvious, if not extreme character. The best example is perhaps 'descendit de coelis' (bars 77–84), which Haydn sets as a descending sequence (both on the motivic level and that of the sequence itself – the choral basses are asked to sing low D), followed by a hushed resting-point on the 'lowest possible' chord and then by an explosion a twelfth higher on a variant of the original motif. The opening movement is dominated by a motto theme on the words 'Credo in unum Deum', stated at the outset by the chorus and repeated at once by solo soprano. Such mottos are common (MacIntyre, pp. 361–3);[37] what is remarkable here is that the motto henceforth is sung only by the solo soprano, in different keys and contexts, and usually followed by a new orchestral ritornello rising towards the heavens (bars 18–20 and 21–4 in the dominant, 40–2 and 43–6 in the subdominant and 85–8 and 88–92 in the tonic to round off the movement). Motto and ritornello thus together constitute a linchpin of the overall form, whose import, however, only gradually becomes evident.

The Largo middle section – Haydn's slowest tempo – is notated as a single movement, without double-bar or change of metre or key signature, and is accompanied throughout only by soft strings. Nevertheless it comprises two complete but run-on movements:[38] 'Et incarnatus' in C minor for tenor and 'Crucifixus' in F minor for alto and bass. The former is introduced by an eight-bar *accompagnato*, before the leisurely but ornate aria proper begins in bar 102 (the violins applying their mutes), based on a common thematic type (MacIntyre, p. 371 and Ex. 8–12). It is very clearly in binary form (bars 102–14 and confirming ritornello in 114–15; 116–29 and 129–30). The strong closure at the end is only confirmed by the seamlessly developing but distinct modulating transition (bars 131–2) to the 'Crucifixus'. This movement contrasts not only in key and singers, but also introduces an arpeggiated ostinato in the violins instead of simple repeated notes as before. It is also more chromatic, with spectacular leaps down to the lowest bass notes on 'sub Pontio Pilato' and 'passus'. The despair of the

---

[37] Especially given the syntax: the word 'Credo' can logically precede any or all of the numerous doctrinal assertions in the text as a whole.

[38] On run-on movements, see Webster, *Haydn's 'Farewell' Symphony*, pp. 13–14, 186–94.

text is wonderfully conveyed by modulations into 'dark' flat-side keys and an obvious but effective final word-painting on 'sepultus est', when the bass himself provides the low tonic pedal underneath the dissonant strings above.

The third and final movement is a complex, two-part structure. The first part comprises two subparts, chorus alone (bars 156–213), then tenor solo alternating with chorus (bars 213–78); the second part is the concluding fugue on 'Et vitam venturi saeculi, Amen' (bars 279–386). In the first subpart almost every text-phrase engenders new motifs and textures; the rising motifs on 'Et resurrexit' and 'Et ascendit in coelis' are again obvious but effective, as are the contrasts on 'judicare vivos et mortuos' and 'et resurrexit mortuorum' (bars 184–97, 271–8). Characteristic of Haydn's treatment of sacred vocal texts is an emphasis on 'little' words, such as 'et' and 'non', where this highlights (or even creates) the rhetorical sense: here, on 'cuius regni *non* erit finis' (bars 202–4).[39] The tenor introduces the second subpart with 'Et in spiritum sanctum' and the doctrinal text proceeds – until the solo soprano suddenly interjects her motto from the *first* movement (varied to fit the prevailing $\frac{3}{4}$ metre; bars 255–61). This is not merely a recollection, but a through-composed gesture *par excellence*, for this is the decisive 'I believe' that prepares the climax of the entire Credo. The chorus rushes through the remaining lines, in order to prepare the concluding 'Et vitam venturi'.

There has always been unanimity about this unique and overwhelming fugue. I therefore close by quoting (for the first time in English) the appreciation in an early review of the first published edition of the Mass (1807), attributed to Friedrich Rochlitz. The 'Resurrexit', he writes,

> moves without pause into a fugue with a character all of its own; in the entire realm of such fugues we possess only a few examples of this kind, and only from men of the richest imagination and most impressive

[39] Compare the treatment of 'non' earlier, bar 60, as well as 'tu' in the 'Quoniam', bars 659–62 and so forth; see also below, on the *Te Deum*. A stunning late example is found in the Credo of the 'Nelson Mass', where the entire final section (from 'Et resurrexit' on) is dominated by motivic repetitions of 'Et' that insist on the content of the Creed: 'I believe in one God . . . *and* that Christ was resurrected . . . *and* ascended to Heaven . . . *and* . . .'. I was made aware of this (and much else) by Tom Beghin, 'Haydn's Musical Reading of the Credo-Text', unpublished paper, Cornell University (1992).

combinatorial powers – a fugue executed in its entirety by the voices, to which is set a true basso continuo in the style of a counterpoint to a cantus firmus, which for ten full pages never loses its secure course [in constant quavers] even for a moment, while the violins, as unshakable as [the bass] counterpoint, imitate each other in passages built on the theme and the countermotives. . . . And all this is held together through no fewer than 108 bars, with such a degree of security and power, so firmly, cogently, tersely and yet so freely, grandly, wonderfully – that one cannot study the score without joyful admiration, or hear the work without the greatest enthusiasm.[40]

Carl Maria Brand comments in the same vein that 'this powerfully driving current does not hesitate even for a moment, always keeps the distant goal in view; who cannot believe this to be a symbol of the unwaveringly firm belief that Haydn here indicates with both hands?'[41] One need only add that the fugue theme itself is unique,[42] with its dotted rhythm on '[ven-]tu-ri sae-cu-li' and cross-accent on 'A-men'; its vitality combines with the 'running' quaver bass, flashing semiquaver tremolo violins and 'wide-leap', syncopated countersubject to create an entire textural world, to which the trumpets add thematic statements and fanfares, including a climax on c^3 at the end in conjunction with the choral climax on a^2 (bar 382). It is not merely the energy, kaleidoscopically changing textures and the local harmonic directedness that never flag; the overall form as well is coherent throughout. Among other things, this fugue contains a veritable compendium of sequences, including an amazing fourfold structure in bars 327–52 that touches on 'all possible' related keys and yet never loses its goal-directedness.[43]

Rochlitz and Brand write from another age; neither possessed a vocabulary with which to describe the through-compositional function of

[40] *Allgemeine musikalische Zeitung* 30 (April 1808), cols. 472–3; quoted from Brand, *Die Messen*, p. 93.

[41] Brand, *Die Messen*, p. 91. More recent appreciations, such as that by Landon, *Chronicle and Works II*, pp. 231–2, are clearly inspired by those quoted here.

[42] MacIntyre, personal communication; compare *The Viennese Concerted Mass*, Ex. 8–19, pp. [415–16].

[43] To be precise: bars 327–32, 332–42, 342–6, 345–52 (with a subtle overlapping in 345–6) – not to mention the preceding vast sequence of thematic entries, bars 306–27.

Example 2.6a *Te Deum*, third movement, bars 123–9

Haydn's fugue as the climax of the entire Credo. But they understood something without which all technical exegesis would fail: its effect can be described (if at all) only in a language of superlatives.

*

Haydn's late *Te Deum*[44] comprises three movements, in an ABA', fast–slow–fast pattern: a freely constructed sonata-form movement; a short middle movement in the minor; and a two-part conclusion. The long text is declaimed with such vigour and economy that the work lasts barely eight minutes in a good performance, even though it finds room for a double fugue and a substantial coda on the last two lines. At the beginning, Haydn quotes the eighth psalm-tone (in the form G–A–C–C–C–C–D–C), which, although partially hidden during the orchestral introduction,

---

[44] This work has not yet appeared in *JHW*. There are two modern critical editions, by H. C. Robbins Landon in Diletto Musicale (Vienna, 1959) and by Denis McCaldin (Oxford: Oxford University Press, 1992); and two good recordings in historical style, one with the English Concert and Choir conducted by Trevor Pinnock (Archiv 423–097–2), the other with the Tölzer Knabenchor and Tafelmusik conducted by Bruno Weil (Sony SK 66–260). An appreciation, with extensive examples, can be found in Landon, *Chronicle and Works IV: Haydn: The Years of The Creation, 1796–1800* (London: Thames and Hudson, 1977), pp. 604–15.

Example 2.6b *Te Deum*, third movement, bars 169–73 and 180–93

becomes overwhelming in the choral entry, in powerful octaves.[45] Again he singles out key 'little' words for rhetorical emphasis. In the initial 'Te Deum laudamus' (We praise Thee, O Lord) the initial 'Te' is twice stated out of context, both rhythmically and in that it enters on C (that is, *before* the psalm-tone fragment). In the dominant key, 'tibi' alone becomes a subject for imitation (bars 21–3); and at the recapitulation (bar 59) the 'Tu' of 'Tu Rex gloriae' (Thou, King of glory) is treated like the initial 'Te'. In the third movement the 'nos' of 'sine peccato nos custodire' (Guard us from sin) is similarly emphasized (see Ex. 2.6a), while near the end an almost identical effect appears on 'non' in 'non confundar in aeternum' (Let me not be confounded for ever; Ex. 2.6b).

The three movements are run on: the opening movement breaks off on a dominant seventh to prepare the shattering unison C that begins the minor-mode 'Te ergo quaesumus' (compare the beginning of the 'Representation of Chaos' in *The Creation*), which in turn cadences by elision into the final movement. But a more subtle through-compositional point involves the two passages just quoted. Landon justly praises the conclusion (Ex. 2.6b), with its disorientating imitative syncopations on 'confundar',

---

[45] Haydn's first intention had been to begin immediately with the chorus; that is, with what is now bar 9.

Example 2.6b (*cont.*)

which die away *piano*, until the sudden outburst on 'non' and the headlong rush to the climax. The latter, a marvel of terseness, comprises additional syncopations on 'confundar' (now diatonic), leading to a powerful homophonic cadence, and a tonic pedal plus long-held notes on '[ae-]ternum'.[46]

---

[46] Compare Michael Haydn, as quoted in note 23. Such abrupt endings are characteristic of Haydn's invocations of sublimity in late vocal works; see below, p. 67.

Example 2.6b (*cont.*)

These elements relate to processes that reach back into the opening movement. Although the exposition (bars 9–38) is metrically neutral, in the middle section (bars 38–58) *fz* syncopations appear throughout in the violins (initially g^2 in bar 39); in the climactic double fugue similar syncopations dominate all the countersubjects and thus lead directly into the coda. In addition, however, this passage is subtly prepared by the one given as Ex. 2.6a: the implicitly syncopated diminished-seventh leap in the soprano in bar 127, directly following 'nos', anticipates the explicitly syn-copated vocal bass in bar 180, directly preceding 'non' (Ex. 2.6b; compare the beginning of the same passage in bars 169–70, where the relationship is much more audible). Indeed, the two diminished-seventh chords are enharmonically equivalent: just as 'non' in bar 183 is almost identical to 'nos' in bar 127 (a seventh-chord fermata supporting f^2 in the soprano), so is the larger motivic context. The 'only' difference is that whereas in bars 127 and 169–82 we were in the minor and on a diminished-seventh chord – in fear of sin and confusion – now we are on the diatonic home dominant seventh and will precisely *not* be confounded: we are saved, as we enter eternity in a blaze of C major.

*

I will discuss Haydn's last completed composition, the 'Harmoniemesse' of 1802, in the context of the musical sublime. Whereas a traditional, 'rhetorical' sense of the sublime had often been applied to vocal music and even to the symphony in the mid-eighteenth century,[47] a newer sense developed in the period bounded roughly by the mid-1780s and the death of Beethoven: in Mozart's and Haydn's late orchestral music, in *Don Giovanni* and *Die Zauberflöte*, in Beethoven's 'heroic phase' and, later, the *Missa Solemnis* and the Ninth Symphony.[48] Squarely in the middle of this repertory, both chronologically and substantively, stand Haydn's late Masses and oratorios, in which the sublime is a central aesthetic element.[49]

The primary artistic resource associated with the sublime is *incommensurability*. In Haydn such effects (not surprisingly) are engen-

---

[47] Carl Dahlhaus, 'E. T. A. Hoffmanns Beethoven-Kritik und die Ästhetik des Erhabenen', *Almanach für Musikwissenschaft* 38 (1981), 79–92; Bathia Churgin, 'The Symphonies as Described by J. A. P. Schulz: A Commentary and Translation', *Current Musicology* 29 (1980), 7ff.

[48] See Sisman, 'Learned Style and the Rhetoric of the Sublime in the "Jupiter" Symphony', in Stanley Sadie, ed., *Wolfgang Amadé Mozart: Essays on his Life and his Music* (Oxford: Oxford University Press, 1996), pp. 213–38; Michel Garda, *Musica sublime: Metamorfosi di un'idea nel Settecento musicale* (Milan: Ricordi and Lucca: Libreria musicale italiana, 1995) – I thank Dr Garda for supplying me with this volume immediately upon publication. Surprisingly, neither study pays any attention to sacred vocal music, which in the later eighteenth century was still the natural location (as it were) for the musical sublime.

[49] Webster, 'The *Creation* and the Sublime', initial section.

dered primarily by musical contrast. However, mere contrast does not suffice to create sublime effects; rather, it must occur in an unusual and exposed context, or its elements appear simultaneously or in an unusual or 'pointed' combination. Previously, Haydn's most common location for such effects had been the slow introduction, especially in the London symphonies, where he avoids clear melodies and periodic phrasing in favour of short, irregular phrases and contrasting motifs, juxtaposed in unexpected or apparently incommensurable ways.

As is well known, many of Haydn's Kyries begin with slow initial sections that in some respects resemble such introductions.[50] The Kyrie of the 'Harmoniemesse', although a single-tempo sonata form, begins with a rather long, slow (Poco adagio) orchestral introduction (see Ex. 2.7). In the first eight bars contrast is ubiquitous: soft vs. loud, diatonic vs. chromatic (the unexpected G♭ in the fifth bar) and so forth. To be sure, things then proceed less disruptively, until, in the middle of a quiet descending sequence in the winds, the entire chorus and very large orchestra burst in *fortissimo*, on a completely unexpected diminished-seventh chord. This 'gestural shock' subsides at once, but this only enhances the sublime effect: like a thunderbolt (the characteristic rhetorical trope for the sublime), it is as astonishing as it is inexplicable, and it resonates long afterwards, both in our inner ear and in its consequences for the music.[51]

Another class of sublime passage comprises tonal and generic discontinuities or disruptions. These differ from gestural shocks primarily in that they seem to function on a larger scale: for example, in an unexpected and violent contrast between entire movements. The 'Agnus Dei' of the 'Harmoniemesse' begins in the remote key of G major, which eventually works its way around to the dominant of G minor. Here, the *pianissimo* close is run on without pause to a *fortissimo* outburst on D in the winds and brass, which leads to the 'Dona nobis' (see Ex. 2.8). Although the tonal transition is not unusual (D is the common tone between the dominant of

---

[50] However, most writers on Haydn's late Masses overstate their closeness to his London symphonies, presumably owing (yet again) to the exaggerated prestige of instrumental music (and especially of sonata form).

[51] Note the gestural similarity between this choral entry and that in the *Salve regina* in G minor (see Ex. 2.2). In his late music it also appears even in lieder; for example 'O tuneful voice' and 'She never told her love'.

Example 2.7 'Harmoniemesse', Kyrie, bars 1–8 and 14–18

G and the tonic B flat), this outburst is at once astonishing and confusing. The dominant of G is stripped down to its root; after three bars F is added on top, but the sonority is still incomplete; only after three more bars do the chorus and strings enter, on a complete B flat triad. However, the most startling stroke (literally) is in the timpani, which anticipate this act of completion by entering on B♭ one bar before the chorus. This at once grounds the passage in what we instantaneously know must be the tonic, yet – because the timpani are both indistinct in pitch and enter 'too soon' – we cannot at first quite grasp.[52] Surely Haydn intended this overwhelming moment as an invocation of revelation – of the Last Judgement.[53]

5

Haydn himself understood his late sacred vocal music in terms of the sublime.[54] The 'Representation of Chaos' from *The Creation* is not merely a programmatic overture, but the initial member of a larger process whose completion points beyond itself, which begins in mystery and ends in triumph with the creation of Light. The sublime carries through *into* the light, uniting instrumental and vocal music in expressing the idea of the origins of the universe and of history. This musical process had the broadest and deepest sources in, and reverberations through, European culture.[55] Similarly, the final chorus of *The Seasons*, after leading to a fugue that interprets a textual prayer for strength in terms of doubt – it is based on a difficult, implicitly dissonant subject and is densely argued – suddenly opens out, sooner than we expect and yet with unimaginable breadth and power, on to a plain subdominant, the portal to the heavenly gates through which we are about to pass.[56] As in the ending of the *Te Deum*, the final cadence follows immediately, with breathtaking swiftness. This too is a hallmark of Haydn's dynamic sublime: the goal, whether it is salvation or the Last Judgement, comes at the end, abruptly, as something both teleologically ordained and experienced.

Thus Haydn's two great oratorios (collectively) begin with the creation of the world and end with a musical image of the end – of salvation. These works (especially *The Creation*) actually created history; they helped create music's new-found status as the highest and most Romantic art, albeit in a form that at the same time maintained its traditional aesthetic

---

[52] However different they may be in character, I cannot help noting the analogy between this 'premature' entry and that of the horn at the recapitulation of the first movement of the 'Eroica' Symphony.

[53] Haydn often singles out the word 'judicare' for special treatment.

[54] As in note 13.

[55] See Hans-Jürgen Horn, 'Fiat lux: Zum kunsttheoretischen Hintergrund der "Erschaffung" des Lichtes in Haydns Schöpfung', *Haydn-Studien* 3 (1973–4), 65–84.

[56] Webster, 'The *Creation* and the Musical Sublime', penultimate section.

Example 2.8 'Harmoniemesse', Agnus Dei, bars 41–53

function as mimesis. Although his late Masses and other church works were subject to the constraints of their liturgical contexts and of generic traditions, they were driven by the same urges and exhibit the same fervour. From this perspective, Haydn's late triumphs can themselves almost seem sublime, both in elementary human terms and in the course of history. They became the touchstone of an entire music-historical period: a period for which we have no name, because it links, rather than divides, the Enlightenment and Romanticism. We could do worse than to think of the entire great flowering of music between 1780 and 1815 as the age of Haydn's sublime. In Haydn's own mind, however, the governing image in these works was that of salvation. His achievement was to create convincing musical expressions of its realization.

Example 2.8 (*cont.*)

3 Sentiment and sensibility in *La vera costanza*

JESSICA WALDOFF

Although Haydn is not best remembered as an opera composer, one of his chief responsibilities while in the service of Prince Esterházy was the composition, direction and production of opera. During this period he composed sixteen Italian operas (of which eleven survive) for première at Eszterháza, as well as several operas for the Castle's marionette theatre. He twice witnessed the completion of a splendid opera house at Eszterháza: the original theatre was built in 1768 and opened with Haydn's *Lo speziale*, but burned to the ground in 1779; it was rebuilt and reopened in 1781 with Haydn's *La fedeltà premiata*, which was composed specially for the event. While operas had been staged at Eszterháza only on an occasional basis during the first half of Haydn's tenure there, in 1776 the Prince initiated a regular season that rivalled those of opera houses in major European centres. Haydn served as the director of this venture, helping to select, cast and produce (adapting where necessary) an enormous repertory of contemporary works. Indeed, when asked in the same year to submit an autobiographical letter to *Das gelehrte Österreich*, an Austrian literary journal, Haydn neglected to mention any of his symphonies, sonatas or quartets by name, choosing instead to present himself as a composer of vocal music with several operas to his credit:

> *Inter alia* the following compositions of mine have received the most approbation:
>
> The operas — *Le pescatrici*
> *L'incontro improvviso*
> *L'infedeltà delusa*, performed in the presence of Her Imperial and Royal Majesty [Maria Theresa].
>
> The oratorio   *Il ritorno di Tobia*, performed in Vienna.

70

The *Stabat mater*, about which I received (through a good friend) a testimonial of our great composer Hasse, containing quite undeserved eulogiums.[1]

To enhance the picture of himself as a successful composer of large vocal works, he observes that his compositions have been performed in Vienna, recognized by royalty and praised by the celebrated Hasse. Haydn's desire to present himself as a composer of vocal music, especially opera, could not be more clear. Over the next fifteen years he conducted over one hundred operas, many of which received multiple repetitions in a single season. For example, in 1783 – the year in which Joseph II spared no expense in establishing the famous Italian opera troupe in Vienna that included Francesco Benucci, Nancy Storace and Michael Kelly (and in which Mozart eagerly sought an opera commission to no avail) – Haydn conducted 105 performances of ten different operas at Eszterháza, including nine performances of his own *La fedeltà premiata* and nineteen of his *Orlando Paladino*.[2]

Of all Haydn's operas, *La vera costanza*, which was composed for the 1778/9 season, is perhaps the one that best reveals his immersion in the late eighteenth-century culture of sentiment and sensibility. The opera is based on a libretto of Francesco Puttini, which was then circulating in the setting by Pasquale Anfossi that had premiered in Rome in 1776. When Haydn and his associates chose this libretto for Eszterháza, they must have been well

---

[1] H. C. Robbins Landon, *Haydn: Chronicle and Works II: Haydn at Eszterháza, 1766–1790* (Bloomington: Indiana University Press, 1978), p. 398 (translation adapted). The clause 'performed in the presence of Her Imperial and Royal Majesty' appears in the original to the right of *L'incontro improvviso*, but it was in fact *L'infedeltà delusa* that was performed before the Empress in 1773 (see Landon, *Haydn: Chronicle and Works II*, p. 398, n. 9, and *Joseph Haydn: Gesammelte Briefe und Aufzeichnungen. Unter Benützung der Quellensammlung von H. C. Robbins Landon*, ed. Dénes Bartha (Kassel: Bärenreiter, 1965), p. 81, n. 17).

[2] Dénes Bartha, 'Haydn's Italian Opera Repertory at Eszterháza Palace', in William W. Austin, ed., *New Looks at Italian Opera: Essays in Honor of Donald J. Grout* (Ithaca, NY: Cornell University Press, 1968), pp. 194–5; see also Dénes Bartha and László Somfai, eds., *Haydn als Opernkapellmeister: Die Dokumente der Esterházy-Opernsammlung* (Budapest: Verlag der Ungarischen Akademie der Wissenschaften, 1960).

aware of Anfossi's setting, which had already enjoyed success both in Italy and abroad.[3] Indeed, the tenor who took the part of Count Errico in the Esterházy company, Andrea Totti, had sung Anfossi's role in the Venice production at the S. Moisè Theatre in 1776.[4] Many modern commentators have complained that the opera is hindered by poorly drawn characters and the slow progression of an unlikely plot. They believe, as H. C. Robbins Landon and David Wyn Jones do, that 'Haydn's choice [of libretto] was not a happy one and [that] the textual changes made by Pietro Travaglia, the Eszterháza set designer, stopped short of rectifying its deficiencies'.[5] But I intend to argue that the merits of Haydn's choice are many. Chief among these is the fact that the story of *La vera costanza* is a sentimental one, and as such it properly centres on a heroine of low birth, a fisherwoman, Rosina, whose virtue triumphs in the end when her constancy is recognized and rewarded. The similarities between this story and that of Samuel Richardson's wildly popular *Pamela, or Virtue Rewarded* are quite transparent.

Haydn and his collaborators must also have been aware of the vogue for 'Pamela' operas that followed the unprecedented success of Richardson's sentimental novel (first published in 1740), both in England and on the Continent. Operas based loosely on this novel held the stage from Piccinni's *La buona figliuola* (1760), which is based on the libretto Goldoni adapted directly from the English novel, through Anfossi's *La finta*

[3] There is no truth to Dies' colourful theory that *La vera costanza* was written at the request of the Emperor for production in Vienna as early as 1777 (according to Griesinger) or 1776 (according to Pohl). See Horst Walter, 'On the History of the Composition and the Performance of *La vera costanza*', in Jens Peter Larsen, Howard Serwer and James Webster, eds., *Haydn Studies: Proceedings of the International Haydn Conference, Washington, D. C., 1975* (New York: Norton, 1981), pp. 154–7, and the Preface to his edition in *JHW*.

[4] See Claudio Sartori, *I libretti italiani a stampa dalle origini al 1800* (Cuneo: Bertola & Locatelli, 1990–), nos. 24607 (Eszterháza, 1779) and 18582 (Venice, 1776) (pp. 460 and 418 respectively). Daniel Heartz suggests that Barbara Ripamonti, who created the role of Rosina in Haydn's opera in 1779 and again in 1785, had also played in the Venetian production in 1776; see *Haydn, Mozart, and the Viennese School: 1740–1780* (New York: Norton, 1995), p. 395. But neither *JHW* nor the 1776 Venice libretto (*La pescatrice fedele*), or any other source, seems to confirm Ripamonti's participation.

[5] H. C. Robbins Landon and David Wyn Jones, *Haydn: His Life and Music* (Bloomington: Indiana University Press, 1988), p. 123.

giardiniera (1774) – based on the same libretto Mozart set in 1775 – to Paisiello's *Nina* (1790).[6] Piccinni's opera, the first and most successful of the 'Pamela' subgenre, had by 1790 received over seventy different productions in Italian, English, French and German. (Indeed, *La buona figliuola* was performed at Eszterháza in 1776 and 1778.) True to contemporary values, these operas centre on the moral worth rather than social status of the individual and represent, in the words of Mary Hunter, 'the virtue of constancy and its eventual reward' which constitutes the moral focus of all 'Pamela' operas.[7] Viewed in this way, Haydn's and Travaglia's choice of libretto proves to be a 'happy one' indeed, offering a modish plot centring on a sentimental heroine, a theme that expresses the concerns and ideals of the age of sensibility more generally and a chance to compose in the new sentimental singing style (which I will come to below). The result is a compelling portrait of the familiar sentimental heroine that makes a departure from earlier realizations of the type, and that illustrates particularly well Haydn's sensitivity to matters of plot and characterization.

In order to situate Haydn's *La vera costanza* in both the immediate context of the popular 'Pamela' operas and the larger context of the cult of sensibility, it is necessary to consider the critical reception of this and other Haydn operas. The prejudice against Haydn's operas has been too deep and the perception that he was a poor dramatist too widespread for either to be discounted without due consideration. The uncomfortable legacy of these misconceptions has been to inhibit analysis of these works, and for this reason it seems both necessary and appropriate, especially in a book of this kind, to attempt to dispel some of the familiar notions about Haydn the opera composer.

Haydn the dramatist?

The facts of Haydn's situation at Eszterháza offer us a portrait of a dramatist who was at this time fundamentally involved in opera at every level – from the selection and adaptation of repertory to the demands of

---

[6] See Mary Hunter, '"Pamela": The Offspring of Richardson's Heroine in Eighteenth-Century Opera', *Mosaic* 18/4 (1985), 61–76. Although Paisiello's first setting of *Nina* dates from 1789, it was the enlarged, two-act version of 1790 that became popular throughout Europe.   [7] *Ibid.*, 67.

mounting productions one after another during the season to the challenge of composing new operas for his theatre, at a rate of one each year. Posterity, however, has not chosen to remember Haydn as a composer and director of opera. This position is summed up succinctly by Christoph-Hellmut Mahling:

> Naturally Haydn *also* composed opera, but he probably never considered himself primarily an opera composer. . . . Otherwise he surely would have applied himself more intensively to opera. . . . Unlike Gluck or Mozart, he never felt compelled to participate in the public musical life of the day as an opera composer, let alone to succeed in it. This is reflected both in the form and the design of his operas, as well as in the types he preferred.[8]

The implications are that Haydn composed opera without real commitment to the genre (which seems at the very least unlikely), that he had no desire for public recognition of his achievement (which we know was not the case) and finally that his operas are in some way different. To a certain extent this long-held view may be regarded as understandable, if unfortunate. The study of Haydn's operas has been conducted primarily in the shadows of his own instrumental music, where his dramatic instincts go unchallenged, and the operas of Mozart and Gluck. Neither critical context has served Haydn well.

His operas have also suffered from the fact that his celebrated London symphonies, *The Creation* and *The Seasons*, not to mention many other of his best-known compositions, post-date his operatic career at Eszterháza. It is particularly regrettable that his last opera, *L'anima del filosofo, ossia Orfeo ed Euridice* (1791), commissioned for the King's Theatre during his first trip to London, was never performed. If this production had reached the stage, opera might have played a role in the international acclaim the two London trips brought Haydn and perhaps have appealed to scholars for this reason. But the most damaging effect on our view of Haydn's operas has been caused by the inevitable comparisons with Mozart and Gluck (and their well-established traditions of criticism and appreciation). 'If you judge Haydn's operas by Mozartian or Gluckian criteria', Andrew Porter suggests, 'they cannot stand up to that competition'.[9] Yet many critics who

---

[8] See 'Haydn as an Opera Composer', discussion in *Haydn Studies* (see note 3), pp. 257–8. [9] *Ibid.*

readily acknowledge Mozart's supremacy make the comparison anyway. For example, Marc Vignal attempts to secure second place for Haydn: 'the only relevant point left seems to me to ask whether there is, in the late eighteenth century, anything nearer to those sublime masterpieces [Mozart's operas] than *La fedeltà premiata*, written well before'.[10] Landon, on the other hand, transforms the inevitable comparison with Mozart by imagining, contrary to Harold Bloom, that the elder(!) composer suffered under the anxiety of influence. 'There seems little doubt', he writes, transferring the critics' discomfort to Haydn himself, 'that Haydn's decision to stop writing operas after *Armida* was in part caused by the emergence of Mozart as the supreme operatic composer of the time'.[11] Not content with second place for Haydn, Eva Badura-Skoda goes the furthest in imagining a way in which Haydn might attain the premier position: '*If Mozart had not lived*, I would say that Haydn, not Gluck, was the greatest opera composer of the second half of the eighteenth century' (emphasis mine).[12]

But this repeated comparison of Haydn's operas with those of Mozart and Gluck is not so much inappropriate as ill-conceived. The problems engendered by this view are several. First is the widely held notion that Haydn is a poor dramatist. 'The first master dramatist among symphonists and string quartet writers of the Classical period', writes Peter Branscombe (with Caryl Clark), 'reveals limited feeling for the ebb and flow of dramatic action and symphonic build-up in his works written for the stage'.[13] Georg Feder suggests that the success of the operas lies not in the sphere of drama but 'rather in the music and the theatrical effectiveness of many individual scenes';[14] Landon and Jones assert that Haydn was 'a composer who lacked an overwhelming dramatic instinct'.[15] However, several of the charges levelled at Haydn – long stretches of recitative, the conflict between action and

[10] Marc Vignal, '*La Fedeltà Premiata* in Holland (1970)', *Haydn Yearbook* 8 (1971), 298.

[11] H. C. Robbins Landon, 'The Operas of Haydn', in Egon Wellesz and Frederick Sternfeld, eds., *The New Oxford History of Music VII: The Age of Enlightenment, 1745–1790* (London: Oxford University Press, 1973), p. 196.

[12] 'Haydn as an Opera Composer', p. 256.

[13] S. v. 'Haydn', II, *The New Grove Dictionary of Opera*, p. 676.

[14] Georg Feder, 'Einige Thesen zu dem Thema: Haydn als Dramatiker', *Haydn-Studien* 2 (1969–70), 130.

[15] Landon and Jones, *Haydn: His Life and Music*, p. 136.

a long succession of arias, the uncritical acceptance of a third act that was usually shorter and far less consequential to the drama than the previous two – are not unique to Haydn and Eszterháza but common to all *opere buffe* of this period. Insertion arias, revisions and additions to the operas in the repertory attest to Haydn's knowledge of and interest in operatic drama.

The second supposed problem is the selection of librettos. With notable exceptions made for the three Goldoni librettos that Haydn set (*Lo speziale* [1768], *Le Pescatrici* [1770] and *Il mondo della luna* [1777]), it is generally thought that Haydn and his collaborators neither chose good libretti nor adapted them well. In the case of *La vera costanza*, for example, Landon and Jones claim that the libretto required alteration (which it did not receive): 'Much of the action is slow-moving as well as complex, too much motivation is taken on trust, and above all, the dialogue lacks the sparkle and wit typical of Goldoni and Coltellini'.[16] But it seems to have been the practice of Haydn and his collaborators to accept libretti as they came, making only those changes absolutely necessary for production at Eszterháza. There is no question that all the libretti chosen had been successfully set by other composers and had already proved their dramatic viability elsewhere. Extensive revisions were apparently not thought to be necessary and Haydn's practice in this matter needs to be viewed in the context of eighteenth- rather than twentieth-century taste and expectations.

The third and most complex problem is that of the particular performance circumstances at Eszterháza, which set Haydn's operas apart from those of his contemporaries in terms of venue, as well as matters of form and style. Haydn writes, or so the myth goes, in 'isolation' for the tastes of his Prince and with neither the anxieties nor the particular requirements of a metropolitan house, its singers and its audience. Here, for example, is Landon:

> When talking about his operas to his biographer Dies, Haydn once said that they were all rather long. 'Nothing was too lengthy for my Prince', he added. This is, indeed, typical . . . in the quiet evenings at Eszterháza there was time to sing long, beautifully worked-out *adagio* arias, delicately orchestrated

---

[16] *Ibid.*, p. 123. The libretto is in fact very little changed from the version upon which it is based, the Venice libretto of 1776.

with intricate string writing and soft woodwind colour. There was time for many arias, which succeeded one another in profusion. Yet this prodigious length could bring the action to a standstill dramatically.[17]

Haydn himself appears to attest to these difficulties in the well-known letter of 1787 to the commissariat in Prague, Franz Roth, in which he responds to a request for one of his operas:

> You ask me for an *opera buffa*. Most willingly, if you want to have one of my vocal compositions for yourself alone. But if you intend to produce it on the stage at Prague, in that case I cannot comply with your wish, because all my operas are far too closely tied to our personnel (at Eszterháza in Hungary), and moreover they would not produce the proper effect, which I calculated according to local conditions. It would be quite another matter if I were to have the great good fortune to compose a brand new libretto for your theatre. But even then I should be risking a good deal, for scarcely any man can brook comparison with the great Mozart.[18]

Haydn seems to confirm the difficulties modern-day critics have assumed by making a point of the fact that the operas were written specially for the circumstances at Eszterháza. What is more, Haydn appears to contribute to the notion that his operas cannot bear comparison with Mozart's. But before jumping to that conclusion, one ought to recall the rest of the letter:

> If I could only impress on the soul of every friend of music, and on high personages in particular, how inimitable are Mozart's works, how profound, how musically intelligent, how extraordinarily sensitive! (for this is how I understand them, how I feel them) – why then the nations would vie with the each other to possess such a jewel within their frontiers. Prague should hold the dear man fast – but should reward him too. . . . It enrages me to think that this incomparable Mozart is not yet engaged by some imperial or royal court! Forgive me if I lose my head: but I love the man so dearly.[19]

---

[17] Landon, 'The Operas of Haydn', p. 191.

[18] Landon, *Chronicle and Works II*, p. 702 (translation adapted); *Gesammelte Briefe*, pp. 185–6. Given that this letter appears to confirm the notion that Haydn's operas cannot bear comparison with Mozart's, it is worth remembering that the autograph for this letter does not survive and that the oldest surviving source for it is Franz Niemetschek's biography of Mozart (Prague: Herrlische Buchhandlung, 1798).   [19] *Ibid.* (translation adapted).

Here Haydn reveals his concern that his talented friend has been unable to find a permanent position and his expressions of admiration and exasperation are equally heartfelt. Given that the year is 1787, that Haydn has not written any new operas since *Armida* (1783), that he does not need a commission from Prague and that he writes so effusively about Mozart with a particular purpose, his comparison of what he could write for a metropolitan centre like Prague and what Mozart could write may not mean exactly what the single line 'scarcely any man can brook comparison with the great Mozart' would seem to imply.

In an earlier letter of 1781, written at a time when Haydn was actively engaged in the composition of opera, his attitude was very different. He writes to Artaria in response to the success of his *Stabat mater* in Paris and implies precisely the success his operas might find if only they could be performed in one of the great European centres:

> They were amazed to find me so exceptionally pleasing in vocal
> composition, but I am not amazed, and they have heard nothing yet; if only
> they could hear my Operette [meaning his short opera] *L'isola disabitata*
> and my most recently composed opera, *La fedeltà premiata*, for I assure you
> that such work has not yet been heard in Paris, and perhaps not in Vienna
> either. My misfortune is that I live in the country.[20]

This letter is reminiscent of one Mozart sent to his father two years later (in 1783), expressing his own frustration with the scene in Vienna and his eagerness to write an Italian opera: 'Well, the Italian opera buffa has started here again and is very popular. . . . But indeed I should dearly love to show what I can do in an Italian opera!'.[21] There is no reason why we should so readily accept Mozart's desire to write opera but question Haydn's. As for Haydn's letters of 1787 and 1781, the truth probably lies somewhere in between the very different implications of the two. By the end of his life, as reported by Georg August Griesinger, the isolation Haydn complains of in the early letter ('My misfortune is that I live in the country') appears

---

[20] The translation is taken from Heartz, *Haydn, Mozart, and the Viennese School*,
p. 399. See also Landon, *Chronicle and Works II*, p. 447; *Gesammelte Briefe*,
pp. 96–7.

[21] 7 May 1783; *The Letters of Mozart and his Family*, trans. and ed. Emily
Anderson, 3rd edn, ed. Stanley Sadie and Fiona Smart (London: Macmillan,
1985), p. 847.

differently to him: 'I was set apart from the world, there was nobody in my vicinity to confuse and annoy me in my course, and so I had to become original'.[22] The implied relationship between isolation (freedom from influence) and originality has become crucial to our perception of his musical genius. And it might be argued that this isolation benefited the operas as well.[23] The extent to which Haydn in 1787 viewed his operas as inferior to Mozart's or to those of any of his contemporaries is impossible to determine. But it would be interesting to know what Haydn's response would have been if he had received the letter from the commissariat in 1781.

One cannot help noticing the irony here, since it is Mozart's 'mature' operas that have been made the standard for Haydn's, all but one of which were produced earlier, between 1762 and 1782. Obviously, Haydn could not have been influenced in the 1770s by what had not yet been written. And yet it is in comparison to these later works of Mozart's that Haydn's operas are seen to fail in matters of plot, verse, dramatic action, tonal planning and so on. But surely nothing in Haydn is more implausible than *Così fan tutte* or longer in performance than the uncut version of *Le nozze di Figaro*. Indeed, one remembers that *Così* has not always been regarded as one of Mozart's greatest works, that critics long believed the story of *Die Zauberflöte* and the dramatic action of *La clemenza di Tito* (with its long succession of arias) to be untenable, and that most eighteenth-century operas are cut (including *Figaro*) before they ever reach the twentieth-century stage, because it is assumed that modern audiences will not stand for the long recitatives and the sheer number of arias.

Still, the question remains – if Mozart's operas are not the appropriate context for studying Haydn's operas, what is? With the recent sea change in the field of late eighteenth-century opera studies and the shift of emphasis from a small core of 'mature' works by Mozart and Gluck to the works of

---

22 Vernon Gotwals, *Joseph Haydn: Eighteenth-Century Gentleman and Genius* (Madison: University of Wisconsin Press, 1963), p. 17; this book is a translation with commentary of Georg August Griesinger's *Biographische Notizen über Joseph Haydn* (Leipzig: Breitkopf und Härtel, 1810) and Albert Christoph Dies' *Biographische Nachrichten von Joseph Haydn* (Vienna: Camesinaische Buchhandlung, 1810).

23 As Pierluigi Petrobelli suggests in 'Goldoni at Eszterháza: The Story of his Librettos set by Haydn', in Eva Badura-Skoda, ed., *Joseph Haydn: Bericht über den Internationalen Joseph Haydn Kongress, 1982* (Munich: Henle, 1986), p. 317.

their contemporaries, there was certainly a chance for Haydn. The goal of this effort, however, has been a more historically informed view of opera altogether in the period. Much of this scholarship now emphasizes the importance of new approaches to genre, questions of historical contexts and cultural (and critical) biases and new information regarding the social, economic and ideological aspects of Mozart's Vienna and other European centres of opera. The gains for opera studies have been tremendous. Given the nature of these developments, however, it becomes clear why the resurgence of interest in Mozart's contemporaries has done comparatively little for Haydn's operas. For they were never a part of the international exchange that shaped the development of opera; they were neither commissioned for nor celebrated in major European centres. Although a few of his operas received performances in Vienna in Italian, and in Pressburg, Budapest, Cologne, Brünn and other cities in German, they remain outside the main developments in opera. And thus if one looks to Haydn's operas to find the influence of Piccinni's *La buona figliuola*, the extraordinary popularity of Paisiello's *Il barbiere di Siviglia* or the grand scale of Martín y Soler's *Una cosa rara*, one looks in vain.

But while Haydn did not play an influential role in the operatic commerce of his day, he certainly benefited from that commerce. He had ample opportunity to familiarize himself with the operas of his day through his visits to Vienna, through his contact with composers and singers, through performing so much of the popular repertory year in and year out at Eszterháza and through the extensive holdings in the Prince's library, which, according to Daniel Heartz, 'provided the equivalent of an international forum'.[24] As Landon points out, Haydn's isolation 'operated in one direction only: Haydn's operas did not get out, but those of everyone else came in'.[25] He knew the operas of his Italian contemporaries intimately. And thus while it is perfectly understandable that those interested in the traffic of Italian opera have overlooked Haydn's works, which for the most part remained close to Eszterháza, it is difficult to understand why more Haydn scholars have not sought to study his works in this larger context.

[24] Heartz, *Haydn, Mozart, and the Viennese School*, p. 400.
[25] Landon, 'The Operas of Haydn', p. 183.

Haydn's 'Pamela' and the cult of sensibility

For students of literature, the importance of Richardson's *Pamela* is well known. Regarded by some as the first true English novel, it tells the story of a young servant girl, Pamela Andrews, who successfully resists her master's repeated attempts to seduce her. She so impresses him with her virtue that he ultimately comes to love her for it and marries her over his sister's objections. First published in 1740, *Pamela* was an immediate success. Its moral mission is acknowledged by the author on the title page: 'to cultivate the Principles of Virtue and Religion in the Minds of the YOUTH of BOTH SEXES'.[26] Within a year the novel was already in its fifth edition; it had been translated into French; it had engendered four plays and several versions in poetry; and it had been answered by such works as John Fielding's parody, *Shamela*. The growing eighteenth-century interest in sentiment had found a heroine in Pamela.

For students of opera, the importance of Richardson's novel is equally great. In her seminal article of 1985, '"Pamela": The Offspring of Richardson's Heroine in Eighteenth-Century Opera', Mary Hunter argues persuasively that Goldoni's and Piccinni's opera of 1760 and other works based, however loosely, on the 'Pamela' story constitute a subgenre of *opera buffa*.[27] In the Prologue to his *The Maid of the Mill* (1765), Isaac Bickerstaffe writes: 'There is scarce a language in Europe, in which there is not a play taken from our romance of Pamela'.[28] These fashionable 'Pamela' operas, in their turn, produced many transformations of the sentimental heroine, including characters outside the 'Pamela' story, such as the Countess in *Figaro*, who make an appeal to sentiment. The influence of the figure of the

---

[26] See the title page for Richardson's *Pamela: or, Virtue Rewarded* (London: C. Rivington in St Paul's Church-Yard and J. Osborn in Pater-noster Row, 1741), reprinted in the Riverside *Pamela*, ed. T. C. Duncan Eaves and Ben D. Kimpel (Boston: Houghton Mifflin, 1971), p. 1. *Pamela* was originally published in 1740.

[27] See Mary Hunter, '"Pamela": The Offspring of Richardson's Heroine'; 'The Fusion and Juxtaposition of Genres in Opera Buffa 1770–1800: Anelli and Piccinni's "Griselda"', *Music and Letters* 67 (1986), 363–80; and 'Some Representations of *opera seria* in *opera buffa*', *Cambridge Opera Journal* 3 (1991), 89–108. See also William C. Holmes, 'Pamela Transformed', *Musical Quarterly* 38 (1952), 581–98.

[28] *The Maid of the Mill: A Comic Opera* (London: printed for J. Newberry *et al.*, 1765). This is one of several English 'Pamela' operas.

sentimental heroine therefore is not restricted to the 'Pamela' operas and may be understood as central to the development of opera more generally in this period. *La vera costanza* offers Haydn's most compelling treatment of the familiar sentimental figure, who poses a question of identity central to the social, economic and ideological concerns of the age of sensibility.[29]

At the same time that various philosophies valued reason and thought as the highest motivators of human acts, the cult of sensibility celebrated instinct and feeling as the primary inducements to virtue. While Hobbes' *Leviathan* (1651) of the previous age had represented man as innately selfish, driven by self-interest and a lust for power, authors of 'sensibility' sought to show that benevolence, sympathy and empathy are innately human and that it is natural to be moved by sentiment to virtuous thoughts and deeds. For these authors, the highest 'sensibility' is accessible to those of noble, middle and lower classes alike, and thus the chambermaid and the garden girl become appropriate subjects for literature. In the new sentimental comedy, as Oliver Goldsmith tells us in 1773, the characters, 'though they want humour, have an abundance of sentiment and feeling'.[30] Notions of pathos in literature go back at least as far as Aristotle's *Poetics*, where drama is celebrated for its ability to move us (and where *peripeteia*, recognition and pathos are named as the three elements of plot). 'What is new in the eighteenth century', however, as Janet Todd tells us, 'is the centrality of sentiment and pathos'.[31] In its day, the exaltation of sentiment was the central goal of much poetry, fiction, drama and music. We must remember that Dr Johnson instructs one to read Richardson 'for the sentiment',[32] and that Rousseau not only represents himself as a man of extreme sensibility in his *Confessions* but includes an entry for 'sensibility' in his music dictionary. The vogue for sensibility was both pervasive and interna-

---

29 Of all Haydn's operatic heroines, Rosina is closest to the 'Pamela' model. Many, however, receive sentimental treatment; of special interest in this context are Eurila in *Le pescatrici*, Costanza in *L'isola disabitata* and Celia in *La fedeltà premiata*.

30 Oliver Goldsmith, 'An Essay on the Theatre: or, A Comparison between Sentimental and Laughing Comedy' (1773), in *Collected Works of Oliver Goldsmith* III, ed. Arthur Friedman (Oxford: Clarendon Press, 1966), p. 212.

31 Janet Todd, *Sensibility: An Introduction* (London: Methuen, 1986), p. 3.

32 James Boswell, *The Life of Samuel Johnson* (London: Penguin, 1986), p. 159.

tional. What is more, it was a part of everyday life. In his *Memoirs* the tenor Michael Kelly – who made his operatic debut in Dublin in 1779 (at the age of fifteen) in a production of *La buona figliuola*, but is better known for having created the roles of Don Basilio and Don Curzio in *Figaro* – describes his parting with Mozart prior to leaving Vienna: 'I could hardly tear myself away from him, and, at parting, we both shed tears'.[33]

It is in this context that the craze for *Pamela* comes to Italy with its translation in 1744–5. Goldoni produces first a drama, *Pamela nubile* (1750), and then a libretto (1756) based on the novel. In the process, he introduces several changes into the story. The Pamela character is renamed Cecchina and given a new occupation, as a garden girl. Her master and suitor, the Marchese, unlike his predecessor Mr B–, has honourable intentions from the first and is loved by her in return. His sister and her noble fiancé, however, are horrified by his affection for one so beneath his station, but a happy resolution is brought about in the end (in a conventional recognition scene), when it is discovered by means of a blue mark on her breast that she is in fact the long-lost daughter of a German nobleman. (Although, in Richardson's England, a servant girl could marry a member of the upper class or even a nobleman and thereby attain his rank and station, in most Italian cities the nobleman, which is what Goldoni translates Richardson's upper-class master into, would forfeit his rank and disgrace his family by such a marriage. This discovery of birthright is therefore crucial to the Italian version of the story, as Goldoni suggests in his preface.[34]) In this way Cecchina's inner nobility, the Marchese's love for her, her sentimental singing style and the desired marriage itself are all legitimized by a discovery of identity.

The astonishing success of Piccinni's opera set off a rage for 'Pamela' operas, which, however different they may be in other respects, share certain essential characteristics:[35] (1) a sentimental heroine who is (or appears to be) of low birth; (2) a central triangle of 'Pamela', her noble suitor

[33] Michael Kelly, *Reminiscences*, ed. Roger Fiske (London: Oxford University Press, 1975), p. 140.

[34] See Goldoni's 'Preface' to *Pamela, Commedia di Carlo Goldoni/Pamela, A Comedy by Charles Goldoni* (London: J. Nourse, 1756).

[35] See Hunter, '"Pamela": The Offspring of Richardson's Heroine' and 'The Fusion and Juxtaposition of Genres' for the arguments summarized here.

Text 3.1ᵃ Cecchina's 'Una povera ragazza' from *La buona figliuola*

(*ottonario*)

Una povera ragazza,	A poor girl,
Padre e madre che non ha,	without father or mother,
Si maltratta, si strapazza . . .	so mistreated, so abused –
Questa è troppa crudeltà.	this is too much cruelty.
Sì, signora, sì, padrone,	Yes, my lady, yes, my master,
Che con vostra permissione	Who, with your permission,
Voglio andarmene di qua.	would like to depart from here.
Partirò . . . me ne andrò	I shall leave . . . but where shall I go
A cercar la carità.	to find pity.
Poverina, la Cecchina,	Poor Cecchina,
Qualche cosa troverà.	where can such a thing be found.
Sì, signore, sì, padrona,	Yes, gentleman, yes, mistress,
So che il Ciel non abbandona	I know that the Heavens have not abandoned
L'innocenza e l'onestà.	innocence and honesty.

ᵃ The translation of this aria is mine. The translations of the arias below (all from Haydn's *La vera costanza*) are adapted from Lionel Salter's translation of the whole libretto, in the liner notes to the Dorati recording (Philips 432 424-2).

and the sister (or other female) who intervenes; (3) a happy ending in which the lovers are united and the virtue of the heroine is recognized and celebrated by all; and, most important, (4) a sentimental singing style for the 'Pamela' figure that sets her apart from the *buffa* style of the lower orders to which she supposedly belongs, as well as from the high style of the *seria* characters. The sentimental singing style is perhaps best exemplified by Piccinni's Cecchina, who is generally regarded as the progenitor of the type. Her music draws upon the traditions of both *seria* and *buffa* but places her in neither category. She retains the nobility of the high style without a hint of its complexity; at the same time she makes a direct and immediate appeal that is neither comic nor simple.[36] Several features of Cecchina's aria, 'Una povera ragazza' (see Text 3.1), are characteristic: the exposed, sweet melody, the andante tempo, the muted strings and the overall effect of the accompaniment – constant in its materials and mood yet at a distinct remove from the voice (see Ex. 3.1). Not all of these characteristics need

[36] See Hunter, '"Pamela": The Offspring of Richardson's Heroine', 66.

be present for a sentimental characterization, of course, but the quality of the melody and its appropriateness to the 'genuine' sentiments expressed may be considered essential to the sentimental style. In the second verse Cecchina turns very effectively to G minor (ii in the tonic of F). The gesture is simple, but the pathos it creates, especially on the words 'Poverina, la Cecchina', must have been one reason for the dramatic success of the number (see bars 15–18).

Since Italian *opera buffa* has a very different origin and *modus operandi* from the epistolary novel, it should not be expected that the sentimental heroine would spring fully formed into Italian opera from the head of Richardson. Two female figures already established in the genres of Italian opera also influence the 'Pamela' figure. The first, drawn from the *commedia dell'arte*, is the scheming servant girl Serpina in Pergolesi's *La serva padrona* (1733), who plots to marry her master. To contemporary audiences, the sentimental heroine must have appeared to be a fully developed, human reincarnation of this comic type. As I am not the first to suggest, this association may have played a role in Goldoni's transformation of Pamela from chamber maid to garden girl, which not only changes the nature of her servitude, but connects her to nature in a highly visible way. The similarities of status and situation are thus made subordinate to important differences, especially the heroine's virtuous nature, allowing the scheming servant girl to become a foil for the 'Pamela' figure. The second female figure related to Pamela, and predating her in Italian opera, is that of the patient Griselda (the subject of many operas from 1701 onwards). Before this opera opens, the peasant (or fisherwoman) Griselda has already married a king (or nobleman), who in the course of the opera puts her through a cruel set of trials to test her virtue and to prove to his fellow noble men and women that she is worthy of being his wife (and their queen, in some versions).

Among many sentimental heroines in late eighteenth-century opera, two became enormously popular and influential and in Table 3.1, I set these two 'Pamelas', Piccinni's Cecchina and Paisiello's Nina, alongside Haydn's Rosina to make clear the crucial differences in their stories. That of the first operatic Pamela, Cecchina, centres on the discovery of hidden identity. Haydn's Rosina merges aspects of the new 'Pamela' and the older Griselda stories, with the heroine married before the opera opens and subjected to the whims and cruelties of her noble husband before her virtue carries the

Example 3.1 Piccinni: *La buona figliuola*, Cecchina, 'Una povera ragazza', bars 4–18

day. The third, that of *Nina*, appears nearer to the end of the century. Though Nina is the daughter of a Count, her virtue is proven by means other than birthright. She is beloved of all the townsfolk and known for her kindness and good deeds. When her father breaks her engagement and shortly afterwards news reaches her that her beloved may be dead, Nina goes mad.[37] When her father relents and her beloved Lindoro reappears,

[37] For a discussion of madness in Dalayrac's *Nina* and Paisiello's *Nina* see Stefano

Example 3.1 (*cont.*)

Nina's sanity is restored. The persistence of the sentimental heroine both in the 'Pamela' operas and in other operas of the period reflects the eighteenth century's confidence in the new idea that human destiny was no longer controlled by birthright, and that all men (and even some women) could attain equality through education, industry and individual merit.

La vera costanza is the first of the group of three *opere semiserie*, including *La fedeltà premiata* (1781) and *Orlando Paladino* (1782), that is generally regarded as marking Haydn's most interesting and complex operatic writing.[38] All three show evidence of the move from comedy towards the popular and more complex ideals of the *dramma giocoso*: all three involve

Castelvecchi, 'From *Nina* to *Nina*: Psychodrama, Absorption and Sentiment in the 1780s', *Cambridge Opera Journal* 8 (1996), 91–112.

[38] For treatments of this opera, among others, see Hunter, *Haydn's Aria Forms: A Study of the Arias in the Operas Written at Eszterháza, 1766–1783* (Ann Arbor: UMI Research Press, 1982), pp. 358–66; Caryl Leslie Clark, 'The Opera Buffa Finales of Joseph Haydn', Ph.D. diss., Cornell University (1991), pp. 163–219; and Reinhard Strohm, 'Zur Metrik in Haydns und Anfossis "La vera costanza"', *Joseph Haydn: Bericht über den Internationalen Joseph Haydn Kongress, 1982*, pp. 279–95.

Table 3.1 Three 'Pamela' figures in late eighteenth-century opera

Cecchina	Griselda	Nina
Examplar of virtue and constancy who is legitimized in the end by the discovery of noble birthright.	Exemplar of virtue and constancy who is of low birth but married (and so legitimized before the opera begins).	Exemplar of virtue of noble birth whose constancy drives her to madness. Her sanity is restored by the return of her lover and her father's consent to their union.

buffa, seria and *mezzo carattere* figures; all feature the new 'sentimental' strain; and all merge *buffa* and *seria* elements in ways that suggest a blurring of social distinctions crucial to the moral message they seek to dramatize. The story of *La vera costanza* centres on Rosina, a virtuous fisherwoman, who was secretly married five years earlier to Count Errico, who then abandoned her. Unbeknownst to him, they have a child. As the opera opens, Errico's aunt, the Baroness Irene, suspects his fondness for Rosina and schemes to prevent the match by marrying the Count to a woman of his own rank and Rosina to the foolish Villotto. The emotional turmoil that ensues tries Rosina's constancy and patience, brings Errico to the point of madness and ultimately leads to a powerful denouement in which he recognizes Rosina's child as his own and (re)discovers his love for her. The quest for identity here is not represented as a matter of disguise or hidden birthright, but rather as a drama of moral constancy and inner nobility that marks a significant shift in the characterization of the sentimental heroine. The first 'Pamela' opera dramatizes a quest for identity that is resolved when inner nobility is confirmed by birthright. Rosina, however, was born a fisherwoman; her nobility is confirmed by her moral character alone.

The difference between the heroine of the Cecchina type and of the Griselda (or Rosina) type leads to a crucial difference in the tale. In Piccinni's setting of the Goldoni libretto, despite the central importance of Cecchina and her effect on the audience, the key to the story and its denouement lies not in her character alone but in the outside confirmation of her identity as defined by birthright and social status. Although she stands at the centre of the opera as an example of 'virtue in distress', she is both visually and musically an object rather than a subject of the plot, more acted upon than acting. In *La vera costanza*, on the other hand, although Rosina is objectified as 'virtue in distress', the key to the story and its denouement lies precisely in her character. The virtuous fisherwoman remains true to herself in the face of adversity, unwilling no matter what the pressures to betray her errant husband, her son or what she believes is right. She is not saved by a convenient plot twist or an accident of birth, but by her own fortitude. She possesses the power not merely to move the audience, but to bring about a much-desired shift in the plot. Sentiment is thus empowered to tap into the sensibility many in the late eighteenth century believed was innately human, to produce clarity from confusion, and finally to set things right both morally and socially. The difference between the two heroines is one of empowerment: while Cecchina is the central object of her story, Rosina is the central agent in hers. It goes without saying that the difference I have just described is located first and foremost in the libretto. But the new possibilities this opens up for the characterization of the sentimental heroine are very great indeed and they are not missed by Haydn.

Haydn's transformation of the sentimental heroine

That Haydn's Rosina, as a sentimental heroine of the lower classes, must be understood in terms of the familiar 'Pamela' type, there can be no doubt. She is also associated, as Cecchina was, with nature in a highly visible way. She is presented at home in natural surroundings, the entire action takes place out of doors and we are told that she was wooed in the mountains, at the seashore and in the forest ('Fuggo allora ogni incontro, egli mi siegue, al monte, alla marina, alla foresta' [recitative before No. 8]). Near the end of Act II, when she has finally resolved to leave with her son to avoid further persecution, she takes her farewell of the shore and the woods in her aria, 'Care spiagge, selve, addio' (No. 30b), addressing nature in the second person as if it were her only friend and neglecting to take any leave of her brother or her confidante Lisetta (see Text 3.2). The stage directions for this aria place Rosina in front of a partly ruined tower – one of the age's favourite symbols for representing nature's power over man. Unlike Rosina's earlier arias (and the rest of the opera), this number is set for strings alone, as was Cecchina's sentimental aria. The slow tempo, the muted strings, the exposed pathetic melody and the 'cantabile' marking all characterize 'Care

Text 3.2 Rosina's 'Care spiagge' from *La vera costanza*

(*ottonario*)

Care spiagge, selve, addio;	Dear shores and woods, farewell;
Io mai più vi rivedrò.	I shall never see you more.
Se vedete l'idol mio,	If you see my beloved,
Dite pur che la Rosina	tell him that poor Rosina
Poverina, se n'andò.	has gone from here.
Ah non pianger, mio tesoro,	Ah, do not weep, my treasure
Che di pena moro, oh Dio,	for I die of grief, oh God,
E resister più non so.	and can resist no longer.

spiagge' as 'sentimental' (see Ex. 3.2). The most affecting phrase of this aria comes at the moment when Rosina describes herself as 'la Rosina poverina'; set off by a fermata, her melodic phrase rises poignantly and cadences in the dominant (see bars 53–60). Cecchina's description of herself as 'Poverina, la Cecchina' in 'Una povera ragazza', it will be remembered, was also especially pathetic, though the effect was achieved by very different musical means (compare Ex. 3.1, bars 15–18).

Rosina's first aria in Act I, 'Con un tenero sospiro', also makes allusions to the sentimental style, though it is more complex than 'Care spiagge'. Rosina has just confided to Lisetta her story of how five years earlier the Count wooed her, married her and left her. Despite his betrayal, Rosina still loves him and her recollection of his affection leads directly to the aria, which begins with her happy memories. The first two verses recall the past, while the third contrasts these happy memories with the harsh reality of the present (see Text 3.3). Anfossi's setting of this text in F major makes an interesting comparison with Haydn's. Anfossi sets the entire text, past and present, in a single tempo (see Ex. 3.3a). He presents new melodic material for each verse and prolongs the arrival in the dominant until Rosina has completed the entire text for the first time. The mood of the third verse is acknowledged by a strong pedal on V of V and a rapid alternation of *piano* and *forte*, and by a preponderance of quavers in the vocal line on the repetitions of 'Che crudel destin spietato: / Che tiranno infido cor!' that seem to suggest Rosina's agitation (see Ex. 3.3b). Anfossi continues with a repetition of the entire text, again emphasizing the third verse, which this time appears over a dominant pedal and cadences (several times) in the tonic.

Example 3.2 *La vera costanza*, Rosina, 'Care spiagge', bars 43–60

Text 3.3 Rosina's 'Con un tenero sospiro' from *La vera costanza*

(*ottonario*)

Con un tenero sospiro,	With a tender sigh
Ah, Rosina, mi diceva;	he said, 'Ah, Rosina!'
E la mano mi stringeva,	and clasped my hand,
Tutto affetto, e tutto ardor.	all affection, all ardour.
Poi con viso languidetto,	Then with a pale face
Con le lagrime sul ciglio	and tears in his eyes,
La baciava con rispetto,	he kissed it with respect,
E spargea di pianto ancor.	and shed more tears.
Come, oh Dio! potè l'ingrato	How, oh God! could the ingrate
Qui lasciarmi in abbandono?	leave me here forsaken?
Che crudel destin spietato:	What a harsh, cruel fate:
Che tiranno infido cor!	what a tyrannical, faithless heart!

Haydn's setting, in A major, portrays the two distinct moods of the text in two tempos: andante (lines 1–8) and allegro (lines 9–12). His attempt here to create a sense of past and present is not unlike Mozart's depiction of the Countess's happy memories in 'Dove sono'. Rosina recalls the happy time when the Count loved her and spoke to her with tenderness. She repeats his words, which Haydn renders with a musical sigh (punctuated by a quaver rest) that multiplies and gains an appoggiatura as Rosina indulges in her memories (see Ex. 3.4a). The second verse moves to the dominant. The third verse (see Ex. 3.4b) represents a sudden return from pleasant recollection to present misery with a *forte* arrival in the new tempo. Rosina now sings an unadorned melody in straight crotchets; as she repeats it, she emphasizes the words 'qui lasciarmi in abbandono' with minims and, with a further repetition of 'Oh Dio, in abbandono', she pauses on a pair of fermatas that elongate 'abbandono'. Lines 11–12 follow with a sudden turn to the parallel minor. (See bars 83ff. in Ex. 3.4b.) Her sense of betrayal is heightened by a diminished-seventh chord on the word 'spietato', the sudden *forte* and the silence created by the fermata that separates these two lines. Haydn now repeats the first verse (text and melody) in the new tempo, which necessarily produces a reinterpretation of the original tune. The third verse, complete with its sudden turn to the minor, is then repeated. Because Haydn does not set the entire third verse in minor, the effect of 'Che

Example 3.3a Anfossi: *La vera costanza*, Rosina, 'Con un tenero sospiro', bars 10–20

Example 3.3b Anfossi: *La vera costanza*, Rosina, 'Con un tenero sospiro', bars 28–52

Example 3.3b (*cont.*)

crudel destin spietato' is all the more striking. A brief comparison of the differences between Haydn's aria, Anfossi's setting of the same text and Piccinni's setting of 'Una povera ragazza' will illustrate nicely the distinction made above regarding the special characterization of Haydn's Rosina as the subject, rather than the object, of her opera.

In 'Una povera ragazza', it will be remembered that the second verse of the aria, in which Cecchina sings her famous line, 'Poverina, la Cecchina', is set in the minor and that the aria presents a sustained pathetic mood. Cecchina does not describe the particular circumstance that threatens her,

Example 3.4a *La vera costanza*, Rosina, 'Con un tenero sospiro', bars 14–26

but presents instead a musical portrait of sweetness, blamelessness and suffering. Her only hope is divine intervention – 'So che il Ciel non abban-dona / L'innocenza e l'onestà' – and her main dramatic task is to appear worthy of it. Anfossi's setting of 'Con un tenero sospiro', though its text speaks of particular events, reveals a similar conception of the sentimental heroine. Anfossi's Rosina, like Cecchina before her, uses the aria to create a sustained impression of her pitiable state. The emotional events of the text are made subordinate to the prevailing mood of the aria; the cohesiveness of the sweet and plaintive Andantino makes an immediate and unproblem-atic claim upon audience sympathy. Haydn's Rosina also makes a claim upon audience sympathy, but she does so by very different means. Haydn's setting does not centre on the goal of creating a pathetic mood.[39] Instead he chooses to dramatize the events of the text, to make them come alive in the

---

[39] Haydn does use the minor for precisely this purpose, elsewhere, however. See, for example, Rosina's transformation of the Baronessa's pastoral melody into the parallel minor at bar 84 of the Act I finale.

Example 3.4b *La vera costanza*, Rosina, 'Con un tenero sospiro', bars 63–90

music and on the stage. Rosina's recollection is sweet, without being 'pathetic'; the Count's words are set off as if she is replaying the scene for us; the shift to the Allegro returns her abruptly to the present; and the sudden turn to the minor at the words 'Che crudel destin spietato' vividly portrays the shock and horror she feels. At the climax of the aria we experience Rosina's sudden awareness of her situation. Haydn uses the minor not to create a mood of pathos for his sentimental heroine, but to dramatize the remembered and psychic events described in the text. Haydn's setting offers a dramatic re-enactment of everything Rosina is feeling and it is her experience as dramatized in the music (and not merely a musical description of her character) that earns her the sympathy of the audience.

Haydn here expands the possible ways of representing the sentimental heroine in music, but in Rosina's Act II aria 'Care spiagge' he relies primarily on the method used to characterize Piccinni's Cecchina, even to the point of employing an exposed setting of the famous 'poverina' phrase in his own aria. The importance of this textual description of the heroine as 'poverina' and its musical depiction is of course crucial to the central theme of both operas. Cecchina and Rosina call upon our sympathies by alluding to the apparent desperation of their situations. Cecchina at this moment has just been informed that she is to be sent away to work for the Marchesa's sister and she is rebuked by her mistress for not being grateful. Rosina believes she has no other hope of avoiding a bigamous marriage to Villotto and her husband's cruel treatment than to flee the only home she has ever known. These women are truly *poverine*. But one recognizes that the 'poverina' type might easily be portrayed as a cliché. One poverina inspires sympathy, but several of them in a season might well begin to suggest comedy rather than pathos. For example, as Don Giovanni eavesdrops on Donna Elvira in 'Ah! chi mi dice mai' (No. 3), he is moved to pity by her story of betrayal and says to Leporello: 'Poverina! Poverina!' The comedy is heightened by the fact that Don Giovanni is the one responsible for putting Elvira into her present pitiable situation and is truly the last person, once he has recognized her, to show her any pity or understanding. On the other hand, Elvira, as a *mezzo carattere* figure, certainly makes a claim on our sympathies and both the nature of her situation and her evident depth of feeling draw on the sentimental type. Mozart and Da Ponte here acknowledge a popular phenomenon with both humour and pathos.

Text 3.4 Lisetta's 'Io son poverina' from *La vera costanza*

(*senario*)

Io son poverina,	I am a poor girl,
Nè ricca nè bella,	neither rich, nor beautiful,
Ma sono buonina,	but I am good-natured,
Son tutta bontà.	I'm all goodness.
Eppur con gli amanti,	Yet with lovers –
Che fiero destino!	how stern a fate! –
Son tanto infelice,	I'm so unlucky,
Non trovo pietà.	I find no pity.
Ingrato Masino,	Ungrateful Masino,
Mi vedi languire,	You see me languishing,
Vuoi farmi morire,	you'd have me die,
Che ria crudeltà!	what wicked cruelty!

Puttini and Haydn, too, make some sport with the 'poverina' type. While Rosina is the true sentimental heroine of *La vera costanza*, Lisetta is clearly aware of the phenomenon and eager to play the role herself. Her very first line, upon stepping out of the boat, is 'Chi mi regge, poverina!' (Who will help me, a poor girl!). Later in Act I, when she is alone with Masino for the first time, she introduces herself to him with the aria 'Io son poverina' (I am just a poor girl). The irony would not have been lost on the elite audience at Eszterháza. To Masino she says, 'I am a poor girl', but to the audience she seems to boast, '*I* am the *poverina*'. In the course of the aria, Lisetta offers a fairly good portrait of the 'poverina' type, though it is coloured by her true *buffa* status in both text and music and by the fact that her description doesn't really fit her own situation (see Text 3.4). Her claims of suffering are surely exaggerated. Masino, though he seems an unwilling suitor, has done nothing to warrant the imagined sufferings of the third verse. The disjunction between her description and the actual state of affairs is heightened by Haydn's setting when he turns to the parallel minor for the third verse. Haydn here exploits the slippage between the reality represented on the stage and the very real fact of the stage, with its character types, suspended disbelief and potential for back-stage rivalries. Both Rosina and Lisetta are of the lower classes, but Rosina is elevated in the opera by her status as *prima donna* and *prima* 'poverina'.

Example 3.5a *La vera costanza*, Lisetta, 'Io son poverina', bars 4–18

Lisetta, on the other hand, is strictly *buffa*. In the course of her only aria, Lisetta betrays not only a knowledge of Rosina's situation – she was the only witness to Rosina's earlier Act I aria, 'Con un tenero sospiro' – but also her awareness of Rosina's status in the larger world of the opera house. She copies the subject matter and shape of a sentimental aria, but several *buffa*

Example 3.5b *La vera costanza*, Lisetta, 'Io son poverina', bars 37–44

features betray her as an impostor (see Ex. 3.5a). She chooses an allegretto, rather than an andante tempo, she slips into patter trying to make her point to Masino on 'son tutta bontà', with special emphasis on the 'tutta', which is sung six times together in rapid succession in semiquavers and then repeated (bars 14ff. in Ex. 3.5a). Later, in framing the contrast between her deserving good nature and her inability to find pity, she again turns to patter, embellishing the text with a great quantity of 'no's to precede 'non trovo pietà'. Her turn to the minor on 'Ingrato Masino' (see Ex. 3.5b) is very moving, as was Cecchina's in 'Una povera ragazza', but while Cecchina used the minor to reflect the real pathos of her situation, and Rosina used it very effectively in the aria Lisetta heard earlier to punctuate the cruelty of her fate (Rosina's phrase climaxes on a diminished seventh, sustained by a fermata), Lisetta uses the minor as simply another tool in her bag of tricks, an allusion to the cruelty she is describing, but has never in fact experienced. When neither her accusations nor their minor setting appear to have the desired effect on Masino, she returns easily to her original strategy, text and melody. Her aria offers neither the evidence of virtuous suffering nor the progression of emotion that Rosina's earlier aria clearly displays. Lisetta, like Sandrina and Paoluccia in *La buona figliuola* and Serpetta in *La finta giardiniera*, is eager to usurp the role of the sentimental heroine (even

101

if only in jest and for the duration of an aria), but these would-be *poverine* serve to remind us that the sentimental heroine was a well-defined and easily recognized type on the late eighteenth-century stage. This sort of sly wit would be unthinkable if the story, the character type and the conventions of the opera house were not understood by all.

Within these conventions, however, Haydn's Rosina, as I have already suggested, marks a significant departure from the earlier 'Pamela' type, one that requires Rosina to take an active role in her own destiny, something Haydn dramatizes effectively in the music. Rosina sings several passages of reflective recitative, which Haydn sets as *accompagnato*; one of these (No. 30a), the recitative directly preceding 'Care spiagge', is even organized by a repeating motif with which Rosina seems to be in dialogue. The Count and Rosina are the only characters in this opera to sing *accompagnato*. In Rosina's case, what this means is that, although she is of low birth, her thoughts are given the texture generally reserved for serious contemplation (and usually for *seria* characters). The pathos of her situation is thus joined by a sense of determination. Nowhere is this more apparent than in her Act II aria, 'Dove fuggo'.

Text 3.5   Rosina's 'Dove fuggo' from *La vera costanza*

(*ottonario*)

A	Dove fuggo, dove m'ascondo,	Where can I flee, where can I hide myself
	Senza aita, e senza scorta?	without help and without guidance?
B	Vado . . . resto . . . mi confondo,	I'll go . . . I'll stay . . . I'm confused.
	Ah non ho chi mi conforta,	Ah, there is no one to comfort me,
	Chi m'uccide per pietà.	no one who will kill me for mercy's sake.
C	E pensando al caro figlio,	And thinking of my dear son,
	Tutta, oh Dio, gelar mi sento:	Oh God! I feel myself freeze.
	Ah che sol per lui pavento,	Ah, only for him do I fear;
	Ah lui sol temer mi fa.	ah, only for him am I afraid.
	Eh si vada;	Oh, I must go –
D	più non teme	this afflicted,
	Un'afflitta sventurata,	unfortunate, reviled, lost soul
	Avvilita, disperata,	has no more to fear
	Del destin la crudeltà.	from the cruelty of fate.

The text of 'Dove fuggo' (see Text 3.5) is in straight *ottonario* and offers a representation of distress and confusion. In lines 1 and 2 Rosina wonders whether to flee. In line 3 she vacillates between going and staying. At line 6 she thinks of her son and her fears for him. At line 10 she makes a decision to go. There is no change in metre at this moment, and her decision could have been obscured or even contradicted by the music. But Haydn chooses to emphasize it, to make this decision the goal of his setting. The aria is in F minor and draws heavily upon the *agitato* topos to create a sense of distress, with repeated driving motifs in the accompaniment and a breathless melody. While often the *aria agitata* is devoted to the representation of a single mood, Haydn sets each new thought in the text to new music. The aria is through-composed and conceived in two sections: the first sets lines 1–9, the second lines 10–13. The dramatic progression from the first section to the second is similar in some ways to that found in two-tempo arias.

The first section begins with the F minor *agitato* melody that sets 'Dove fuggo' (see Ex. 3.6a, which includes the opening ritornello). At the first new thought, 'vado… resto…' (bar 65), the music makes a turn towards the relative major, A flat, and takes up a new theme, which I have called B. Word-painting shows how Rosina's senses freeze at the thought of her son as the music makes a sudden turn to A flat minor (see Ex. 3.6b, bar 92); the words at this point, 'Oh Dio, gelar mi sento', are set syllabically to minims that derail the melody (C) begun at bar 86. She starts the text over from the beginning at bar 103, while the music is still in a state of development-like confusion, but this time the words 'vado. . . resto' lead to a fermata and silence. Rosina resumes with the thought of her son and makes her way through the text; but even once the dominant of F minor is clearly articulated, a strong cadence that would firmly re-establish the tonic is avoided. At bar 125, still not having arrived at a point of resolution, Rosina represents her dilemma with the repetition of four words: 'fuggo, m'ascondo, vado… resto…', culminating in another portentous fermata (see Ex. 3.6c). Out of this confusion come clarity and resolution, with the words – set only once – 'Eh si vada' (Oh I must go). Now, finally, we have a strong arrival in the tonic, new music (D) representing this decision, and the remaining lines of text. Haydn dramatizes Rosina's new-found resolution with a driving and intense rising melodic line and the second section now proceeds without any hint of confusion or harmonic development. In fact, the setting of lines 10–13 proceeds at breakneck pace with no rests in the vocal melody, a feat that is all the more remarkable the second time through

Example 3.6a *La vera costanza*, Rosina, 'Dove fuggo', bars 50–80

Example 3.6b *La vera costanza*, Rosina, 'Dove fuggo', bars 86–104

(beginning in bar 142, not shown) with its extensions and repetitions of text. The text could easily have been set without the strength of resolution with which Haydn imbues 'Eh si vada'. With the shift from the first section to the second, Rosina's appeal to sentiment – the sense of distress so clearly created by the *agitato* topos – gives way to clarity of thought and the ability to take action.

The power of sensibility in the plot

The centrality of Rosina's virtue to both plot and theme is also demonstrated by the effect her character produces on the others, especially the Count, whose abandonment of her lies at the heart of the opera. The fact

Example 3.6c *La vera costanza*, Rosina, 'Dove fuggo', bars 125–40

that he married her five years earlier (over all social objections) and is still drawn to her in ways he himself does not fully comprehend underlies the entire sequence of events. His characterization, which has been called 'weak' by more than one commentator, is in fact crucial to the working-out of the sentimental plot.[40] For it is his need of conversion to the principles celebrated by the cult of sensibility that makes possible this drama in which Rosina's constancy and goodness are called upon to bring such a conversion about. 'If women had far less power in society than men', Janet Todd suggests, 'they grew great in moral importance'.[41] In her recent book, *The*

---

[40] See Hunter for the characterization of the Count, *Haydn's Aria Forms*, pp. 363ff.; see also Clark, 'The Opera Buffa Finales of Joseph Haydn', pp. 182–7 and 208–19, for the role of the Count in the episodic quality of the plot.

[41] Todd, *Sensibility: An Introduction*, p. 18.

Culture of Sensibility, G. J. Barker-Benfield observes that such a conversion was in fact the goal of much sentimental fiction. Richardson's work 'expressed the moral power of literate women and the potential conversion of men to the values for which women stood. This was the central thrust of the emerging literature of sensibility'.[42]

Modern commentators have difficulty accounting for the Count's behaviour towards Rosina, which is hostile and cruel one moment, remorseful and tender the next. It seems to represent a puzzle that can only be explained as an oversight on the part of Puttini, Anfossi and/or Haydn. Jones and Landon suggest that he is 'palely drawn'; Caryl Clark that he is 'aloof' and 'unpredictable'.[43] Even Hunter writes that 'he is one of the least interesting characters in the opera: his changes of heart regarding Rosina are apparently unmotivated, and he is without self-consciousness or any evidence of an inner life'.[44] 'To the very end', Clark contends, for example, 'the Count (unlike Rosina) remains a wooden "operatic" character, a character lacking in psychological depth and devoid of the kind of believable "humanness" expected of Mozartian heroes'.[45] But I would argue that the Count possesses the greatest sign of an inner life and a humane and virtuous nature that the age can bestow – an excessive sensibility. The Count's seemingly irrational and inexplicable behaviour, his contradictions and outbursts, are the product of his highly volatile and sensitive nature, which, when considered in the context of the cult of sensibility, proves him to be worthy of the virtuous Rosina after all.

From the first, the Count appears to be violently in love. Before he ever appears on stage, we learn from Rosina's narrative of their courtship that she only agreed to marry him because he drew his sword and threatened to stab himself, crying out, 'Either Rosina or death' ('O Rosina, o la morte'). His love for Rosina has apparently been evident enough in his demeanour for the Baroness to suspect it and seek to prevent its consummation, and her suspicions are confirmed by the fact that the Count does not arrive at the fishing village in the boat with the others, but has been

[42] G. K. Barker-Benfield, *The Culture of Sensibility: Sex and Society in Eighteenth-Century Britain* (Chicago: University of Chicago Press, 1992), p. 168.

[43] Clark, 'The Opera Buffa Finales of Joseph Haydn', p. 209.

[44] Hunter, *Haydn's Aria Forms*, p. 364.

[45] Clark, 'The Opera Buffa Finales of Joseph Haydn', p. 209.

there all along, presumably to be near Rosina. In Act I he goes so far as to threaten to kill Villotto, if he persists in his attentions to Rosina. At the same time, however, the Count's menacing presence seems to belie his strong feelings; his potential for violence suggests that his love is the product of an unbalanced and perhaps even disturbed sensibility. The Count's volatile and unpredictable emotions turn against Rosina in Act II and ultimately threaten to tear him apart. Twice in Act I, at moments when the Count seems repentant and on the brink of reuniting with Rosina in a private *tête-à-tête*, the entrance of other characters produces a sudden change in his feelings. The conflict between the demands of nature and the dictates of society in these scenes is blatant. Alone with Rosina in natural surroundings, the Count experiences the return of his proper and passionate feelings (they are after all sanctioned by marriage), but when interrupted by the others and the social rebuke that their witnessing presence seems to imply, the Count changes abruptly, encouraging Villotto's suit to protect himself from his own feelings in the first instance (Recitative, No. 13) and taking an interest in the portrait of a young woman of noble birth that the Baroness presents to him in the second. In Act II the Count actually instructs Villotto to kill both Rosina and her brother. This last turn to violence ultimately exacerbates his inner conflict to the point of madness. In his mad scene, the recitative and aria 'Ah, non m'inganno ... Or che torna il vago Aprile' (which appears in Haydn's opera as an insertion aria, taken directly from the Anfossi setting), the Count has visions of strange music, of Orpheus looking for his Eurydice, and imagines that he 'sees' Rosina approaching. But the Count's madness is temporary only, and his faculties are restored in the Act II finale, when he is reunited with his true family, his wife and son (as opposed to his family by birthright, that of his aunt). This reconciliation is twofold: the reunion of the Count and Rosina brings about the recovery of his senses. His violent actions, both the protestations of love and the rages against it, all attest to the same fact – his true sensibility.

In her *Eighteenth-century Sensibility and the Novel*, Ann Jessie Van Sant offers the following definition of 'sensibility':

> an organic sensitivity dependent on brain and nerves and underlying a) delicate moral and aesthetic perception; b) acuteness of feeling, both emotional and physical; and c) susceptibility to delicate passionate arousal. Though belonging to all, greater degrees of delicacy of sensibility – often

to a point of fragility – are characteristic of women and upper classes. Excessive delicacy or acuteness of feeling produces an impaired or diseased state. [46]

The acuteness of feeling that is the precondition of sensibility, that makes so poignant the sufferings of Rosina, Cecchina and their contemporaries in fiction, drama and opera, is thus also the key to nervous disorders, hysteria and madness. The Count, as a member of the upper class, is susceptible to both the acuteness of feeling and the 'diseased state' to which such acuteness of feeling may eventually lead. 'In the writings of [eighteenth-century] physicians', according to John Mullan, 'the body also displays the effects of a privileged sensitivity. . . . A privileged delicacy or refinement can forbode illness'.[47] Richard Mead, writing in 1751, cautions that 'The affections of the mind, commonly called *passions*, when vehement and immoderate, may be justly ranked among diseases; because they disorder the body various ways'.[48] As Janet Todd explains,

> a susceptible organism could easily become erratic and deranged. So hysteria, an especially female disease, became prominent in eighteenth-century England – just as melancholia or hypochondria grew common in sensitive men – and formed the subject of numerous treatises, notably by Robert James (*Medical Dictionary*, 1743) and George Cheyne (*English Malady*, 1733).[49]

The Count may be understood as just such a 'susceptible organism'; his irrational acts and eventual madness need to be understood in the context of this eighteenth-century view of sensibility.

The Count's Act I military aria, in which he advises Villotto on how best to conquer women, perfectly exemplifies his 'erratic and deranged' state. In it he draws on the popular *seria* metaphor in which love is a battlefield. The preceding *accompagnato* shows the Count to be in control

---

[46] Ann Jessie Van Sant, *Eighteenth-century Sensibility and the Novel: The Senses in Social Context* (Cambridge: Cambridge University Press, 1993), p. 1.

[47] John Mullan, *Sentiment and Sociability: The Language of Feeling in the Eighteenth Century* (Oxford: Clarendon Press, 1988), p. 16; see also his last chapter, 'Hypochondria and Hysteria: Sensibility and the Physicians', pp. 201–40.

[48] Cited in Mullan, *Sentiment and Sociability*, p. 233.

[49] Todd, *Sensibility: An Introduction*, p. 19.

Text 3.6 The Count's 'A trionfar t'invita' from *La vera costanza*

(*settenario*)

Allegro C	A trionfar t'invita Già la guerriera tromba, Vanne con alma ardita Quel core a debellar.	The warlike trumpet already calls you to victory; go with a bold spirit to subdue that heart.
	Ripara quell'assalto, Ritrati con arte, Accorri in quella parte, Per vinta già si dà.	Repel that assault, withdraw with skill, charge in that place which is already conquered.
Adagio $\frac{3}{4}$	Vedi in quel vago viso Amor che scherza e vola; Mira in quei labbri il riso, La grazia e la beltà.	You see in that fair face love sporting and playing; look at the smile on those lips, the grace and the beauty.

	Digli, che a suoi bei rai . . .
	  (*Villotto si accosta.*)
		Say that at her fair glances . . .
		  (*Villotto draws near.*)

Allegro C	Perfido, olà, che fai? Pensa, che tu, che lei . . . Ch'io ti farò tremar.	Ho, traitor, what are you doing? Do you think that you, that she . . . that I will make you tremble.
Presto assai	Oimè! Che smania orribile! Mi perdo, mi confondo; E fuori già del mondo Da un turbine, da un vento Mi sento trasportar.	Alas! What dreadful frenzy! I am lost, I am confused; and already I feel transported from this world by a gale, by a whirlwind.

as he spins out his elaborate simile: he sets the scene for Villotto, detailing the sights and sounds of the camp, the call to arms and the arrival of the 'fair foe' ('la bella nemica'). The orchestra, complete with timpani, backs him up in every particular. This recitative and aria is one of the opera's greatest spectacles, a virtuoso display for Haydn as much as for his tenor. The aria (see Text 3.6) begins with a military tune in C major (see Ex. 3.7a, which includes full orchestration) and moves to the dominant for the second verse, as might be expected. But at the moment the Count imagines Rosina's face, a sudden shift to adagio and $\frac{3}{4}$ derails his *bravura* aria (see Ex. 3.7b). With the first line of the fourth stanza, the Count's verse-making abilities fail him and he turns violently to Villotto as the music moves from adagio to

Example 3.7a *La vera costanza*, Count, 'A trionfar t'invita', bars 52–63

Example 3.7b *La vera costanza*, Count, 'A trionfar t'invita', bars 90–6

allegro, calling him a traitor ('Perfido, olà, che fai?'). The Count now presses on to presto assai as his violent reaction to Villotto turns inward: the outburst 'Oimè! che smania orribile!' is vividly represented in the parallel minor (see Ex. 3.7c). The confusion of which the Count speaks is brought to life by the *agitato* rhythm in the strings; the sense of being transported by a whirlwind ('E fuori già del mondo / Da un turbine, da un vento / Mi sento trasportar') is dramatized by a striking rising chromatic line in both voice and orchestra. As the Count repeats the text, a diminished-seventh chord on 'Oimè!', a repetition of the haunting chromatic ascent, and a long melisma painting the word 'trasportar' (bars 158ff.) intensify the sense of an 'acuteness of feeling' that is fast approaching a deranged state. Indeed, he appears to be at least half-way there. This showpiece *bravura* aria has been irrevocably interrupted. There is no return to the original C major ideas and music, nor is there any resolution of the tensions raised by the number. The musical form is entirely dependent on the passions of its text, without which its rapid shifts of tempo and mode would make no sense.

Example 3.7c *La vera costanza*, Count, 'A trionfar t'invita', bars 108–41

Example 3.7c (*cont.*)

Example 3.7c (*cont.*)

The Count's erratic and overwrought behaviour reaches its climax in his mad scene in Act II. For the student of Haydn's operas, it is perhaps unfortunate that this important moment was not set by Haydn, who instead retains Anfossi's setting of both the preceding *accompagnato* and aria. Haydn's reasons for keeping Anfossi's aria are not known. It seems likely that he did so in accordance with the wishes of his singer (Andrea Totti had played the Count in the 1776 Venice production of the Anfossi opera), but he must also have thought well of the scene.[50] One interesting effect of Haydn's choice is that the opera's only mad scene is also the only number in the opera not composed by Haydn. As a result, its distinct musical character and style might be thought to serve a dramatic purpose; its thinner orchestration and texture and its overwhelmingly homogenous and homophonic accompaniment stand in striking contrast to Haydn's setting of the rest of the opera. The Count's madness therefore appears out of context, for his aria literally transports him to another world – that of a different opera. Whether the effect is by design or not, it suits the dramatic situation perfectly.

The restoration of the Count's senses now becomes the goal of the plot. In a moving scene in the Act II finale, the Count, while looking for Rosina, meets Rosina's son. He immediately feels a tumult of emotion for him, the significance of which he does not fully understand. Rosina appears on the scene and the Count now recovers Rosina, his love for her and his son (the product and proof of that love) simultaneously. The ensuing duet is very similar in form to the duet they sang in the Act I finale: Rosina takes the Count's tune to express acceptance of his affection and they sing *a due* before being interrupted by the others. The conclusion of their duet in the first finale is in some ways the more compelling, for it is the first time the lovers sing *a due* and seem in fact to be lovers. But the recognition drama that is acted out in the Act II finale, which is preceded by the Count's mad scene and its attendant recognition, assures us that the reconciliation we are witnessing is the real thing. For if the mad scene has in fact purged the Count of the dangerous side of his passions, the reunion with Rosina that is

---

[50] Anfossi's *La finta giardiniera* (1774), which was produced at Eszterháza in 1780, also features a tenor lead, Count Belfiore, whose madness has the effect of isolating and purging the excessive qualities of sensibility. This Count too was played by Totti.

possible now must necessarily be complete in ways that the earlier reunion could not be. However true to his own heart the duet in Act I was, the disturbing passions to which the Count was still susceptible were only barely submerged; indeed, they erupt in the very next scene of the finale. The reconciliation in the Act II finale cannot be threatened by the arrival of the others or by any trick of the Baroness's because the Count is now cured of his 'diseased state'.

The brief events of Act III further attest to the restoration of his senses. The Baroness sends each of the lovers a letter suggesting the other's infidelity, but the trick fails to send the Count into a jealous rage. The necessity for a short third act centred on a duet for the lovers, typical of *opere buffe* at this time, was surely the rationale for the scene. But this third duet, which Clark suggests is 'present out of tradition rather than necessity (as is Act III itself)', is in fact necessary in terms of the plot.[51] The proof that the Count is restored to his senses and proper sensibilities, not for the moment but for good, is confirmed only when we see this third occasion for a mad rage avoided without threat of violence. Clark suggests that the reunion at the end of *La vera costanza*, like that in *Figaro*, is insufficient to assure us of the Count's changed nature.[52] But within the conventions of the drama of sensibility, the ending of *La vera costanza* offers precisely this assurance. The two Counts and the forces that act on them are completely different. Count Errico's madness, entirely unlike Count Almaviva's insensitivity, is physiological and is itself meant to be understood as proof of his depth of feeling. Madness here is not of the type found in Shakespeare's Ophelia or King Lear. It is a temporary state brought about by the very acute sensitivity – a disorder of the nervous system – that makes him emotionally worthy of the sentimental Rosina in the first place, a condition that can be cured by a proper channelling of the diseased feelings (which must be purged from the body).

The Count's apparently changeable nature is thus crucial to the story. The restoration of his love and of his senses become the same goal in the course of the plot. The Count's rehabilitation attests to the power of the sentimental heroine and the goals of sentimental fiction and theatre in ways that are perfectly attuned to the procedures and morals of *opera buffa*. As

[51] Clark, 'The Opera Buffa Finales of Joseph Haydn', p. 208.   [52] *Ibid.*

Wye Jamison Allanbrook reminds us, 'The Enlightenment faith, was, of course, a faith in universal reason and human perfectibility, a faith in the possibility of discovering for society a model of the divine harmony of nature. It is with this faith that our modern impatience lies'.[53]

Conclusion

Leaving aside the source problems created by the loss of the original score in the Eszterháza fire of 1779, *La vera costanza* has suffered more generally from the tired conception that Haydn's operas are '*sui generis*', that they are so in part on account of their having been composed especially for performance at Eszterháza (a view to which Haydn himself unwittingly contributed), and that as a result they cannot bear comparison with the 'mature' works of Gluck and Mozart.[54] But once the context for analysis has been shifted from the so-called Mozartian ideal to a smaller circle of contemporary 'Pamela' operas that treat versions of the same story, characters and themes, both *La vera costanza* and its sentimental heroine appear in a new light. Haydn's complete musical characterization of sentiment (Rosina) and sensibility (the Count) show him to have been in deep sympathy with the spirit of the age. Many of the features that have been lamented by critics – especially the extreme pathos, which has been called 'exaggerated' and 'unbelievable'[55] – should rather be understood as central to the dramatization of the 'Pamela' plot. For it is precisely these features of Haydn's opera that must have been valued in the age of sensibility. It must be remembered that this opera was revived at Eszterháza with great success in 1785 and was subsequently produced in German in Pressburg, Vienna, Budapest and Brünn. It was translated into French in 1791 and given as *Laurette* in Paris, where it was published in full score. And thus *La vera costanza* was still in the repertory when Dalayrac's *Nina* was first produced

---

[53] Wye J. Allanbrook, 'Mozart's Tunes and the Comedy of Closure', in James M. Morris, ed., *On Mozart* (Cambridge: Cambridge University Press, in association with the Woodrow Wilson Center Press, 1994), p. 172.

[54] 'Haydn as an Opera Composer', p. 256. The phrase '*sui generis*' is Porter's.

[55] For the characterization of the opera as a whole see, among others: Heartz, *Haydn, Mozart, and the Viennese School*, pp. 394ff.; Landon and Jones, *Haydn: His Life and Music*, pp. 123ff.; and Landon, *Chronicle and Works II*, pp. 528ff.

in 1786. Both Paisiello's and Dalayrac's *Nina* operas premiered in Vienna in 1790. Paisiello's *Nina* was to rival Piccinni's *La buona figliuola* in longevity and popularity, remaining in the repertory until 1830.

In the context of this history, Haydn's 'Pamela' should be recognized as a thoughtful, up-to-date and highly individual realization of a figure important to the age. The sentimental heroines of *La buona figliuola*, of Haydn's *La vera costanza*, of Paisiello's *Nina* and of other contemporary operas each represent something different about the way identity is perceived. And the differences between Rosina and Nina are as revealing as those between Rosina and Cecchina. Nina, whose madness is forced on her, even though it eventually brings about the resolution she longs for, takes the 'Pamela' figure a long way into the Romantic sensibility. 'Illness', as John Mullan shows, '[becomes] the last retreat of the morally pure'.[56] The emotion that empowers Nina also *over*powers her and she is rendered all the more pathetic, having lost her senses. But Haydn's Rosina, in her knowledge of herself, her conscious belief in the righteousness of her actions and her ability to take action for the preservation of her character – to think for herself – is still very much a child of the Enlightenment. The extreme pathos that romanticizes Nina is not hers. Nor is the confirmation of virtue by birthright. The different sentimental heroines reflect the multiple sensibilities of the period. Haydn's contribution to the eighteenth-century fascination with the 'Pamela' figure is a distinct, responsive and highly inventive musical characterization. His Rosina is a testament to the moment in the history of the cult of sensibility when it had come to value individual feeling, virtue and internal achievement over external measures of social worth. Inner nobility had become its own reward.

[56] Mullan, *Sentiment and Sociability*, p. 16.

4 Haydn as Romantic: a chemical experiment with instrumental music[1]

DANIEL K. L. CHUA

The early Romantics,[2] it is said, formulated the idea of absolute music. If this is so, then its emergence at the close of the eighteenth century was muttered rather than announced by them. In fact, the Romantics were so reticent on the subject that they did not even name absolute music 'absolute music'; that task was left to Wagner in the 1840s.[3] The Romantics, however, did call instrumental music 'pure music', and this can be read as 'absolute', for they used the term to imply that instrumental music, as the essence of music, is the spirit of creativity itself. Music is pure *poesis*, claims Tieck;[4] it is the 'centre and circumference of all the arts'.[5]

---

[1] This article has been developed from papers given in the colloquia series of King's College London, the University of Chicago and the University of Wisconsin. The material is also drawn from a book that the author is currently preparing on instrumental music.

[2] It is important to distinguish between the early and late Romantics (or idealists); see Andrew Bowie, *Aesthetics and Subjectivity* (Manchester: Manchester University Press, 1990), pp. 41–4. I use the term 'Romantic' to refer to the early Romantics only.

[3] It appears that Wagner first used the term in passing in a programmatic commentary on Beethoven's Ninth Symphony designed for the Dresden Palm Sunday concerts. He subsequently consolidated the term's political and historical significance in his 'Zürich writings' of 1849–51. See Klaus Kropfinger, *Wagner and Beethoven: Richard Wagner's Reception of Beethoven* (1974), trans. P. Palmer (Cambridge: Cambridge University Press, 1991), p. 115; Carl Dahlhaus, *The Idea of Absolute Music*, trans. R. Lustig (Chicago: University of Chicago Press, 1989), pp. 18–19; and Thomas S. Grey, *Wagner's Musical Prose: Texts and Contexts* (Cambridge: Cambridge University Press, 1995), pp. 1–2.

[4] Wilhelm Heinrich Wackenroder and Ludwig Tieck, 'Symphonien', in *Werke und Briefe von Wilhelm Heinrich Wackenroder* (Berlin: Verlag Lambert Schneider, 1938), p. 255.

[5] Friedrich Schlegel, *Literary Notebooks, 1797–1801*, ed. H. Eichner (London: The Athlone Press, 1957), no. 1416.

But what did this 'Romantic music' sound like to the Romantics? By the time someone like Schumann stylized Romantic philosophy as music, it was too late. When the Schlegel brothers, Novalis, Tieck and Schelling were writing in the late 1790s, Schumann was not even a gleam in his father's eye. There was no 'Romantic music' as we know it, only what we call 'Classical music'. What the Romantics heard were the symphonies of Stamitz or Haydn and they renamed the music as their own. E. T. A. Hoffmann, in his celebrated review of Beethoven's Fifth Symphony, simply appropriates Haydn and Mozart as Romantic composers in retrospect.[6]

The idea of absolute music is therefore not 'Classical' but 'Romantic'. The commonly held notion of Haydn, Mozart and Beethoven as *Classical* composers of *absolute* music has confused the meaning that the early Romantics attached to instrumental forms. Although musicology acknowledges the early Romantics as the originators of absolute music, it perceives absolute music Classically through the organicism of the idealists (or later Romantics) who were not advocates of absolute music. We therefore base our understanding of absolute music on a philosophical tradition that is opposed to it.[7] In fact, the early Romantics could not have conceived of instrumental music as either organic or Classical: first, because organicism implies a perfect synthesis of the parts with the whole which cannot be attained within the Romantic system, where the absolute is expressed negatively in the form of fragments – hence their fascination with the ironic and the sublime; and, secondly, because Classical implies an aesthetic of perfection which the early Romantics idealized as a Golden Age of Antiquity. This they then projected into the future as unreachable Utopia – hence their sense of interminable yearning.[8]

[6] E. T. A. Hoffmann, 'Review of Beethoven's Fifth Symphony', *Allgemeine musikalische Zeitung*, 12 (1810) in *E. T. A. Hoffmann's Musical Writings: Kreisleriana, The Poet and the Composer, Music Criticism*, ed. D. Charlton, trans. M. Clarke (Cambridge: Cambridge University Press, 1989), pp. 236–8.

[7] See, for example, Georg Wilhelm Friedrich Hegel, *Vorlesungen über die Aesthetik* (Frankfurt am Main: Suhrkamp, 1970), III, 213–18. There are two English translations of his *Aesthetics*, the 1920 translation by F. P. B. Osmaston, reissued as *The Philosophy of Fine Art* (New York: Hacker, 1975), and T. M. Knox's translation, *Aesthetics: Lectures on Fine Art* (Oxford: Clarendon Press, 1975).

[8] See Ernst Behler, *Irony and the Discourse of Modernity* (Seattle: University of Washington Press, 1990), pp. 73–110; and Peter Szondi, *On Textual Understanding and Other Essays*, trans. H. Mendelsohn (Manchester: Manchester University Press, 1986), pp. 57–68.

So what meaning did the early Romantics attach to instrumental music? What does a Romantic reading of the Classical style look like? In this essay I focus in particular on the Romantics' appropriation of a music that is Haydnesque in medium and method, to elucidate how the epistemological shift created by their discourse transformed the meaning of instrumental music. I suggest that absolute music, at its inception, was perceived as absolute not because it was organic but because it was ironic.[9] Haydn's humour inevitably comes to mind; his musical pranks capture those contradictions of an ironic wit that distances the listener from her absorption in the work with a knowing smile. But it would be a mistake to turn Haydn's humour into a paradigm of Romantic irony, because the Romantics did not focus on Haydn in particular but on modern instrumental music in general. I have therefore included an analysis of a Mozart symphony, as a counter-example of how the 'Classical style' can be ironic without being a joke. Romantic irony, after all, is no funny matter; in fact, the meaning of its humour is deadly serious. The early Romantics wanted an aesthetic revolution in the face of despair. It was for this reason that they philosophized over instrumental music to transform the meaning of their world in the wake of the French Revolution.[10] This was a radical epistemological shift that involved nothing less than a movement of music from the *ancien régime* of the body to the spirit (*Geist*) of freedom, that is, a movement from the passive to the active, from sentiment to irony, or, to borrow Schlegel's metaphor, from a material biology to the chemical processes of life.

Body language

To shift instrumental music from a material to a transcendental aesthetic was no easy matter. By the beginning of the eighteenth century music had fallen from the celestial spheres to roam the body; sound was explained by Newtonian physics and its meaning by physiology. Music was *seen* as

[9] On Romantic irony see, for example, Szondi, *On Textual Understanding*, pp. 57–73, and Kathleen M. Wheeler, *German Aesthetic and Literary Criticism: The Romantic Ironists and Goethe* (Cambridge: Cambridge University Press, 1984), pp. 17–24.

[10] See Maurice Blanchot, 'The Athenaeum', *The Infinite Conversation*, trans. S. Hanson (Minneapolis: University of Minnesota Press, 1993).

motion and its effect was somatic. The fusion of physics and physiology resulted in a peculiar form of sonic passion: sound *moved the body*. And to be moved was literally to move – emotion was motion. The visibility of musical movement that the new discourse had brought into focus through the vibrations of strings and tubes was internalized as a physiological experience. Cosmic harmony was now a matter of pulsating nerve fibres and dilating blood vessels. Almost every music theorist of the eighteenth century believed in a kind of parallel tracking between the musical movement of sound and the emotional movement of the body.[11]

At first such a somatic experience of sound was a problem because the body at the beginning of the eighteenth century was not a living organism but a mechanical structure of levers, pumps and sieves.[12] In fact it was no different from an inorganic object. 'To think', for Descartes, may have grounded the self in the 'I am' of being, but it also severed the body from the soul in the act of reflection, creating an ontological fissure at the very core of self-realization.[13] The Cartesian, writes Charles Taylor, 'discovers and affirms his immaterial nature by objectifying the bodily'.[14] The mind (the rational soul) had to disengage its nature from ordinary experience and divide itself from the flesh as a disembodied entity in order to find its new epistemological footing as an external observer. The body became purely material, something to be reconstructed by the rational soul as mere mechanism and mere extension, emptied of all spiritual essences. In this way the Cartesian mind banished the animistic principles that had inhabited the Renaissance body with a functionalism that left its own flesh as good as dead. This is why some historians of science claim that biology was impossible before *c.* 1750; life simply could not be explained by laws different to those of the inanimate world.[15]

---

[11] See, for example, Johann Mattheson, *Der vollkommene Capellmeister*, trans. E. C. Harriss (Michigan: UMI Research Press, 1981), pp. 104–5; and Daniel Webb, *Observations on the Correspondence between Poetry and Music* (London, 1769), pp. 150–1.

[12] See Thomas L. Hankin, *Science and the Enlightenment* (Cambridge: Cambridge University Press, 1985), pp. 113–19.

[13] See René Descartes, *Meditations on First Philosophy*, trans. J. Cottingham (Cambridge: Cambridge University Press, 1986), pp. 16–23 and 50–62.

[14] Charles Taylor, *Sources of the Self* (Cambridge: Cambridge University Press, 1989), p. 146.   [15] See Hankin, *Science and the Enlightenment*, pp. 113–19.

So, although sound resided in the body, the body itself could not validate musical meaning, since the thinking ego had basically mechanized it to death. If any life existed in instrumental music it was merely that of 'a marionette or a mechanical doll'.[16] For sound to have any real meaning at all it would have to ground itself in the *cogito ergo sum* of Cartesian ontology; it had to inhabit the mind. But how? Given its inability to represent concepts, how was music supposed to think? This was why music needed a voice, for the voice signified a rational presence, the thinking 'I am' that was the very identity of the self. Vocal music was the only kind of music that could authenticate its own being; the soul, as it were, inhered within it. As for instrumental music, it was derided as 'body without soul', which, in Cartesian thought, is to declare it 'a dead thing'.[17] So instrumental music merely moved mechanically in the body, in the raw data of the senses, without migrating to the analytical processes of the mind and without any external validation.

However, it is clear that by the later eighteenth century instrumental music had developed the ability to distinguish between the living and the dead. In fact, the mechanical became the butt of a great deal of 'Classical' joking. Instrumental music managed to have the last laugh at an old ideology that had brandished it as a 'mechanical doll'. It depicted such ticktocking machines as something to be tinkered with, using the elasticity of its own tonal momentum to pull the precision of the movement around;[18] sometimes it even smashed the mechanism to pieces, as with the unexpected hammer blow in Haydn's 'Surprise' Symphony. The surprise of the symphony is in the human hand which comes to tamper with the self-wound motions that the music signifies with its clockwork tune. Conscious life had seeped into the score, and the mechanical was merely a play of signs for the organic (Ex. 4.1).

Or take, as another example, the minuet in the C major Quartet, Op. 54 No. 2; this piece was actually incorporated into a musical clock at

---

16 Nöel-Antoine Pluche, *Le Spectacle de la nature, ou Entretiens sur les particularités de l'histoire naturelle, qui ont paru les plus propres à rendre les jeunes-gens curieux, et à leur former l'esprit* (Paris, 1732–50), VII (1746), p. 115.

17 Johann Christoph Gottsched, *Auszug aus des Herrn Batteux schönen Künsten aus dem einzigen Grundsätze der Nachahmung hergeleitet* (Leipzig, 1754), p. 202. Nöel-Antoine Pluche shares the same opinion; see *Le Spectacle de la nature*, pp. 114–15.

18 On tonal elasticity and mechanical motion see Daniel K. L. Chua, *The 'Galitzin' Quartets of Beethoven* (Princeton: Princeton University Press, 1995), pp. 175–88.

Example 4.1 Symphony No. 94 in G major, second movement, bars 1–16

Eszterháza,[19] but it must have been a very odd clock, since the music sounds like a madman trying to struggle out of a symmetrical straitjacket of regular four-square phrases. Each phrase wreathes restlessly in and out of keys, cadencing clumsily and twisting chromatically this way and that within a very tight intervallic space. Dynamically too it is restricted to *piano* with the odd *sforzandi* punctuating the texture. There is life in the machine waiting to get out – hence the peculiar ending. Suddenly, the mechanism bursts into life: *forte, crescendo, fortissimo* (bars 41–6). An unexpected flourish rips through the awkward angularity of the minuet, brushing aside its restricted motions for a breath-taking gesture that sweeps over the entire range of the quartet to wipe out the mechanical (Ex. 4.2).

Clearly, instrumental music was not only alive but kicking away its old mechanical self to show off the new biology that the aesthetic had bestowed upon it.[20]

It was the rise of experimental physiology in the 1740s that threw a spanner into the anatomical works, replacing a system of blind mechanism with a dynamic of change and activity, growth and regeneration. Life was no longer a matter of structure but of vital function. Tissues and nerves, as the physician Théophile de Bordeu claimed, contained invisible forces of 'sensibility'.[21] In this way, bodily sensations became connected with the impulse of life and even its very consciousness. Knowledge need no longer be divided up hierarchically between a passive body and an active soul; rather 'all the faculties of the soul . . . could have their origins in sensation itself'.[22] The body could stir the mind to action and desire could modify the cogitating ego. Cartesian psychology was turned upside down, and the body could at last stand on its own two feet.

---

19 See H. C. Robbins Landon, *Haydn: Chronicle and Works II: Haydn at Eszterháza, 1766–1790* (London: Thames and Hudson, 1978), p. 637.

20 For further discussion see Janet M. Levy, '"Something Mechanical Encrusted on the Living": A Source of Musical Wit and Humor', in W. J. Allanbrook, J. M. Levy and W. P. Mahrt, eds., *Convention in Eighteenth- and Nineteenth-Century Music* (New York: Pendragon Press, 1992).

21 See Hankin, *Science and the Enlightenment*, pp. 124–7, and Dorinda Outram, *The Body and the French Revolution* (New Haven: Yale University Press, 1989), p. 54.

22 Etienne de Condillac, *Traité des animaux* (1755), quoted in Ernst Cassirer, *The Philosophy of the Enlightenment*, trans. F. C. A. Koelln and J. Pettgrove (Princeton: Princeton University Press, 1951), p. 101.

The consequence for the rational soul was a crisis of existence. Not only was it physically robbed of its domination, but its very existence was thrown into question by the physiological experiments of scientists, such as Bordeu, who dispersed the centre of control across the entire network of nerves and ganglions, without even privileging the brain.[23] If the material of the body is alive, then the soul might as well be dead. As a result, instrumental music found itself appropriated as a symbol of the secular self; it became the very vibration of sentient identity. After all, what was disturbing for the Cartesian about instrumental music was the way it took hold of the body with a plurality of affects that did not emanate from a single, rational being. But once the self has had its soul disassembled and disseminated throughout the nervous system, instrumental music could easily bristle across the sensory surface of the secular body. As a mirror of the self, music could celebrate its materiality as purely instrumental.[24]

The body of *Empfindsamkeit* became the index of one's moral sensibility; through music, the body automatically vibrates.[25] The body cannot lie – it is always authentically connected up with the object of its emotions. And, as Janet Todd notes, this sympathetic movement breaks through the typology of the sentimental novel, with its dashes, mutilated letters, torn sentences, missing chapters, stuttering speeches.[26] It also breaks through the pages of Haydn's music, such as in the cluttered and fragmented notation of the slow movement of his Sonata No. 62 in E flat major (see Ex. 4.3). In a sentimental reading of this movement the extreme harmonic digression (bars 9–12), chains of dissonances (bars 11–12), stuttering ornaments (bar 14), the dotted and jerky motifs, sudden disruptions (bar 19), extreme dynamics and isolated gestures are not so much the rhetorical

---

[23] See Outram, *The Body and the French Revolution*, pp. 56–67.

[24] See, for example, Denis Diderot, 'Lettre sur les sourds et muets à l'usage de ceux qui entendent et qui parlent' (1751), in *Œuvres complètes*, ed. H. Dieckmann and J. Varloot (Paris: Hermann, 1978) and *D'Alembert's Dream* (1769), in *Diderot's Selected Writings*, pp. 187–8; the latter is in the form of a play, in which the main characters are Diderot, D'Alembert and, pertinently, the physician Bordeu. On music and monism see, for example, Johann Nikolaus Forkel, *Allgemeine Geschichte der Musik* (Leipzig, 1788–1801), I, 1–15.

[25] Johann Gottfried Herder, *Kalligone* (Weimar, 1800), trans. Peter Le Huray and James Day, *Music Aesthetics in the Eighteenth and Early Nineteenth Centuries* (Cambridge: Cambridge University Press, 1981), pp. 253–4.

[26] See Janet Todd, *Sensibility: An Introduction* (London: Methuen, 1986), p. 5.

Example 4.2 String Quartet in C major, Op. 54 No. 2, third movement

classifications of some musical grammar as mutilated figures that cannot speak clearly under the stress of emotions. The body obtrudes through the gaps in the score and it smothers any tidy classification of affects in the sincerity of its movement.

But are these disruptive gestures sentimental or ironic? Mark Evan Bonds suggests that 'the striking juxtaposition of E major' in this move-

128

Example 4.2 (*cont.*)

ment against the E flat major of the outer movements creates an ironic distance; the composer seems to meddle with the artwork to prevent the body
from absorbing itself into the music.[27] E major, it seems, can be read both as
bodily disturbance and ironic dislocation. But this need not be an either/or

---

[27] Mark Evan Bonds, 'Haydn, Laurence Sterne, and the Origins of Musical Irony',
Journal of the American Musicological Society 44 (1991), 72.

Example 4.3 Sonata No. 62 in E flat major, second movement, bars 1–21

contradiction. In the same way that the sentimental novels of Laurence Sterne, with which Haydn's music was often compared,[28] are self-absorbed to the point of doubling back on themselves as ironic commentaries, so Haydn's disruptive gestures can be read as simultaneously sentimental and ironic. Inherent in the sentimental style is the body's own undoing; the early Romantics simply used the ironic aspects of sentimentality to dematerialize music into the spirit realm.

By the 1780s revolution was in the air. The body could not just lie passively in the movement of time, vibrating with its delusions of natural innocence; it needed the action of a *Geist* that would capture the spirit of the age and master nature as its own history. The fusion of body and soul, on which the empirical aesthetic of *Empfindsamkeit* depended, was split by a Kantian aesthetic in a replay of the body–soul duality of Cartesian thought. This time, however, instrumental music was no longer on the side of the body – it had soul. Although Kant himself left music in the body,[29] he actually hoisted aesthetics out of the empirical world and relocated it in the transcendental realm.[30] The early Romantics merely carried further the logic of Kant's aesthetics to include instrumental music. For them, such music was a mysterious out-of-body experience; or as Wackenroder puts it, music has to demonstrate 'the movement of our soul, disembodied'.[31] But how?

If Newtonian physics at the beginning of the eighteenth century denounced instrumental music as mechanically dead and the emergence of biology in the 1750s rendered it physiologically alive, then it was left to the birth of modern chemistry in the 1780s to disembody music as pure spirit (see Ex. 4.4). 'Irony', says Schlegel, 'is chemical inspiration'.[32] It was this inspiration that breathed life into absolute music. But what is this Romantic connection between chemistry, irony and music? It begins as a *Lebenskraft* (life-force) experiment.

---

[28] *Ibid.*

[29] Immanuel Kant, *Critique of Judgement* (1790), trans. J. C. Meredith (Oxford: Oxford University Press, 1973), pp. 196–9.

[30] See Dieter Henrich, *Aesthetic Judgement and the Moral Image of the World* (Stanford: Stanford University Press, 1992), pp. 29–56, and Paul Crowther, *The Kantian Sublime: From Morality to Art* (Oxford: Clarendon Press, 1989).

[31] Wackenroder and Tieck, *Phantasien über die Kunst*, in *Werke und Briefe*, p. 207.

[32] Friedrich Schlegel, *Kritische Schriften und Fragmente* [1794–1818], ed. E. Behler and H. Eichner (Paderborn: Ferdinand Schöningh, 1988), V, 58.

Life-force

At some point at the very close of the eighteenth century, Alexander von Humboldt stuck a silver rod up his anus and a zinc disc in his mouth and basically electrocuted himself. It was quite an experience, so his 1797 treatise, *Versuche über die gereizte Muskel- und Nervenfaser nebst Vermuthungen über den chemischen Process des Lebens in der Thier- und Pflanzenwelt*, tells us; the shock on his body produced strong convulsions and sensations that included 'pain in the abdomen, increasing activity of the stomach and alteration of the excrement'. Humboldt's idea was to include his entire body in a galvanic chain so that he could experience himself as the object of one of his experiments. Such experiments, which included the galvanization of his eyes, teeth and tongue, were designed to investigate *Lebenskraft* in terms of what Humboldt called a vital chemistry, in which the stimulus of excitable matter produced 'chemical alterations and combination' (*chemische Mischungsveränderung*).[33]

For the early Romantics, chemical activity signified the productive power behind an organic structure. It was life, the very movement of spirit in the sense of a creative, poetic force, that unites the parts to the whole. But the Romantic circle in Jena, which included Humboldt, knew that this *Lebenskraft* was an elusive force that always evaded analysis. It took shape as an organic form through such complex interactions of chemical processes that it was impossible to pin it down; the vital process, as Humboldt noted, was always in flux, and to complicate matters further, it constantly altered its activity with the external stimulus of the experimenter. Life could only be inferred as a formative impulse from the chemical activity, but to catch it in a static state would merely kill the organism as a dissected specimen. And yet it seemed that life refused to manifest its processes unless the experimenter tampered with it, altering and mutilating the organism in some way, by slicing up a polyp, for example, to see the action of its regeneration. So instead of employing the instrumental reason of the Enlightenment that distances the subject from the object, the Romantics conceived their inves-

---

[33] Alexander von Humboldt, *Versuche über die gereizte Muskel- und Nervenfaser nebst Vermuthungen über den chemischen Process des Lebens in der Thier- und Pflanzenwelt* (Berlin: Rottman, 1797), quoted in Joan Steigerwald, 'Lebenskraft in Reflection: German Perspectives in the Late Eighteenth and Early Nineteenth Centuries', Ph.D. diss., King's College London (forthcoming).

tigation of life as an active *participation*, even to the point of experimenting on the experimenter. In Humboldt's experiment, for instance, he is both the subject and the object; he is both outside and inside the experiment as the observer and the observed. But not only does Humboldt divide himself, he also attempts to synthesize the subject–object antithesis by reflecting upon the contradictions of this schizophrenic process – he observes himself observing himself as object. So he is not only inside and outside the experiment, he also rises above it in a self-reflexive manoeuvre that detaches him from his own participation in the experimental process. It is this higher synthesis of opposites that initiates the ironic glance of German Romanticism.

Reflection on life always leads to irony because the investigation of the self necessarily involves the endless oscillation between the self as subject and object. Romantic irony is an infinite process, for the subject, in the act of synthesizing its own identity, realizes its inability to perfect the synthesis and has to incorporate that failure as part of the process of self-knowledge; the synthesis is annulled, but in doing so, the subject creates another consciousness, which looks down on a new synthesis that can only replay the same situation again. And so on, *ad infinitum*. In this infinite movement of irony, the subject comes into a sovereign awareness of its own conscious activity and redeems its life negatively as a transcendental idea. 'An idea', says Schlegel,

> is a concept perfected to the point of irony, an absolute synthesis of absolute antithesis, the continual self-creating interchange of two conflicting thoughts.[34]

Evidently, the coherence of the ego can only be grasped ironically as constant contradiction. Like Humboldt's self-experiment, one has to tamper with the ego, dividing it to tease out the signs of life.

'The object of music is life', notes Schlegel.[35] Music was regarded by the Romantics as the very modality of *Lebenskraft*; its movement is not a blind chemistry, but the self-conscious activity of a subject that knows itself as a living form and multiplies itself as contradiction in the attempt to grasp

---

[34] Friedrich Schlegel, *Athenaeum Fragments*, no. 121; in *Philosophical Fragments*, trans. P. Firchow (Minneapolis: University of Minneapolis Press, 1991), p. 33.
[35] Friedrich Schlegel, *Literary Notebooks*, no. 1496.

that knowledge. It is within this infinite movement that instrumental music weaves itself as the formative impulse (*Bildungstrieb*) that yearns towards the impossible ideal of perfect synthesis. The Romantics described this tension between the 'real and the ideal'[36] as the interaction between the chemical and the organic; or, to use Humboldt's terminology, life consists of 'Form und Mischung' – a vital communication and constant contradiction between organic structure (*Form*) and chemical mixture (*Mischung*).[37] But what exactly is the difference between the chemical and organic in this vital aesthetic of music? Schlegel explains:

> Understanding is mechanical, wit is chemical, genius is organic.[38]

This tiny fragment elucidates the nature of aesthetic life-forms: to analyse art is to kill its life as dead mechanism – 'understanding is mechanical'. However, 'wit is chemical': to experience life is to enter its chemistry as a self-experiment in which the subject and object find a chemical affinity that is the process of wit in action; chemical wit is that which synthesizes the heterogeneous and chaotic elements as a sudden ironic revelation that lifts the subject into a momentary intuition of organic form. But since wit is an ironic movement, aesthetic life is a perpetual chemical motion that is infinite and can never grasp its final form. Hence, only 'genius is organic', for only the genius is able to discover the organic universe within himself and to deposit its form as art. The moment this happens, however, the ironic

---

[36] On the 'real and ideal' see Friedrich Wilhelm Joseph von Schelling, *System of Transcendental Idealism* (1800), trans. Peter Heath (Charlottesville: University Press of Virginia, 1978), pp. 38–43 and 49; *Ideas For a Philosophy of Nature* (1797), trans. E. E. Harris and P. Heath (Cambridge: Cambridge University Press, 1988), pp. 49–51; and Ian Biddle, 'F. W. J. Schelling's *Philosophie der Kunst*: An Emergent Semiology of Music', in Ian Bent, ed., *Music Theory in the Age of Romanticism* (Cambridge: Cambridge University Press, 1996).

[37] Humboldt, *Versuche*, quoted in Steigerwald, 'Lebenskraft in Reflection'. Schlegel uses the concept of 'Mischung' in his discussions on the novel as a genre. See Friedrich Schlegel, 'Letter on the Novel', in *Dialogue on Poetry and Literary Aphorisms*, trans. E. Behler and R. Struc (University Park: Pennsylvania University Press, 1968), p. 101; hence Schlegel's comment in his *Literary Notebook*, no. 1359, that '[t]he method of the novel is that of instrumental music'. Also see Anthony J. Cascardi, *The Subject of Modernity* (Cambridge: Cambridge University Press, 1992), pp. 110–12.

[38] Schlegel, *Athenaeum Fragments*, no. 366; in *Philosophical Fragments*, p. 15.

disappears in the perfection of the organic. To know the organic is to enter an aesthetic paradise removed from the chemical chaos of the world.

It is precisely this tension between the chemical and the organic that divides the early Romantics as a subset of German Idealism. An idealist constructs systems that are a perfect synthesis of organic forms and therefore no longer require the infinite movement of ironic chemistry, whereas for the Romantics life can only be ironic, because the organic is Utopian. 'An organic age', writes Schlegel, 'will follow a chemical one'.[39] And for Schlegel, the revolutions of his age are a chemical process of history, dissolving and recombining elements as fragmentary annotations that are only 'brief notes' on an age which is unable 'to draw the profile of the giant'. If one is *inside* the process of history, there is no way of grasping the total form from the *outside*; the chaotic chemical combinations of the Romantic age are simply 'preliminary exercises' that try to catch a glimpse of the organism of history, sporadically bursting through the surface with an ironic glance. Thus it is the task of the Romantic to embrace the infinite contradictions of these exercises as an end in themselves, so that humanity might participate in the chemical aesthetic that constitutes the *Bildungstrieb* of an age to come.

Chemical analysis

The 'Classical style' is a chemical style, born in a chemical age of revolution, indeed, born in the age when chemistry itself became a science.[40] Its processes mirror the interaction of 'Form und Mischung' teased out by Humboldt in his work on vital chemistry, for its 'Classicism' is always in dissolution, which is why it was known as the 'mixed style'.[41] It was this constant mixture of seemingly immiscible elements that divided the critics; its detractors heard a mess of contrasts, whereas its admirers heard in the

---

[39] Schlegel, *Athenaeum Fragments*, no. 426; in *Philosophical Fragments*, p. 87.
[40] On the birth of modern chemistry see Hankin, *Science and the Enlightenment*, pp. 81–112.
[41] See, for example, Johann Joachim Quantz, *Versuch einer Anweisung die Flöte traversière zu spielen* (Berlin, 1752), trans. E. R. Reilly as *On Playing the Flute* (London: Faber, 1966), p. 341; and V. Kofi Agawu, *Playing with Signs* (Princeton: Princeton University Press, 1991), pp. 29–30.

Example 4.4 Mozart: Symphony No. 41 in C major, K. 551, finale, bars 1–8

chaos a unifying force behind its chemistry. The mixed style lives or dies according to the definition of its form; it is dead as long as the form is thought of as a mechanical unity of identity and uniformity, but alive if the form is inferred from a chemical impulse that both generates and encapsulates the structure as constant process and ironic contradiction. For example, here is the opening phrase of Mozart's 'Jupiter' Symphony (Ex. 4.4).

It is a mixture; the learned style and *opera buffa* are forced to coexist in a juxtaposition of the sacred and secular; contrapuntal law is forced to make comic conversation.[42] This contradiction of *topoi* is the basis for an ironic movement that annihilates any simple conceptualization of meaning, creating a process of infinite synthesizing. But this cannot be disclosed by a

---

42 The opening four notes are derived from Gregorian chant and were used by Mozart in a *Missa brevis* (K. 192) to the words 'Credo, credo'. For further information, see Neal Zaslaw, *Mozart's Symphonies: Context, Performance Practice, Reception* (Oxford: Clarendon Press, 1989), pp. 537–44.

mechanical dissection that only demonstrates the patterns of harmonic, motivic and textural identity. An analysis that controls the object with an instrumental reason always produces an anatomy of music that alienates the critic. What the Romantic ego wants, however, is not a clinical analysis but a dissolution of itself into the chemistry of sound, resulting in a *confusion* of object and subject as the ego flickers in and out of the work. In the symphony the Romantic ego can experience itself as an experiment of *Lebenskraft*; it 'lives in the work',[43] as E. T. A. Hoffmann puts it, not as the passive body of *Empfindsamkeit* that merely vibrates with each tingle, but as a self-conscious being that deliberately waits to divide itself from the process in an act of ironic alienation. Thus the alienation that is always necessary to grasp the form from the outside is no longer instrumental but ironic. The Romantic ego does not need to organize the symphony from the outside, but can simply reside in the mixture as it awaits its own ironic resurrection. Mozart's little phrase can spawn a play of difference and plurality with all its titillating twists and turns because there might be a sudden eruption of wit in the mixture that will provide a momentary flash of unity. It will not divulge the entire form, but it will give a glimmer of the form in process. The mixture of the opening phrase is a promise to reveal the secrets of the symphony's vital chemistry.

But what is this chemical wit that resides in music? For a start it is not *in* music: it *is* music. The pure play of signs in instrumental music was considered by the Romantics as the very grammar of ironic wit. Music could combine the most incompatible elements into a play of resemblances that could reveal the chemical activity of life in process. Music was the joker in language; it functioned as a capricious spirit that made unexpected affinities between words, messing up the attempts to make meaning for an autonomy of play. 'Wordplays are something very social' notes Schlegel, 'conversations up to [the point of] irony. Wordplays are a logical and grammatical music in which there must be fugues, fantasias and sonatas'.[44] Musical logic is therefore an ironic movement for Schlegel, hovering over words as giant inverted commas that suspend the truth of representation to

---

[43] E. T. A. Hoffmann, *Kreisleriana*, no. 4 of the *Fantasiestücke in Callots Manier* in Giorgio Pestelli, *The Age of Mozart and Beethoven*, trans. E. Cross (Cambridge: Cambridge University Press, 1984), p. 292.

[44] Schlegel, *Literary Notebooks*, no. 1144.

trip up language in its attempt to say something determined. Music's autonomy is not in its formal construction, but is an internal activity that remains hidden until an unexpected affinity bubbles to the surface of consciousness as an ironic revelation.

As the very grammar of wordplay, music is not an occasional play of wit. The stock witticisms of the 'Classical style', with its false recapitulations, surprise crashes and deferrals of closure, are merely sporadic pranks in a music that is ironic throughout in its chemical make-up. And this need not be peculiar or even particularly funny, as if a few jokes would galvanize the musical organism into giggles. Rather, wit is a process that functions as a kind of motivic development which is concerned with the mixing of disparate elements, dissolving and combining them in a perverse logic that can align them all into a single ironic smile. It is a quintessentially Haydnesque technique; even an insignificant upbeat can be severed by Haydn and reconnected into different syntactical configurations until the tiny anacrusis contradicts itself by becoming the final cadence of a work, as in the finale of Op. 54 No. 1. Or take again the finale of Mozart's 'Jupiter' Symphony. This movement, as with many 'Classical' structures, is not concerned so much with thematic unity as with the disintegration, contradiction and realignment of themes. The movement is made up of tiny detachable fragments that are forced into a chemical play of form and mixture which throws up all kinds of contrapuntal and thematic affinities. Not only are the fragments broken down in the process, but they are disfigured and warped by harmonic progressions that seem to pull the structure out of shape.

Clearly, the music is not developing blindly but struggles with its own processes in order to catch a momentary glimpse of itself as organic. It does not merely want to function: it wants to know how it functions, just like the new language of chemistry that Lavoisier had formulated in the 1780s: the musical compounds need to describe their own process of composition in the same way as water is H_2O. Thus in the coda, the contrapuntal apotheosis that ingeniously intertwines the disparate fragments into a single texture is a self-reflexive move that reveals the chemical make-up of the movement; the music comes into a contrapuntal self-consciousness; it suddenly knows itself as the intellectual force that activates the structure of the work. But this moment of self-knowledge is a textural disruption. The revelation is not the teleological goal of a symphony working out its material, as if this

Example 4.5 Mozart: Symphony No. 41 in C major, K. 551, finale, bars 158–64: motifs *a* and *b*

were an ineluctable organic process; it is more a play of wit that side-steps the coherence of the form to give an inkling of the absolute behind the clever connections of chemical affinity. Thus unity is not inherent *in* the work as an objective formula, but is disclosed by the work as an intellectual stance that is an ironic glance thrown back over the structure. 'Wit', writes Schlegel, 'is already a beginning towards universal music'.[45]

Thus chemical wit is not the wordplay itself but that which plays with words – the vital force that is caught by the web of irony. In the chemical mixture of the 'Jupiter' Symphony, the Romantic critic stumbles upon an all-knowing smile that will suddenly detach itself from the process to give an intuition of the form. This process of structural consciousness is particularly evident at the point of recapitulation. For a start, it is in the wrong place – it is simply too early. Mozart truncates the development, and he makes this obvious by suddenly blocking the harmonic and motivic momentum that had been pushing the development section forward with considerable violence. This violence is one of chemical chaos, made up of two fragments taken from the first group which are juxtaposed together – the initial motto (*a*) and the scalic motif (*b*) that asserts itself with a military precision (Ex. 4.5).

Because both fragments are harmonized as antecedent structures, they propel the music towards a closure that is constantly denied as they push from one dominant to another around the cycle of fifths. At first it is only the military motif (*b*), in canon with itself, that spirals flatwards from A minor to F major. Then the whole process reverses itself, employing both fragments to retrace the harmonic steps, only to overstep its A minor origin into a sharpward move towards E (Ex. 4.6). And just to make it clear, Mozart inverts motif (*b*) to signal the point of harmonic reversal.

[45] *Ibid.*, no. 2012.

Example 4.6 Mozart: Symphony No. 41 in C major, K. 551, finale –
harmonic structure of the development

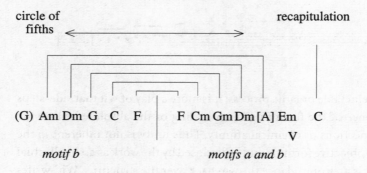

circle of   recapitulation
fifths

(G) Am Dm G C F   F Cm Gm Dm [A] Em   C

                                           V

   motif b   *motifs a and b*

Thus the harmonic arch is destabilized as the music insists on lingering for some ten bars on the dominant of E minor, as if it were a kind of false
preparation for some trick reprise.[46] What cannot happen is a tonic recapitulation (C major), despite the syntactical gestures towards a reprise of some
kind. And besides, the timing is askew; the development has not run its
course. But here lies the double bluff: the recapitulation does happen – as if
by magic.

At the centre of the movement, Mozart sets up a slippage between
form and content. And it is precisely this gap between structural closure
and harmonic function that is bridged by the smile of irony (see Ex. 4.7).
Just before the reprise, from bar 219, Mozart unfolds a diminished chord as
a dissonant reinforcement of E minor, but the opening motto (*a*), which has
already been transformed by the development section into semitonal
shapes, appears in the bass as a chromatic line that magically alters the tonal
function; the harmonic activity is purely chemical, turning the diminished
chord into new compounds with each semitonal step. In fact, the progression seems to have lost some of its logical calculations in the deft movement
of the chemical connections. And, appropriately, it is the chemical affinity
between the two antagonistic fragments (*a* and *b*) that conjures up the harmonic transformation and eventually turns the antecedent aggression of

---

46 This harmonic strategy is not uncommon; see, for example, Haydn, String
    Quartet in C major, Op. 76 No. 3, first movement, bars 65–79.

Example 4.7 Mozart: Symphony No. 41 in C major, K. 551, finale, bars 218–27

the military motif into a consequent phrase. This then slips softly into the recapitulation with an ironic smile that resolves the structure as sheer serendipity.

In a space of just six bars the movement untwists itself into the recapitulation in the face of this very impossibility. It is not an ineluctable progression, but a sudden revelation. The music rises above its chemical activity; this ironic consciousness is not *in* the music but hovers above it as a kind of critical self-commentary that detaches itself from the process to annotate its own structural antagonisms. And because the wit arises contingently out of the developmental chaos, the form and function are reconciled without really resolving the process of development. The development is not worked out with a mechanical appetency; it is simply erased by a turn of wit. The unexpected resolution is paradoxically a disruption of the formal procedures; but that is the way of irony – it annihilates

141

the structure to reveal the *Lebenskraft* that unites the chaotic activity of its vital chemistry. The music at the point of recapitulation is given an all-knowing glance that assures its consciousness of the organic process of its own formation (*Bildung*). As Karl Solger says concerning irony:

> the spirit of the artist must unite in one single glance all the tendencies of his work, and this glance, hovering over the whole and yet also cancelling out everything, this glance we call irony. The entire being and essence of art is resolved in irony.[47]

Conscious life form

Irony, I suggest, is the distinguishing feature of the 'Classical style'. But what Charles Rosen calls the 'Classical style' is problematically just the music of Haydn, Mozart and Beethoven.[48] Can these three composers legitimately represent the period? – for the 'Classical style' itself, as a categorization of the whole period, is not specifically ironic. Perhaps the three composers should be thought of as embodying a different style rather than colonizing the entire epoch. They are not the sole exponents of the 'Classical style'; rather the Classical language, which takes its vocabulary from Italian opera and *style galant*, is merely a historical texture from which the three composers try to disentangle themselves. Hence Johann Reichardt could call them 'the three pure humorists'.[49] The chemistry of their music is ironic activity, and this is the distinctive mark of a style that has been anachronistically and erroneously named as 'Classical'.[50]

If 'Classical' forms – most notably sonata forms – are to be modelled

---

[47] Karl Solger, *Erwin: Vier Gespräche über das Schöne und die Kunst*, quoted in Wheeler, *German Aesthetic and Literary Criticism*, pp. 23 and 146.

[48] See Charles Rosen, *The Classical Style* (London: Faber, 1971) and *Sonata Forms* (New York: Norton, 1988).

[49] Johann Reichardt, *Vertraute Briefe geschrieben auf einer Reise nach Wien . . . 1808/9*, quoted in Gretchen A. Wheelock, *Haydn's Ingenious Jesting with Art* (New York: Schirmer, 1992), pp. 50–1.

[50] See James Webster, *Haydn's 'Farewell' Symphony and the Idea of Classical Style: Through-Composition and Cyclic Integration in his Instrumental Music* (Cambridge: Cambridge University Press, 1991), pp. 347–57. Unfortunately, because there is no alternative label in the current discourse, I shall use the term Classical style to refer to the style of Haydn, Mozart and Beethoven.

on Haydn, then irony is their definition. His forms are not organic structures, but structures that try to *see themselves* as organic. There is a perpetual tampering with the music's biology to bring the forms into self-reflection. In this sense, the 'Classical style' is a musical embodiment of Kant's *Critique of Judgement*, for its structures focus on the contradiction within themselves as subject and object; this is the necessary condition of self-knowledge, the primary division of *Ur-teil* (judgement) that caused the Romantic ego to tumble down the asymptotic pit of ironic reflection. Because of this fissure, Haydn's forms never coincide with themselves; they always explore an ironic gap in their constant preoccupation with their own dislocated structures. In fact, this self-referential manipulation of form is a sign of their autonomy. But this autonomy is not the kind of self-regulating system that is often associated with the 'Classical style'. After all, Baroque forms also enclose themselves within their own tonal and thematic constructs; a binary or a ritornello structure is no less dynamic in its harmonic processes and no less symmetrical in its formal design than a sonata-form movement – a form, in fact, which owes its processes to these Baroque designs. What distinguishes the sonata processes of Haydn – and, indeed, of Mozart and Beethoven – is that they assert their autonomy by subverting it; they seek to destroy a blind autonomy for an ironic one, and so come into self-consciousness as an anti-aesthetic that demythologizes its own existence. Sonata-type forms are more a way of thought than a method of construction. When, for example, the rondo finale of Haydn's 'Joke' Quartet, Op. 33 No. 2, fails to finalize the work with its abortive gestures of closure, the form negates itself to know itself as an aesthetic illusion. The smile of self-knowledge that hangs in the air after the quartet has disappeared is that ironic lightness of being that happily destroys the aesthetic autonomy for the knowledge of its own sovereignty. But, of course, this ironic consciousness is yet another aesthetic illusion that must be negated in an infinite regression that mimics the trail of concluding phrases that defer the quartet's completion.

Perhaps this quartet is almost too obvious an example of the ironic mismatching of gesture and function in the works of the three composers, but it underlines a principle that is a general procedure of the style. Thus the Classical notion of sonata form as a perfect structure in which form and content are inextricably bound is simply erroneous. Sonata form discovers its identity in the slippage between its external and internal procedures. This means that there is no sonata form that is *in* 'sonata form'. A Classically perfect sonata form is a contradiction, because the very essence of sonata form is contradiction itself. Its ironic consciousness demands that it simultaneously insist on and resist all definitions of its form. Sonata form is only perfect in the Schlegelian sense – perfect to the 'point of irony', that is to the point of imperfection[51] – which means that it is an analytical trap waiting to snap up the innocent theorist. Not everyone will get it, which is why sonata form lives in a confusion of analytical concepts. On the one hand, it refuses the formulaic definitions that seem to work for binary, ternary and ritornello forms. It constantly disrupts its form so that any 'textbook' definition of it will simply miss the point. In fact, Rosen claims that to define sonata form is to kill it:

> Sonata form could not be defined until it was dead. Czerny claimed with pride around 1840 that he was the first to describe it, but by then it was already part of history.[52]

But on the other hand, not to define sonata form is to be left with some amorphous organism that ultimately denies its own species. Any similarity between pieces becomes a matter of feeling, sensibility or practice – some kind of nebulous spirit that organizes the form from the inside. But this will not work. Sonata form not only refuses prescriptive definitions, but confuses any attempt to deduce its structure internally. The rejection of an external mould in favour of a microscopic investigation of what James Webster would call a 'through-composed' work that arises from the particularity of its own configurations is also spurious. After all, the sonata forms of Haydn, Mozart and Beethoven are suspiciously similar. In fact, the concept of sonata form asserts itself as a norm; it is a measure for all kinds of structural deviations in the music of the nineteenth and twentieth centuries. Consequently, it can only be described as a normative principle that refuses normal definition. If, for example, 'the development and recapitulation [can] exchange roles' in the first movement of Haydn's Symphony No. 89, then the form is not going through the motions mechanically, but is self-

---

[51] See Behler, *Irony and the Discourse of Modernity*, p. 84.
[52] Rosen, *The Classical Style*, p. 30.

144

consciously manipulating itself against the norms it sets up.[53] Similarly, the 'off-key' ambiguity that initiates the B minor Quartet, Op. 33 No. 1, and the submediant 'dominant preparation' that heralds the recapitulation in the opening movement of the E major Quartet, Op. 54 No. 3, are designed to create an ironic coherence where there is a formal contradiction. These disruptions become the focus of formal consciousness.

So, like the Fichtean ego that only knows itself in the act of philosophizing, the text of sonata form constantly interferes with its own coherence to render the system ironically infinite in its conscious attempt to grasp its own identity as a compositional act. *Sonata form has to catch itself out as form.* Hence sonata form is *not a form*, in that any external definition of its structure will destroy its essence as consciousness. And yet sonata form *has to be a form* in that its consciousness is only signified by its constant negation of the structure it posits. Sonata form is therefore the double activity of indicating and subverting its structure in an ironic attempt to synthesize the universal and the particular. In Romantic fashion, it strives towards a reconciliation that it knows to be impossible and at best illusory.

By *never* conforming to the structure that it *always* posits, sonata form is able to indicate its own theory of form and to surpass it as a theory beyond theory, so that its definition neither resides in the actual non-conformity nor its virtual formality, but in the gap of negation. 'It is equally fatal', says Schlegel, 'for the mind to have a system and to have none. One will simply have to decide to combine the two.'[54] This is what sonata form does; it is in this space of contradiction that an intellectual unity embraces the work within the giant inverted commas of ironic distance. Sonata form therefore asserts its autonomy in the sovereign knowledge of its own illusions – a mere manipulation of empty signs – and so redeems from nothing its conscious life.

Artificial reality

Irony, of course, existed long before the Romantics brought it into their peculiar philosophical focus. Practice precedes theory, and this also

---

[53] *Ibid.*, p. 157.
[54] Friedrich Schlegel, *Lucinde and the Fragments*, trans. P. Firchow (Minneapolis: University of Minneapolis Press, 1971), p. 167.

applies to the Romantic discourse on music. Haydn's instrumental forms perhaps prepared the path for a Romantic philosophy of music. As Mark Evan Bonds points out, by the 1780s Haydn's music was consistently being compared to the novels of Laurence Sterne,[55] whose ironic pose was openly adopted by the German Romantics.[56] Sterne's *Tristram Shandy* and *A Sentimental Journey* are not really novels but ironic commentaries on the aesthetic process of creating and consuming novels. And Haydn's works follow the same stance of authorial self-consciousness. An anonymous critic in the *Musikalischer Almanach auf das Jahr 1782* compared Haydn to Sterne, calling him 'a musical joker of the high comic; and this is dreadfully difficult in music', he adds. 'It is for this reason that so few people sense that Haydn is making a joke, even when he is making one.' Haydn has 'two different styles', he claims: 'in the works of the earlier period, Haydn often laughed whole-heartedly; in the works of the second period, he contracts his visage into a smile'.[57]

This smile, so the critic claims, seems difficult to manufacture in sound, but instrumental music, with its alienated signs, is perhaps the purest vehicle for the wry curve of ironic distance. Its signs are so far removed from reality that they can only simulate things as illusion. This is perhaps the greatest achievement of Haydn: he was the first to glory in the sheer artificiality of instrumental music. If instrumental music for Rousseau was an art distanced from the origin of humanity and therefore divorced from nature,[58] then Haydn merely affirms this as fact, channelling his creative powers to ironize nature and to destroy all naïve delusions of Eden. In the hands of Haydn, art is no longer artless nature but the artificial simulation of it. For the first time in its history, instrumental music becomes truly instrumental – a tool. It was used as an implement for a perpetual manipulation of the distance between the subject and its object of contemplation. Haydn's instrumental forms were designed to prevent the unmediated absorption of the subject into the piece, so that the body of

---

55 Bonds, 'Haydn, Laurence Sterne'.
56 See, for example, Friedrich Schlegel, *Dialogue on Poetry and Literary Aphorisms*, pp. 95–7. 57 Quoted in Bonds, 'Haydn, Laurence Sterne', 59.
58 See Jean-Jacques Rousseau, *Essai sur l'origine des langues*, in *The First and Second Discourses together with the replies to Critics and Essay on the Origin of Languages*, ed. and trans. V. Gourevitch (New York: Harper & Row, 1986).

Empfindsamkeit could no longer vibrate with the natural laws of music. However much the body wants to discover its innate morality through the sensations of sound, Haydn's music turns around and says 'I am art – a mere illusion. See, here are the hands of the composer.' Almost every element comes under the ironic scrutiny of Haydn; he robs music of what Schiller would define as the naïve – the unreflective state of nature which modern man, divided in himself and from the world, can no longer return to.[59] The music needs to objectify this division by interfering with the alignment of sign and referent, so that, like a *Lebenskraft* experiment, conscious life can be squeezed out from sound. Thus Haydn writes against the objects he posits; his minuets are 'anti-minuets', says Hans Keller, a deliberately artificial simulation of the real thing;[60] his evocations of bucolic drones and folk tunes are quirky, decontextualized objects that dispossess nature of its innocence; his sonata forms are not in sonata form but find their consciousness in the gap of negation. Semiotics for Haydn is not a means of making meaning but of destabilizing representation, whether it involves mimetic signs or internal cross-references in the structure. He simply throws out an A flat major brick in a C major quartet to force the audience out of an Arcadia of natural complacency, making them think twice before falling back into an uncritical mode of thought (see Ex. 4.8).

The A flat major brick shatters the aesthetic illusion to reveal the hand that is manipulating the act of aesthetic consciousness. Haydn's humour, says Jean Paul, can 'annihilate entire key areas' as a kind of pre-emptive strike that negates the form, to bring the process of composition into ironic knowledge.[61] In fact, to emphasize the awkwardness of this A flat intrusion, Haydn cancels it out with a quick cadential shuffle that leaves the phrase lopsided and somewhat disorientating. Of course, there is nothing new about the flattened submediant; there is a sizeable chunk of it in Op. 20 No. 2, where it is used as a cadential device to articulate the end of various sections of the opening movement. But Haydn in Op. 54 No. 2 cannot leave this

---

[59] See Friedrich von Schiller, *On the Naive and Sentimental in Literature*, trans. H. Watanabe-O'Kelly (Manchester: Carcanet Press, 1981).

[60] Hans Keller, *The Great Haydn Quartets* (London: Dent, 1986), p. 237. See also Wheelock, *Haydn's Ingenious Jesting with Art*, pp. 55–89.

[61] Jean Paul Richter, *Vorlesungen über Aesthetik*, quoted in Bonds, 'Haydn, Laurence Sterne', 63.

Example 4.8 String Quartet in C major, Op. 54 No. 2, first movement, bars

innocent cadential cliché alone. He has to invert its function, elongating it like some overblown full-stop in mid-sentence so that it deliberately makes a mess of the cadence. The flattened submediant is therefore forced to initiate a movement of formal self-consciousness that is not 'resolved' until the end of the movement, where the inflated cadence of the opening turns into a correspondingly massive block of C major, via A♭, placed where it should be – at the close and as a structural cadence (bars 185ff.). These thirty bars of cadential gesture at the close elucidate the contradiction of sign and function that had dislocated the opening of the work. Thus Haydn manufactures a disruptive logic of chemical wit that explains the disjunctions and gives a revelation of an organic intelligence behind the quartet. It is an ironic rather than syntactic coherence.

And all this is sparked off by only the third phrase of a quartet that is a catalogue of quirks, with its mischievous gaps, harmonic fissures, asymmetrical structures and stark juxtapositions. It is calculated to force the aesthetic subject to flicker in and out of the work in endless contradictions. Take, for example, the bubble of jollity that bursts into the finale to destabilize the entire structure of the work. For a start, the finale is an Adagio. It pretends to be an enlarged slow introduction, but the long awaited arrival of the Presto is contradicted by its own brevity, and the return of the slow tempo simply confirms the perverse structure of a movement that jars against itself as an immiscible and inexplicable form. It would have been at least amusing if it were not for the deadly seriousness with which the Adagio returns – as if nothing had happened. The entire movement is a web of contradiction, made all the more peculiar by the ironic composure of a composer who stands benignly at a distance to manipulate his audience.

If, in the hands of Haydn, instrumental music makes a defiant stand against the voice of nature as pure artificiality, then it does so as 'an expression of disdain for the world'. That, at least, is Jean Paul's insight into Haydn's humour.[62] This disdain does not arise from a hatred of nature; rather the infinite longing of Romantic irony comes from the knowledge that nature has been lost forever. Instrumental music signals the recognition of reality as a radical alienation, so clearly articulated in Schiller's

---

[62] Quoted in Bonds, 'Haydn, Laurence Sterne', 63.

aesthetics as a division between man and nature, reason and sense, duty and desire, freedom and necessity. It is the function of art, he claims, not only to recognize the division, but to strive to heal it, *without* returning to a naïve state of nature. In German aesthetics, culture becomes nature not by reviving the garden of innocence, but by manufacturing nature through an artificial paradise, cultivated by the fruit of knowledge. Art as artificiality reunites humanity this side of Eden, which is why Kant claims that a naïve art is a contradiction in terms.[63] Any false reconciliation of the aesthetic has to be recognized as illusion, not reality. Thus a Utopian aesthetic in a music that seems to pursue happiness can only be expressed ironically; instrumental music registers the impossibility of manufacturing a second nature even in the very attempt to do so. The 'Classical style' simply knows too much. If you hear only happiness in Haydn, then the joke is on you.

Optimistic pessimism

'Irony', writes George Lukács, 'can see where God is to be found in a world abandoned by God.... [It] is the highest freedom that can be achieved in a world without God.'[64] The Romantics wanted to know the truth, even if the truth is the knowledge that one can never arrive at the truth. I suggest that the idea of absolute music reflects this posture. Haydn's music is not simply the bearer of Enlightenment joy; Haydn is a Romantic. In reading the Classical style Romantically, I have tried to tease out the *Lebenskraft* of absolute music as an ironic spirit that attempts to overcome the apparent failure of God after the Lisbon earthquake and the failure of humanity after the French Revolution; this is what Schlegel calls an 'aesthetic optimism' in the face of *Candide* – that is, an aesthetic optimism in the face of a historical pessimism. It is an aesthetic attempt to prolong the revolutionary ideals without reifying them in reality, lest Utopia should prematurely arrive as yet another disaster of humanity. Hence absolute music should remain ineffable and incomplete as a negative absolute, yearning towards the

---

[63] Kant, *Critique of Judgement*, p. 203.
[64] Georg Lukács, *The Theory of the Novel*, trans. A. Bostock (Cambridge, Mass., MIT Press, 1994), pp. 92–3.

organic as an interim measure in hard times, creating an artificial nature full of contradictions that reflect the uncertainty and the divisions of the modern ego. Thus the unexpected affinities and connections between irony, chemistry, music and philosophy were meant to produce a brave face which could confront the terrifying contradictions bequeathed to the Romantics by the Enlightenment, with a smile manufactured in the laboratory of the aesthetic.

5 Haydn's 'Cours complet de la composition' and the *Sturm und Drang*

MARK EVAN BONDS

The phenomenon known as the *Sturm und Drang* figures prominently in most twentieth-century accounts of Haydn's development as a composer. Théodore de Wyzewa, writing in 1909, was the first to suggest an 'extremely acute crisis' in the composer's personal life, in the year 1772. This 'crisis', according to Wyzewa, manifested itself in a series of unusual minor-mode works, including Symphonies Nos. 44 ('Trauer'), 45 ('Farewell') and 49 ('Passione'), and the slightly earlier (1771) Sonata No. 33 in C minor. Wyzewa could not, however, identify any particular incident that would have caused such a 'Romantic paroxysm', so he invented one. These minor-mode works were 'songs of sorrow' occasioned by the death of a young woman. But 'without a doubt', Wyzewa concluded, the world would 'never know the name of Haydn's "immortal beloved"'.[1]

No one has ever taken Wyzewa's theory of an 'immortal beloved' for Haydn very seriously for the simple reason that there is no evidence to support it. Even Wyzewa himself seems to have found this hypothesis insufficient, for he went on in the same essay to offer a second, complementary explanation for these unusual symphonies. The 'melancholy seriousness' of these works, he argued, was also at least in part a product of the *Zeitgeist* and could be found in contemporaneous music by other composers as well, including Gluck, Mozart, C. P. E. Bach, Vanhal and Dittersdorf. On this basis, Wyzewa drew a parallel with the slightly later literary move-

---

[1] Théodore de Wyzewa, 'A propos du centenaire de la mort de Joseph Haydn', *Revue des deux mondes* 79 (1909), 935–46. Wyzewa's reasoning was based in part on a faulty chronology that placed Symphonies Nos. 44 and 49 in 1772, whereas the former dates from before 1772 and the latter from 1768. All dates given for Haydn's works in the present essay derive from Georg Feder's work-list in *The New Grove Haydn* (New York: Norton, 1982).

ment known as the *Sturm und Drang*, characterized by the expression of extreme emotions and a rejection of formal conventions.

Although the details of Wyzewa's original *Sturm und Drang* hypothesis have been refined and varied over time, its basic shape has remained essentially unchanged down to the present day. The notion of a 'personal crisis', combined with the influence of the *Zeitgeist*, has been invoked on many occasions to explain the unusual nature of a number of pieces written during the late 1760s and early 1770s. For all its demonstrable flaws, Wyzewa's hypothesis has persisted because there *is* compelling musical evidence to suggest that Haydn did in fact enter a critical phase of his compositional career at this time, and that there was indeed something 'in the air' extending beyond Haydn himself. The idea of the *Sturm und Drang* is particularly germane to theatre music of this period, as Daniel Heartz has argued so persuasively.[2] And within the realm of instrumental music, it is difficult to ignore such pronounced similarities as those found among Haydn's Symphony No. 39 in G minor (before 1770), Vanhal's Symphony in G minor, B. Gm1 (1771 or before) and Mozart's 'Little' G minor Symphony, K. 185 (1773). The technical and emotional congruencies of these three works are too detailed and far-reaching to be merely coincidental. It is unclear whether Haydn's or Vanhal's symphony was the first of these three works to appear; assuming that the two subsequent symphonies represent instances of direct modelling, it is striking that two later composers should have been attracted to the same work or the same kind of work.[3]

How this broader tendency relates to Haydn's instrumental music of the late 1760s and early 1770s as a whole, however, remains deeply problematic. In recent years scholars have begun to recognize that the prototypical

---

[2] Daniel Heartz, 'Sturm und Drang im Musikdrama', in Carl Dalhaus *et al.*, eds., *Bericht über den Internationalen musikwissenschaftlichen Kongress Bonn 1970* (Kassel: Bärenreiter, 1971), pp. 432–5; Heartz, 'Sturm und Drang', *The New Grove Dictionary of Music and Musicians*, ed. Stanley Sadie (London: Macmillan, 1980), XVIII, 311–12. See also Joel Kolk, '"Sturm und Drang" and Haydn's Opera', in Jens Peter Larsen, Howard Serwer and James Webster, eds., *Haydn Studies: Proceedings of the International Haydn Conference, Washington, D. C., 1975* (New York: Norton, 1981), pp. 440–5.

[3] On the uncertain chronology of the two earlier symphonies, see Paul Bryan's thematic catalogue of Vanhal's symphonies in *The Symphony, 1720–1840*, Series B, vol. X (New York: Garland, 1981).

Sturm und Drang works are in many respects anomalous. The vast majority of Haydn's compositions from this time are in the major mode, and relatively few of them exhibit the specific musical characteristics typically associated with the style of the *Sturm und Drang*, such as wide melodic leaps, driving syncopations, increased dissonance, fuller textures, and abrupt contrasts in dynamics, texture, harmony and rhythmic motion.

These features, moreover, are by no means exclusive to the late 1760s and early 1770s; indeed, they can be found in individual works throughout Haydn's career.[4] Minor-mode symphonies, which constitute one of the linchpins of the '*Zeitgeist* hypothesis', provide a case in point. Beginning in the mid- to late 1760s, there is indeed a significant increase in the production of such works among symphonists in general. Yet, as Rey Longyear has pointed out, the total number of symphonies in the minor mode actually *increased* over the final decades of the eighteenth century.[5] This phenomenon, in other words, cannot be considered peculiar to the period known as the *Sturm und Drang*.

This is not mere quibbling over labels. The very notion of the *Sturm und Drang* has seriously distorted our view of Haydn the composer by positing a disruption in his career attributable to either a personal crisis or the *Zeitgeist*, or to some combination of the two. This notion of disruption, in turn, has shaped the manner in which we view both his previous and subsequent output, particularly from the mid- and late 1770s. Within accounts of Haydn's career, the years around 1768–72 are often interpreted as a kind of artistic mid-life crisis, a period of 'turmoil' that produced some of his most remarkable music before his years of stylistic 'maturity'. Considered against the 'bold experimentation' of the *Sturm und Drang*, earlier and later works alike (at least through to the early 1780s) are often held to be less ambitious and aesthetically less significant. Sets of published works lacking

---

[4] See R. Larry Todd, 'Joseph Haydn and the *Sturm und Drang*: A Revaluation', *Music Review* 41 (1980), 172–96; Jens Peter Larsen, *The New Grove Haydn* (see note 1), pp. 28–9, 92–3; Leonard Ratner, in his *Classic Music: Expression, Form, and Style* (New York: Schirmer, 1980), p. 21, treats the *Sturm und Drang* as a 'topic', that is, as a particular category of musical gesture, rather than as a period, noting that this manner of writing is 'also present in [Haydn's] later symphonies'.

[5] Rey M. Longyear, 'The Minor Mode in the Classic Period', *Music Review* 32 (1971), 27–35.

a minor-mode work are labelled 'conservative', and there is a general perception that the output of the mid- and late 1770s represents a certain
falling-off in both intensity and quality, not redeemed until the self-pro-
claimed 'entirely new manner' of the string quartets Op. 33, and the 'breakthrough' to the 'Classical style'.[6]

James Webster's recent debunking of the myth of the 'Classical style'
has laid the foundation for a thorough re-evaluation of Haydn's output in
general and his middle-period instrumental music in particular.[7] Webster
identifies the notion of 'Classical style' as the 'master trope' that has governed critical interpretations of Haydn's music for the past century, the
central concept that has shaped our attitudes towards his development as a
composer. Within this trope, as Webster points out, Haydn achieved 'maturity' only after a noble but unsuccessful struggle with Baroque counterpoint in the early 1770s (exemplified by the fugal finales of Op. 20 but
extending, by implication, to the contemporaneous *Sturm und Drang* as a
whole) and a subsequent period of withdrawal over the remainder of that
decade. This 'master trope', as Webster observes, follows the archetype of
the mythical 'quest': after a brief period of ambitious but unsuccessful
experimentation, Haydn withdraws for almost ten years in order to refine
his skills so that he can re-emerge in mature splendour with the 'entirely
new manner' of the Op. 33 quartets. The very idea of a 'Classical style'
demands a demonstration that the works of Haydn's earlier career,
although brilliant enough in their own way, were nevertheless somehow
deficient in that they had not yet achieved the 'perfection' of the 'mature
Classical style'. A period of unsuccessful striving – a grappling with
extremes – was a necessary prerequisite to the eventual 'breakthrough' and
balance achieved with Op. 33.

Not everyone, of course, accepted the 'Op. 33 hypothesis'. Jens Peter

---

[6] See, for example, Karl Geiringer, *Haydn: A Creative Life in Music*, 3rd edn
(Berkeley and Los Angeles: University of California Press, 1982), chapter 14;
Rosemary Hughes, *Haydn*, rev. edn (London: Dent, 1978), pp. 176–7; Charles
Rosen, *The Classical Style: Haydn, Mozart, Beethoven* (New York: Viking, 1971),
p. 23 *et passim*; A. Peter Brown, *Joseph Haydn's Keyboard Music: Sources and Style*
(Bloomington: Indiana University Press, 1986), p. 303.

[7] James Webster, *Haydn's 'Farewell' Symphony and the Idea of Classical Style:
Through-Composition and Cyclic Integration in his Instrumental Music*
(Cambridge: Cambridge University Press, 1991), especially pp. 335–73.

Larsen and H. C. Robbins Landon, in particular, have argued that it was the *Sturm und Drang* that represented Haydn's 'synthesis' of earlier styles into a mature, coherent idiom.[8] But this approach, as Webster notes, merely pushes back by one decade the notion of a 'Classical breakthrough'. Regardless of whether this period is seen as a noble failure or as a breakthrough, it is consistently viewed as a 'crisis', a decisive turning-point in Haydn's 'progress' towards a 'full mastery' of his art.

But there is a second, equally powerful trope at work here as well, one that ultimately derives from Wyzewa's original formulation of the hypothesis and that has permeated the literature on Haydn throughout our century. As his postulation of an 'immortal beloved' suggests, Wyzewa was very much under the sway of contemporaneous Beethoven research.[9] His theory of dual sources – personal and social – for the *Sturm und Drang* represents nothing less than an attempt to impose the premises and methods of Beethoven scholarship on to the music of Haydn.

Drawing on the paradigm of contemporaneous Beethoven scholarship, Wyzewa assumed that direct and significant connections could be made between a composer's life and works. A sudden slew of unusual and emotionally charged works like Haydn's minor-mode symphonies of the late 1760s and early 1770s *had* to have been motivated by a specific biographical incident. That the works inspiring Wyzewa's *Sturm und Drang* hypothesis were those most closely resembling the popular image of Beethoven's 'C minor mood' is scarcely coincidental: a few years before, George Grove had flatly asserted that it was 'impossible not to believe' that Beethoven's C minor Symphony was 'based on his relations' to Theresa Brunswick and that 'the work – the first movement at any rate ... is more or

---

[8] Jens Peter Larsen, 'Some Observations on the Development and Characteristics of Viennese Classical Instrumental Music', *Studia musicologica* 9 (1967), 115–39; H. C. Robbins Landon, *Haydn: Chronicle and Works II: Haydn at Eszterháza, 1766–1790* (Bloomington: Indiana University Press, 1978), p. 324.

[9] Wyzewa himself had written an extended review of a recent monograph on Beethoven's 'Immortal Beloved' only a few months before: La Mara [that is, Ida Maria Lipsius], *Beethovens Unsterbliche Geliebte: Das Geheimnis der Gräfin Brunsvik und ihre Memoiren* (Leipzig: Breitkopf & Härtel, 1909), reviewed in the *Revue des deux mondes* 79 (1909), 456–68. Another book on the same subject had also appeared in 1909: W. A. Thomas-San-Galli, *Die 'unsterbliche Geliebte' Beethovens, Amalie Sebald* (Halle: Otto Hendel, 1909).

less a picture of their personality and connection'.[10] For Wyzewa, Haydn's music from the early 1770s provided sufficient evidence to demonstrate that Haydn had his own 'immortal beloved'. The only piece missing from this biographical puzzle was the composer's self-revelatory love letter.

The idea that the *Zeitgeist* would have constituted a second, congruent source of influence is also basic to the premises of Beethoven scholarship. Untroubled by the chronological disparity between the works under discussion and the literary movement that began to emerge only later, Wyzewa scarcely missed a beat in moving from his account of Haydn's presumed personal crisis to what he called the broader 'intellectual and moral' crisis of European society. Contemporaneous (but unspecified) music by Gluck, Mozart, Vanhal and Dittersdorf provided an 'absolute equivalent' to works like Gottfried Bürger's *Leonore* and Goethe's *Die Leiden des jungen Werthers*, as well as to the writings of Rousseau and Ossian in general.

The attempt to single out a moment of disruption in the composer's career has other parallels to Beethoven criticism. Although Wyzewa did not state so explicitly, he was trying to distinguish, in effect, between Haydn's 'early' and 'middle' periods by using the *Sturm und Drang* as a point of demarcation within the composer's thirty-odd years of service to the Esterházy family. The immediate motivation behind such an attempt is certainly understandable. The first volumes of the ill-fated Breitkopf & Härtel *Gesamtausgabe* of Haydn's works, including the symphonies Nos. 1–40, had been issued only recently, and, like almost everyone else interested in this repertory, Wyzewa was faced with the task of assimilating a considerable body of essentially unfamiliar music by a major composer. As Wyzewa rightly pointed out, the general perception of Haydn's music, particularly his symphonies, was based almost entirely on works from the late period. Against what he perceived to be the relatively carefree, more or less uniform tone of these pre-1772 symphonies, the 'bizarre' minor-mode symphonies Wyzewa knew from other editions stood out in even greater relief.

To varying degrees, all of the premises that Wyzewa drew from Beethoven scholarship had proven useful – for the study of Beethoven's music. The persistence of an early/middle/late periodization is a testimony

---

[10] George Grove, *Beethoven and his Nine Symphonies* (London: Novello, 1896), p. 140.

to its basic utility, for, in spite of its tendency towards over-simplification, this schema has provided an almost unavoidably useful framework for the understanding of Beethoven's development in the very broadest terms. The biographical elements of certain specific works, in turn – such as the 'Eroica' Symphony, the Piano Sonata Op. 81a ('Les Adieux'), and the 'Heiliger Dankgesang' of the String Quartet Op. 132, to name only a few examples – have long provided powerful evidence for a more or less direct connection between the composer's life and works. Equally strong associations of certain works with the *Zeitgeist* are also readily apparent in such compositions as *Fidelio, Wellingtons Sieg* and the Ninth Symphony. An important body of Beethoven's music does demonstrably reflect events in his own personal life or the political and intellectual tendencies of the day, even if the connections are not always as immediate or precise as some commentators would have us believe.[11]

But these basic premises do not apply particularly well to Haydn, whose music cannot be aligned with an 'inner biography', even at a superficial level. Here, the matrix of life, times and works, already problematic enough in the case of Beethoven, becomes even more tenuous. This is not to say that such connections do not exist, and we should of course try to identify them whenever possible, for they can enhance our understanding of the music, its composer and its contexts. At the same time, we should recognize that Haydn's career and compositional output proceeded along a path that was very different in kind from that of Beethoven.

Haydn's music resists clear chronological divisions. Changes in exter-

---

11 On the historical and analytical implications of these assumptions in Beethoven scholarship, see Carl Dahlhaus, *Ludwig van Beethoven: Approaches to his Music*, trans. Mary Whittall (Oxford: Clarendon Press, 1991), chapter 1, 'Life and Work'; and Maynard Solomon, *Beethoven Essays* (Cambridge, Mass.: Harvard University Press, 1988), chapter 7, 'Thoughts on Biography'. In moving beyond this simple tripartite division, recent scholarship has raised important questions about some of the basic premises of periodization in general: see, for example, Maynard Solomon, 'The Creative Periods of Beethoven', in his *Beethoven Essays*, pp. 116–25; James Webster, 'The Concept of Beethoven's "Early" Period in the Context of Periodizations in General', *Beethoven Forum* 3 (1994), 1–27; Tia DeNora, 'Deconstructing Periodization: Sociological Methods and Historical Ethnography in Late Eighteenth-Century Vienna', *Beethoven Forum* 4 (1995), 1–15; K. M. Knittel, 'Imitation, Individuality, and Illness: Behind Beethoven's "Three Styles"', *Beethoven Forum* 4 (1995), 17–36.

nal circumstances tended to affect the genres within which Haydn worked but not his trans-generic style of writing *per se*. The death of Prince Nicolaus and the subsequent departure for England, for example, are events of obvious importance in Haydn's career, yet there is no marked shift in style. The symphonies written for London are of course distinctive in their own ways – many critics consider them more 'public' – but the stylistic differences between these symphonies and others written even a decade before are still fairly subtle, especially when compared to, say, the distance between Beethoven's Second and Third Symphonies, which are often cited as exemplars of the distinction between the composer's 'early'- and 'middle'-period styles. Nor is there any single, external event that decisively demarcates Haydn's long years of service at the Esterházy court. Some commentators have suggested the death of his predecessor, Georg Joseph Werner, and Haydn's ascendance to the position of Kapellmeister in 1766; others have argued that the construction of the opera house in 1776 and Haydn's concomitant engagement with this genre, both as a composer and as a conductor, mark a significant turning-point in his career. Still others have pointed to the composer's own celebrated description from 1781 of the string quartets of Op. 33 as having been written 'in an entirely new manner'. But revealingly, and in marked contrast to Beethoven, none of these divisions has won general acceptance, nor is any of them likely to.[12]

Haydn's development as a composer simply does not mirror Beethoven's. His declaration on Op. 33 notwithstanding, there is no 'breakthrough' in his art. There *are* novel elements in Op. 33, and these should not be underestimated; but the same can be said for almost every major set of works that Haydn ever issued.[13] In the case of Op. 33, Haydn had an immediate commercial need to promote this particular set, yet a great many historians have seized on this statement to satisfy their own need to identify a particular moment that marks the arrival of the 'mature Classical style'. But, as Webster has demonstrated so convincingly, the resulting dichotomy

---

[12] For a convenient summary of attempts to divide Haydn's career into distinct periods, see Elaine R. Sisman, *Haydn and the Classical Variation* (Cambridge, Mass.: Harvard University Press, 1993), pp. 146–50; see also Webster, *Haydn's 'Farewell' Symphony*, pp. 359–62.

[13] See W. Dean Sutcliffe, *Haydn: String Quartets, Op. 50* (Cambridge: Cambridge University Press, 1992), pp. 17–23.

between the 'Classical' ('perfect') style and an earlier, implicitly 'pre-Classical' ('not yet perfect') style has badly distorted the perception of Haydn's output as a whole. Haydn was nothing if not a shrewd business-man, and the venue of his claim – within a letter inviting pre-publication subscriptions to the set – is scarcely the place to expect any artist to offer a detached view of his output. Haydn's assertion is in fact part of a long tradi-tion in which composers promote the element of novelty in their music. A few decades later, Beethoven himself would make a similar claim about both his Opp. 34 and 35 piano variations – again, significantly, in a letter offering the works for sale, this time to a publisher.[14]

In short, the search for discrete stylistic periods within Haydn's career, punctuated by brief but significant episodes of disruption, is part of the larger (and largely inappropriate) 'Beethoven trope'. The works of the so-called *Sturm und Drang* period, as Webster has shown, represent a continuation of earlier tendencies rather than an abrupt shift within the composer's career. For all their significance in Haydn's artistic develop-ment, the years between *c.* 1768 and 1773 do not witness an abandonment of earlier principles or a dramatic change in direction.

*

Rather than a period of disruption in Haydn's compositional output, the late 1760s and early 1770s can be more profitably understood as a period of intense, quasi-systematic exploration. This notion is supported by a hith-erto unknown statement from Haydn himself, one made without any motivation of financial gain. In spite of its brevity, it reveals much about the composer's own view of his earlier career and the nature of the works written during the so-called *Sturm und Drang* years.

---

[14] Letter of 18 October 1802 to Breitkopf & Härtel, in *The Letters of Beethoven*, trans. and ed. Emily Anderson, I (London: Macmillan, 1961), pp. 76–7. Hans-Werner Küthen, 'Beethovens "wirklich ganz neue Manier" – eine Persiflage', in Sieghard Brandenburg and Helmut Loos, eds., *Beiträge zu Beethovens Kammermusik* (Munich: Henle, 1987), pp. 216–24, argues that phrases like 'an entirely new manner' were in fact so common in the musical world that Beethoven's characterization of his own variations is to be understood ironically. See also Glenn Stanley, 'The "wirklich gantz neue Manier" and the Path to It: Beethoven's Variations for Piano, 1783–1802', *Beethoven Forum* 3 (1994), 53–79, suggesting that the 'new manner' was not really as new as Beethoven wanted his publishers to believe.

Haydn's self-evaluation appears within an anecdote related by the Bohemian composer Anton Reicha (1770–1835), who lived in Vienna between 1802 and 1808 and was in close personal contact with Haydn during that time. Sometime around 1814 or 1815, after emigrating to Paris, Reicha wrote a brief treatise entitled 'Sur la musique comme art purement sentimental'.[15] Although clearly intended for publication – the second, cleaner version of the manuscript even includes a title page with the words 'Ouvrage publié par F. Fayolle' – the work was in fact never issued publicly.[16]

Reicha's unpublished treatise is an important witness to the rapidly changing perception of instrumental music's emotional power in the early nineteenth century. The particular passage in question here, however, deals with Haydn's working methods and appears at the end of an account of just how far instrumental music had developed in recent decades at the hands of Mozart and particularly Haydn:

> Haydn étudiait son art sans cesse. A l'âge de 72 ans, je le vis faire des accompagnemen[t]s aux airs écossais, uniquement pour ne pas perdre l'habitude de bien moduler (c'étaient ses propres paroles). Après avoir fait beaucoup d'ouvrages, il recommença à 40 ans, le cours complet de la composition, pour s'affermir dans son art, et en connaître mieux les secrets. Il m'a dit plusieurs fois qu'*il ne faut point passer un seul jour, sans s'occuper de son art* (Principe d'Apelle et de Raphael: Nullus dies sine linea): *Et si l'on ne pouvait pas composer, qu'il fallait étudier.* Quelle leçon pour ces génies prétendus qui croient pouvoir se dispenser d'approfondir leur art! Nous en voyons les heureux effets.[17]
>
> Haydn studied his art ceaselessly. When he was seventy-two, I saw him making accompaniments for Scottish airs, solely so as not to lose the habit

---

[15] Paris, Bibliothèque du Conservatoire, Rés. F. 1645–1646. The entry for Reicha in *The New Grove* dates the manuscript as '?before 1814', but on f. 41 of F. 1645, Reicha refers to 'notre ouvrage sur la Mélodie' (Reicha's *Traité de mélodie*, published by the author in 1814) as covering a particular point in greater detail. The later version of 'Sur la musique comme art purement sentimental' (MS F. 1646), in turn, cites the *Traité de mélodie* by its specific title.

[16] François Joseph Marie Fayolle (1774–1852), better known as a writer on music, was also active as a book publisher around this time.

[17] Anton Reicha, 'Sur la musique comme art purement sentimental', Paris, Bibliothèque du Conservatoire, Rés. F. 1646, f. 27–28. Emphasis in the original. My translation.

of harmonizing well (those were his exact words). After having written many works, he began again, at the age of forty, a complete course in composition, to strengthen himself in his art and to learn its secrets better. He told me many times that *one should never let a single day pass without occupying oneself with one's art* (according to the principle of Apelles and of Raphael: 'Nullus dies sine linea'). *And if one cannot compose, then one must study.* What a lesson this is for those sham geniuses who believe that they can exempt themselves from fathoming their art! We see the happy consequences of this.

On at least one point, Reicha's anecdote confirms something we have long known from other sources: that Haydn studied his art throughout his life. There are multiple references in the early biographies to the 'well-worn' copy of Fux's *Gradus ad parnassum*, and Haydn prepared an abstract of this counterpoint text for use in his own teaching. He worked through treatises by other theorists as well, including Mattheson and Kirnberger.[18]

More significant within Reicha's account, however, is the suggestion that Haydn's approach to composition underwent a profound change as a result of a period of particularly intensive study when the composer was 'about forty years old', that is to say, around the year 1772, directly in the middle of the so-called *Sturm und Drang*.

How reliable is this anecdote? Posthumous accounts of a composer's dicta must always be treated with extreme caution: the welter of spurious reports circulating after the deaths of Mozart and Beethoven from figures like Rochlitz and Schindler are too well known to need rehearsing here.[19]

---

[18] See Denis Arnold, 'Haydn's Counterpoint and Fux's Gradus', *Monthly Musical Record* 87 (1957), 52–8; Alfred Mann, 'Haydn as a Student and Critic of Fux', in H. C. Robbins Landon and Roger E. Chapman, eds., *Studies in Eighteenth-Century Music: A Tribute to Karl Geiringer on his Seventieth Birthday* (New York: Oxford University Press, 1970), pp. 323–32; Mann, 'Haydn's *Elementarbuch*: A Document of Classic Counterpoint Instruction', *Music Forum* 3 (1973), 197–237; F. Sumner, 'Haydn and Kirnberger: A Documentary Report', *Journal of the American Musicological Society* 28 (1975), 530–9.

[19] See Maynard Solomon, 'The Rochlitz Anecdotes', in Cliff Eisen, ed., *Mozart Studies* (Oxford: Oxford University Press, 1991), pp. 1–59; James Webster, 'The Falling-Out Between Haydn and Beethoven: The Evidence of the Sources', in Lewis Lockwood and Phyllis Benjamin, eds., *Beethoven Essays: Studies in Honor of Elliot Forbes* (Cambridge, Mass.: Harvard University Department of Music, 1984), pp. 3–45.

Still, it would be mistaken to dismiss Reicha's account simply because it was written down after Haydn's death. Unlike Rochlitz or Schindler, Reicha seems to have had no motive for financial gain in recording such an assertion; indeed, he seems never to have published any personal account of his contact with Haydn at all. More importantly, the substance of this particular report, as we shall see, is confirmed by the music itself.

Reicha had spent a good part of his youth in Bonn, where he was a friend of Beethoven, and it was there, in 1790, that he first met Haydn, who was on his way to London for the first time. Reicha later moved to Hamburg, where he met Haydn once again when the latter was returning from London after his second English sojourn. After moving to Vienna in 1802, Reicha renewed his acquaintance with the elder composer. In an unpublished autobiographical sketch, written around 1824, Reicha repeated the essence of his encounter with Haydn while the latter was harmonizing 'a Scottish air', and he went on to describe the nature of their subsequent relationship:

> The first time I called, I found him at the piano composing an accompaniment to a Scottish air. When I expressed surprise that he could be bothered with such trifles, he told me it was an excellent lesson in modulation. He was more than seventy years old. We became the best of friends, and later he opened his door practically to only such people as I presented to him.[20]

Even if Reicha was exaggerating the closeness of his relationship to Haydn, we do know that he introduced Cherubini and Baillot to him in Vienna in 1805, and it seems clear that Reicha and Haydn were in fairly close contact over a sustained period.

How literally should we interpret the date implied in Reicha's narrative? Was Haydn referring specifically to 1772 or to a broader period around that time? I suspect that 1772 marks a culmination of the composer's 'cours complet', and that this systematic review of his art – a 'recommencement' of his compositional career – is manifested most clearly in the string quartets of Op. 20 and Symphonies Nos. 45, 46 and 47, all of which can be securely dated to 1772. The 'cours complet' was in all likelihood an extended process, but it seems to have reached an unusual level of intensity in that year,

20 Jacques-Gabriel Prod'homme, 'From the Unpublished Autobiography of Antoine Reicha', *Musical Quarterly* 22 (1936), 345.

sufficient enough at any rate to have stood out in Haydn's memory even late in his life.

The idea of a self-imposed 'cours complet de la composition' is richly suggestive. We do not know the original phrase Haydn actually used, for he would have been conversing with Reicha in German, of course, not French. But we can reasonably assume that he would have been speaking about something along the lines of a 'gründliche' or 'vollständige Komposi-tionslehre'. The phrase 'cours complet de la composition' is not in itself unusual, as witnessed by Momigny's well-known *Cours complet d'harmonie et de composition* (Paris, 1803–6); Reicha himself would later go on to write a treatise entitled *Cours de composition musical, ou Traité complet et raisonné d'harmonie pratique* (Paris, 1816).

Significantly, Reicha presents the phrase 'cours complet de la compo-sition' within the context of the composer's working methods. The idea of a 'complete course' suggests above all else a systematic review of composi-tional techniques. From a pedagogical perspective, the fundamentals of composition consisted of harmony and counterpoint, and there is ample evidence in Haydn's music to reflect the idea of a quasi-systematic review in both areas during the late 1760s and early 1770s. The expansion of his har-monic vocabulary around this time is quite dramatic. Some of the better-known examples of this include the jarring cross-relations in the opening bars of the minuet of the 'Farewell' Symphony; the extraordinary harmonic progression in the coda of the first movement of the String Quartet in F minor, Op. 20 No. 5; and the unexpected excursions from A major to A minor to C major and then back again to A major within the first-move-ment exposition of the String Quartet in D major, Op. 17 No. 6.

Haydn also cultivated unusual tonalities to an unprecedented degree around this time: the 'Farewell' Symphony in F sharp minor, the only eigh-teenth-century symphony in this key, is perhaps the best-known example, but Symphony No. 46 and Sonata No. 23 (?1765–70; now lost), both in B major, also represent a highly unusual choice of key, as do the D flat major slow movement of Sonata No. 31 in A flat major (*c.* 1767–70) and the move-ments in C sharp minor and major in Sonata No. 49 (?*c.* 1770–5).

Even more striking are Haydn's repeated essays in several of the more demanding elements of counterpoint. The three fugal finales of the Op. 20 quartets systematically explore the possibilities of fugues on two, three and four very different kinds of subjects. The first of the two themes in the finale of the Quartet in F minor, Op. 20 No. 5, is a slow-moving 'pathotype' subject with a prominent leap of a descending diminished seventh, reminiscent of several older fugal themes, including examples from Handel's *Messiah*, Bach's *Well-Tempered Clavier* and other works by Caldara and Birck.[21] Haydn's movement is a contrapuntal *tour de force*, with thirty-eight separate entries, including two in inversion, stretto at four different temporal intervals and a canonic entry in the two outer voices just before the end. The finale of the Quartet in A major, Op. 20 No. 6, assumes a more 'modern' style, with two of the three subjects emphasizing syncopated rhythms. The episodes are full of canonic sequences and the themes are inverted toward the end. Three of the four subjects in the fugal finale of the C major Quartet, Op. 20 No. 2, in turn, are extremely brief, and the contrapuntal emphasis here is on the idea of invertible counterpoint rather than imitation *per se*. Easily the most 'modern' of the three fugues in Op. 20, this finale is notable for its gigue-like rhythm, the exposed chromaticism of its principal subject and the juxtaposition of contrapuntal and homophonic textures. In a manner that anticipates the finale of Mozart's 'Jupiter' Symphony (also in C major), Haydn presents fragments of all four subjects in a variety of vertical permutations and eventually inverts the principal subject, using it as a counterpoint against itself in its original or 'prime' form.[22] As in comparable passages of the other two Op. 20 fugal finales, Haydn draws attention to the contrapuntal artifice of thematic inversion by marking the autograph score 'al rovescio'.

On the basis of Haydn's *Entwurf-Katalog* and the paper types of the autograph scores, we can be fairly certain that the original order of these Op. 20 quartets was 5, 6, 2, 3, 4, 1. Three works with fugal finales, in other words, are followed by three works with non-fugal finales.[23] And within the first group, the finales move from a fugue on two subjects in *alla-breve*

---

[21] See Warren Kirkendale, *Fugue and Fugato in Rococo and Classical Chamber Music*, 2nd edn, trans. Margaret Bent and Warren Kirkendale (Durham, N.C.: Duke University Press, 1979), pp. 91, 143.

[22] Mozart followed the outlines of this movement even more directly in the finale of his String Quartet in A major, K. 464, one of the six quartets dedicated to Haydn in 1785; see my 'The Sincerest Form of Flattery? Mozart's "Haydn" Quartets and the Question of Influence', *Studi musicali* 22 (1993), 392–5.

[23] See Webster, *Haydn's 'Farewell' Symphony*, p. 299, n. 30.

metre (No. 5) to one with three subjects in common time (No. 6) to one on four subjects in the compound metre of $^6_8$ (No. 2). Haydn thus systematically explores various possibilities according not only to the number of voices, but also metre and general parameters of style.

Canon, that strictest of all imitative procedures, also plays an unusually important role around this time, in the minuets of Symphony No. 44 in E minor (?late 1760s, canon at the octave), Sonata No. 40 in E flat major (?1773, canon at the octave) and the Baryton Trio Hob. XI: 94 (before 1774, canon at the fifth). The most extraordinary of all canonic movements from this time is of course the 'Minuet al rovescio' from Symphony No. 47 in G major (1772), later re-used in Sonata No. 41 in A major (1773). Here Haydn writes out only one reprise of a two-reprise form, and the performer must play the music 'backward' the second time around.

Explicit counterpoint was certainly not a new element in Haydn's music in the late 1760s, and he would continue to cultivate it throughout his career. Nor was he by any means alone among his contemporaries in using such contrapuntal artifices in instrumental music.[24] Still, there is no other comparable span of years in his career in which he cultivated so many different kinds of counterpoint in so many different genres and works.

Haydn also became intensely interested in variation form and technique at this time. As Elaine Sisman has demonstrated, 1772 marks a 'watershed year' in this regard, for it was around then that Haydn 'reconceived' his 'variation aesthetic', giving variation movements far greater weight and for the first time incorporating them into instrumental cycles as an internal movement. Taking the theme-and-variations movement of Symphony No. 47 as an exemplary manifestation of this new aesthetic, Sisman shows how the two-part invertible counterpoint within the theme itself extends across the movement as a whole. From 1772 onwards, individual variations provided not only a kind of musical commentary on the theme itself, but on previous variations as well.[25]

In a related fashion, Haydn also began to explore the idea of the 'varied reprise' with particular intensity in the early 1770s. Instead of

---

[24] On the continuing tradition of fugue within the realm of chamber music, see Kirkendale, *Fugue and Fugato*.

[25] Sisman, *Haydn and the Classical Variation*, pp. 135–46.

simply marking a repeat sign at the end of a sonata-form exposition, Haydn 'recomposes' this section. This procedure appears in a number of slow movements from string quartets from this period: Op. 9 Nos. 2 and 4 (?1769/70), Op. 17 No. 4 (1771) and Op. 20 No. 6. Along these same lines, only two of the slow movements in the Op. 17 quartets feature a literal reprise.

Haydn's concern with the principle of variation is part of a broader preoccupation with the idea of thematic elaboration. There is a significant increase in the number of so-called 'monothematic' movements around this time – that is to say, movements in which the initial theme of the secondary key area closely resembles the opening theme of the entire movement.[26] As is the case with so many characteristic features of this period, this particular device had long been present in Haydn's music, but one senses at the end of the 1760s and the beginning of the 1770s a more concentrated effort to explore its various possibilities. In earlier works Haydn had usually limited monothematic movements to finales – that is, to shorter movements of a generally lighter, less demanding character. Within an exposition that spans little more than twenty or twenty-five bars, moreover, the device is far less striking and less structurally significant. Around the end of the 1760s, Haydn began to apply it more frequently in opening movements as well. Within the genre of the symphony, for example, he used it in the first movements of Nos. 43, 44 and 46, as well as in the (lengthier) finales of Nos. 41, 46 and 47. Among the string quartets, the device had similarly figured before primarily in finales, but in Op. 17 (1771) he worked it into the opening movement of No. 6, and again into the first movement of Op. 20 No. 5, the finale of Op. 20 No. 4 and even into the slow movement of Op. 20 No. 5. Monothematicism figures in fully half the first movements of the 'Esterházy' Sonatas of 1773 (Nos. 36, 39, 41), two finales (Nos. 36, 38) and one slow movement (No. 39).

This growing interest in monothematicism is symptomatic of a palpable intensification of thematic work in general. For Haydn, this would remain the most protean of all principles by which to extend the size and substance of an instrumental movement. Late in his life, he chastised

---

[26] Although widely used, this term is misleading, for a 'monothematic' sonata-form movement can (and almost always does) in fact have more than one theme.

younger composers for 'stringing together one idea after another and breaking off before they have barely begun'. When Griesinger asked Haydn about his own compositional methods, the composer responded by saying that he 'fantasized' at the keyboard until he had 'seized on an idea'. His 'entire effort' then went toward 'elaborating and sustaining' this idea 'according to the rules of art'. And when asked about his 'theoretical justifications' for this, Haydn, according to Griesinger, insisted that 'a work of music should have a flowing melody' and 'mutually coherent ideas [*zusammenhängende Ideen*]'.[27] These pronouncements are amply borne out by the music itself. At every stage of his career, Haydn explored new ways of developing a thematic idea to the fullest extent possible and of realizing its implications in a sustained and satisfying manner commensurate with its content.

As a means of increasing the elaborative potential of a given theme, Haydn also began to explore the implications of opening ideas that were themselves inherently unstable by virtue of their harmony, texture, phrase structure or some combination of these elements.[28] Endings also became more extended: only in the late 1760s did he begin to expand sonata-form movements through the use of a structurally significant coda. This is an issue of particular significance in the Op. 17 quartets (Op. 17 No. 1, fourth movement; No. 4, first and fourth movements; No. 6, fourth movement) and most spectacularly in the first movement of Op. 20 No. 5, in which the harmonically audacious coda provides the emotional climax of the entire movement.[29]

Indeed, movements in general become larger around this time through the extended use of thematic elaboration. Variation, counterpoint and harmonic inflection, after all, do not exist as ends in their own right, but rather as means of 'elaborating and sustaining' a given idea. And those ideas were now being sustained on a much broader scale now than ever before:

27 Georg August Griesinger, *Biographische Notizen über Joseph Haydn*, ed. Karl-Heinz Köhler (Leipzig: Philipp Reclam, 1975; 1st edn, 1810), p. 78.
28 See Webster, *Haydn's 'Farewell' Symphony*, pp. 127–33.
29 On codas in Haydn's string quartets, see Jürgen Neubacher, *Finis coronat opus: Untersuchungen zur Technik der Schlußgestaltung in der Instrumentalmusik Joseph Haydns, dargestellt am Beispiel der Streichquartette* (Tutzing: Hans Schneider, 1986), pp. 144–50.

one need only compare the size of individual quartet and symphony move-ments from the early 1770s with ones written in the mid-1760s to see that Haydn's sense of dimensions had grown considerably. This is in part a reflection of the changing musical style of the time, of course; still, Haydn's method of achieving this expansion is decidedly different from, say, Mozart's.

Haydn's concern with the elaboration of a basic idea extended beyond the range of individual movements. The manner in which the various move-ments of a work relate to one another also became an issue of increasing concern during the late 1760s and early 1770s. Webster has already shown how the principle of 'through-composition' permeates the 'Farewell' Symphony and a number of other important pieces from this period. Again, this was not a novel idea in the late 1760s: the three movements of Sonata No. 19 in E minor (?c. 1765), for example, feature strikingly similar incipits, and Haydn underscores these thematic connections by eliminating any break between the first and second movements, with the Adagio ending on the dominant and continuing without a pause into the Allegro. But the fre-quency and breadth of such cyclical integration become substantially greater in the late 1760s and early 1770s.[30] The String Quartet in A major, Op. 20 No. 6, offers a good illustration of this tendency. As in the earlier Sonata No. 19, there are clear thematic parallels among all of the work's movements. Here, the connections are emphasized through rhythm, texture and timbre as well as pitch (see Ex. 5.1). The opening movement exploits the rhythmic ambiguities inherent in the compound meter ($^6_8$) by ending the antecedent phrase on a 'weak' beat, and this same rhythmic idea appears in a new guise in the second movement, with the antecedent of the opening theme also ending off the beat. The continuation of the second movement's

---

[30] Webster discusses many instances of this phenomenon throughout his *Haydn's 'Farewell' Symphony*; see especially the analyses in chapter 8. His discussion of the connections between the last two movements of Symphony No. 46 (pp. 267–87) may be supplemented by a discussion of the first movement of that same work in my own 'Haydn, Laurence Sterne, and the Origins of Musical Irony', *Journal of the American Musicological Society* 44 (1991), 57–91. Like the finale, this movement also incorporates the dual strategies of disruption and unanticipated return. On through-composition in general, see also Ethan Haimo, *Haydn's Symphonic Forms: Essays in Compositional Logic* (Oxford: Clarendon Press, 1995).

Example 5.1 String Quartet in A major, Op. 20 No. 6
(a) first movement, bars 1–5
(b) second movement, bars 1–8
(c) third movement, bars 7–20
(d) fourth movement, bars 1–15

(a)

(b)

Example 5.1 (*cont.*)

(c)

opening idea, moreover, bears a distinct resemblance to the opening theme of the first movement. The second reprise of the minuet similarly leaves the first violin exposed in mid-bar (bar 14). The opening of the fugal finale, in turn, incorporates several elements from the first movement: the broadly descending contour from the very opening of the work; the downward turning gesture that first appears in bars 15–16 and figures prominently throughout the first movement; the descending complementary lines of the upper strings (first movement, bars 22–5), with a rapidly moving first violin set off by a slower moving second. Even the three repeated notes at the beginning of the finale's opening theme can be heard as an echo of the prominent three-note accompanimental figure at the beginning of the first movement, re-emphasized, in turn, at the beginning of the minuet (see also bar 17).

Related to the growing integration of multiple movements is a corresponding increase in the weight of the finale. The principle of 'through-composition' necessarily entails a more substantial, culminative finale than

171

Example 5.1 (*cont.*)

(d)

had traditionally been the case. Symphonies Nos. 45 and 46 and the three quartets of Op. 20 with fugal finales provide especially clear examples of finales that sum up and resolve issues raised in earlier movements.[31]

---

31 See Webster, *Haydn's 'Farewell' Symphony*, pp. 183–5, 298–300, 368–72.

Another, still broader contemporaneous development in Haydn's music reflects what might best be described as a heightened awareness of audience. Humorous and ironic elements become increasingly common as Haydn plays with his listeners' understanding and expectation of musical conventions. Once again, it must be emphasized that this is not a new quality in Haydn's music, but there is evidence for a more thorough exploration of various possibilities in the late 1760s and early 1770s. One finds, for example, a veritable flurry of movements incorporating a 'false recapitulation', that is, a return to the tonic key and opening theme within the course of a development that eventually proves not to be the onset of the 'true' recapitulation. This device appears in the first movements of symphonies Nos. 41, 42, 43, 46 and 55, the string quartets Op. 17 No. 1 and Op. 20 No. 4 and the finale of Symphony No. 48, all of which date from the late 1760s or early 1770s.[32] Haydn returned to it again at various times later on in his career, but only in isolated works and never with such intensity.

*

The end of the *Sturm und Drang* has provoked almost as much speculation as its beginning. There is, undeniably, an overall lessening of intensity in Haydn's instrumental music of the later 1770s. One of the predominant explanations for this change rests once again on the premise of a direct link between life and works – specifically, the notion that Prince Nicolaus Esterházy was dissatisfied with Haydn's unusual music of the early 1770s, which in turn led a chastised Haydn to 'retrench'. But as with Wyzewa's hypothesis of an 'immortal beloved', there is no tangible evidence to support this view. From time to time, the Prince's musical 'conservatism' has been deduced from the relatively unpretentious quality of the 'Esterházy' sonatas published in 1774 and dedicated to Prince Nicolaus himself. The contrast with a work like the C minor sonata of 1771 is certainly pronounced. But there is no reason to equate an act of dedication with the (implicitly exclusive) tastes of the dedicatee. By the terms of his employment, Haydn was compelled to receive permission to publish his music, and the dedication to Prince Nicolaus was an intelligent – indeed, a virtually obligatory – diplomatic gesture on the part of the composer, particularly when we recall that

---

[32] See my 'Haydn's False Recapitulations and the Perception of Sonata Form in the Eighteenth Century', Ph.D. diss., Harvard University (1988), chapters 4 and 6.

this was the first publication of Haydn's music that the composer himself authorized. Haydn, moreover, was necessarily concerned with the marketability of these keyboard sonatas and they are accordingly written in a style that appeals to amateurs as well as connoisseurs.

The autograph score of Symphony No. 42 (1771) is also used on occasion to demonstrate a lack of musical imagination on the part of Haydn's patron. In the slow movement Haydn cancelled two bars that are now difficult to decipher but that were probably quite daring harmonically and certainly quite daring texturally, for the first violins would have been playing entirely alone after having already slowed down to a near-static state. Above the deleted bars Haydn added the comment 'Dieses war vor gar zu gelehrten Ohren' (This was for far too learned ears). This has sometimes been interpreted as Haydn's way of saying: 'If I had a better audience, I could have left this as it was'. But such an interpretation runs counter to common sense. We know from his contract that Haydn was required to submit clean copies of all new works to the Prince, and it is in this princely copy that the remark has come down to us today. It is bizarre to think that Haydn would have insulted his employer so openly. Instead, the remark is to be understood as an acknowledgement that this was all 'too learned by half'. In his 'cours complet de la composition', Haydn had caught himself going too far in his exploration of textural, harmonic and formal extremes.

In the end, there is simply no evidence to suggest that the Prince was somehow dissatisfied with Haydn's 'experimentation' at this time. To the contrary, Haydn's oft-quoted statement about being 'forced to become original' is immediately preceded by his acknowledgement that '[t]he Prince was satisfied with all my works... I could make experiments, observe what elicited or weakened an impression, and thus correct, add, delete, take risks. I was cut off from the world, no one in my vicinity could cause me to doubt myself or pester me...'.[33] A more plausible explanation for a general lessening of intensity in Haydn's music in the mid- to late 1770s is that these years represent a period of consolidation after a period of intense and quasi-systematic exploration of many demanding compositional issues. Alternatively, one might see Haydn as having changed the nature of his self-imposed challenge: from examining the fundamentals of harmony,

---

[33] Griesinger, *Biographische Notizen*, p. 28.

174

counterpoint and form to dealing with a style that was more readily accessible to a wider audience.

*

A composer's evaluation of his own work and career is at once both
welcome and suspect. Welcome, because almost any such pronouncement
has at least the potential of revealing the composer's development and
output in ways we might not have otherwise discerned. Suspect, because
composers have repeatedly tried to shape the reception of their works in the
most advantageous possible manner. Whatever its basis in truth, Haydn's
pronouncement about the 'entirely new manner' of his Op. 33 quartets was
driven to at least some degree by the desire to promote a new set of works. By
contrast, his retrospective claim to Reicha that he had 'recommenced' the
study of his art around the age of forty with a 'complete course of composition' was a private acknowledgement to a fellow composer and unmotivated by the prospect of commercial gain. As such, it is an observation that
can help us better approach a particularly remarkable period within an
altogether remarkable career.

The notion of the *Sturm und Drang* persists with good reason.
Something *does* happen in Haydn's music in the late 1760s and early 1770s,
and there are in fact broader manifestations of these same developments
among other composers as well. But what happens in the case of Haydn goes
well beyond the limited repertory of minor-mode symphonies and string
quartets so closely associated with the *Sturm und Drang*. To view this period
as one of intense experimentation puts us closer to the truth, yet even this
formulation remains potentially misleading. 'Experimentation' implies an
attempt to find a solution, a specific answer. And by their very nature,
experiments fail from time to time. For Haydn, there were always multiple
answers to the compositional challenges he took up. Rather than experimentation, with its implied 'solution' in the 'Classical style' of the Op. 33
quartets, our understanding of Haydn's career would be better served by
the metaphor of exploration. From the very beginning of his career, Haydn
sought out a variety of approaches to different compositional problems,
and, having discovered and developed various possibilities, he moved on to
new challenges.

If we perceive Haydn's career as a journey of continuous exploration
rather than as a series of destinations, the late 1760s and early 1770s emerge

as a period of unusually intense and quasi-systematic exploration. Within this framework, it is possible to accept a strong interest in a particular style – characterized by wide leaps, syncopated rhythms and the like – without at the same time restricting this interest to one period alone, and without extending this interest, in turn, to that one period as a whole. The subsequent years of the mid- and late 1770s, moreover, need not be seen as the fallow period for which they are often taken. Nor do we need to postulate a personal or collective 'Romantic crisis' as a necessary impetus for a 'recommencement' of his career around the age of forty. To amplify the composer's own lightly ironic remark: Haydn forced himself to become original at every stage of his career.

6 Haydn's reversals: style change, gesture and the implication-realization model

MICHAEL SPITZER

How would the Western musical canon look to an outsider? Bruno Nettl, the doyen of American ethnomusicologists, reports the following experience:

> Carnatic musicians in Madras, looking interestedly at the foreign musical culture of the West, said to me, 'We have our trinity of great composers, Sri Tyagaraja, Syama Sastri, and Muttuswami Dikshitar, just as you have your trinity,' meaning Haydn, Mozart and Beethoven. But I would like to argue that dualism is a more significant guide to the conceptual framework of the Music Building and its cultural context. Mozart and Beethoven are presented as emblems of the two ends of a continuum not only by the myth-makers; they have been so recognized by musicologists for a long time.[1]

Nettl's encounter rings true: our conceptual framework really does appear to have a blind spot for the master of Eszterháza. Why is this so? Special pleading, the watchword of Haydn studies, seems to address both scholars and listeners at cross-purposes to their needs, alternately preaching to the converted and lecturing to deaf ears. The defensive, frankly partisan, tone which permeates books such as *Haydn's 'Farewell' Symphony*[2] is directed not to the merits of the composer, about which there is not a particle of doubt, but to the extraordinary gap between our critical encomiums and his historiographical neglect. Haydn, in short, is a victim of the way we construct historical narrative, a composer squeezed between his brother

---

[1] See Bruno Nettl, 'Mozart and the Ethnomusicological Study of Western Culture', *Yearbook for Traditional Music* 21 (1989), 8.

[2] James Webster, *Haydn's 'Farewell' Symphony and the Idea of Classical Style: Through-Composition and Cyclic Integration in his Instrumental Music* (Cambridge: Cambridge University Press, 1991).

giants, Mozart and Beethoven. It is helpful to consider this state of affairs in terms of a conflict of models. Haydn's apologists recuperate him into a 'cluster', or 'radial', interpretative scheme, by which the three chief exponents of the Classical style are grouped together as a school (whether this school has a centre, or father-figure, is a different question).[3] Yet, as Nettl argues, our prevailing model may well be binary.[4] Curiously, Nettl's 'Mozart–Beethoven' opposition turns on the subject of food. Referring to a popular Viennese cookbook of the 1930s, Alice Urbach's extremely comprehensive *So kocht man in Wien!* (1936), Nettl discovers that Mozart's name appears with some prominence in recipes for 'Mozartkrapfen' (balls made of chocolate, marzipan and pistachios). Mozart is a *sweet* composer; Beethoven, whose name appears in no known recipe, would clearly be a 'meat and potatoes' man. Why is Mozart so relishable? Because his music 'goes down' better, it is 'a piece of cake' or 'as easy as pie'.[5] Turning back from Nettl's *esprit* to the more formal language of Western music theory, Mozart's style is assimilable to our ears because it relies so comprehensively on readily identifiable conventional units. Beethoven, the composer of laboured musical logic, composes against the grain. Beethoven fights, Mozart fits.

This double paradigm has opened up in recent years into a polarization of theoretical endeavour between ideology-critique (Beethoven = cultural hegemony) and cognitive science (Mozart = psychologically realistic = 'natural'). On the side of ideology, Scott Burnham's *Beethoven Hero* convincingly shows that our reception of Western music, and the analytical tools we have developed to legitimate it, have been largely shaped by the impact of Beethoven's 'heroic' sonata-form movements.[6] Because of Beethoven, we are powerfully beholden to the metaphor of music as motion, process and development. Haydn is the main casualty of this analytical paradigm, for Beethoven has usurped Haydn's position on the

[3] Webster proposes that we view Haydn as 'the central figure in the "First Viennese Modern School"'; *ibid.*, p. 367.

[4] The tension between ternary and binary models is enshrined in the very titles of our textbooks, as witness Charles Rosen's *The Classical Style: Haydn, Mozart, Beethoven* (London: Faber, 1971) and Giorgio Pestelli's *The Age of Mozart and Beethoven*, trans. Eric Cross (Cambridge: Cambridge University Press, 1984).

[5] Nettl, 'Mozart and the Ethnomusicological Study of Western Culture', 10.

[6] Princeton: Princeton University Press, 1995.

'development' side of what Friedrich Blume termed the 'Entwicklung/ Fortspinnung' distinction.[7] Blume saw Haydn and Mozart as epitomizing two contrasting models of musical structure. Whereas Haydn submits his material to processive development (*Entwicklung*), Mozart prefers to arrange independent fragments in mosaic-like structures (*Fortspinnung*). Possession of the *Entwicklung* model passed from Haydn to Beethoven. Not only has Mozart kept control of the *Fortspinnung* model, but recent theory has served to enhance its power considerably. An influential study by Leonard Meyer translates Blume's 'fragment/mosaic' conception into a fully worked-out transaction between 'grammatical simplicity' (simple figure) and 'relational richness' (multi-levelled networks).[8] On the basis of Meyer's work, Mozart's 'grammatical simplicity', his penchant for short, stock, figures, has proved to be ideally suited for computer-based representations of music perception. For example, the theorist Robert Gjerdingen has trained self-organizing neural networks to categorize musical patterns in Mozart's early keyboard works.[9] In fact, a special issue of the journal *Music Perception* was devoted exclusively to the consideration of a Mozart piano sonata, his K. 282 in E flat major.[10]

Why, in the current intellectual climate, would it be literally 'unthinkable' for a Haydn piano sonata to receive such special treatment? There are two answers. First, the one attribute Haydn has made overwhelmingly his own, humour, has failed to find an adequate theoretical framework to

[7]   Blume's arguments, which were originally presented in his 1929 treatise *Fortspinnung und Entwicklung*, are summarized by Carl Dahlhaus in his 'Some Models of Unity in Musical Form', *Journal of Music Theory* 19 (1975), 2–30: '*Fortspinnung* means a process of joining together unrelated, independent elements, a series of motifs, which do not need to be substantively related, and which only become related through their placement in connection with one another. . . . Development [*Entwicklung*] means a process of gradual transformation of a beginning element into further elements, substantively related to it and joined to it. It is a variety of separate motifs which form a chain of inner connections.' Haydn 'tends towards the developmental and Mozart towards the *Fortspinnung* principle' (25).

[8]   Leonard Meyer, 'Grammatical Simplicity and Relational Richness: The Trio of Mozart's G Minor Symphony', *Critical Inquiry* 2 (1975), 693–761.

[9]   Robert O. Gjerdingen, 'Revising Meyer's "Grammatical Simplicity and Relational Richness"', in M. R. Jones and S. Holleran, eds., *Cognitive Bases of Musical Communication* (Washington: Ann Arbor, 1992), pp. 225–43.

[10]   13/3 (1996).

represent it as anything more than a rhetorical trope. Second, the stylistic basis for Haydn's humour, his subversion of listeners' expectations, is more fine-grained than Mozart's 'simplicity'. It emerges not from the manipulation of stock figures, but from the manipulation of the parameters underlying those figures. In this respect, a new book by the music theorist Eugene Narmour, *The Analysis and Cognition of Basic Melodic Structures*,[11] might herald a sea change. Humour, for Narmour, is a serious business. In the form of 'mental play', it is the foundation both for how the mind works and for the nature of aesthetic experience in general:

> The listener's cognitive 'exhilaration' in having all her subconscious inferences validated, or her sense of 'cognitive irony' in having her forecasts proved only partly right, or her 'cognitive shock' at being completely mistaken and thus wholly surprised – such diverse cognitive pleasures are among the main syntactic reasons that *Homo ludens* listens to music or for that matter engages in any kind of communicative mental play: from working crossword puzzles to reading complex poetry, from relishing political cartoons to contemplating allegorical frescos.[12]

Narmour is a disciple of Leonard Meyer, and both theorists believe that musical meaning arises from the interaction of two processes: pattern continuation (or completion) and pattern deflection. But Narmour and Meyer interpret this interaction on different levels. Meyer observes patterns and interruptions on the level of real themes. Narmour, by contrast, is concerned on a more abstract level with the patterns and interruptions of individual parameters which build up these themes. By means of 'syntactic parametric scales' Narmour is able to assess painstakingly the precise degree of closure or openness of each interval, register and rhythm. By comprehending a melody in terms of the interaction of these low-level microstructures, Narmour is then able to predict its implicative or closural properties with greater subtlety than Meyer.

What follows is, to my knowledge, the first extensive application of Narmour's analytical methods to a piece by Haydn. This essay will not specifically address Haydn reception, though I do hope that, by developing

---

[11] Eugene Narmour, *The Analysis and Cognition of Basic Melodic Structures: The Implication-Realization Model* (Chicago: Chicago University Press, 1990).
[12] *Ibid.*, p. 121.

a model more suited to the unique qualities of Haydn's style, it goes a little way towards curing us of our 'blind spot'. I shall be attempting to achieve three separate things. First, a melodic analysis of the first movement of Haydn's Symphony No. 46 in B major aims to provide insights into the composer's comic practice on a more technical level than is usual. Second, I will show how Narmour's methods can help us track Haydn's apparent change of style between 1772 and 1773, when the experimental radicalism of his *Sturm und Drang* symphonies gave way to the *galant* style of the 'Prince Esterházy' piano sonatas. Webster's critique of Haydn periodization[13] keeps 1772–3 as a turning-point, but maintains that this represented changes in genre and style rather than of quality. Haydn drops a 'personally expressive' style, adopts a 'light, theatrical' style, and resumes the composition of opera and incidental music.[14] Webster is surely right in his claim that 'experimentation was a fundamental aspect of [Haydn's] musical personality, throughout his life'.[15] There is, however, a dearth of analytical evidence to attest to this continuity throughout the 'interregnum' between the *Sturm und Drang* period and the Op. 33 string quartets. To help correct this deficiency, the second part of this study focuses on the first movement of the Sonata No. 40 in E flat major. My third argument, which will run like a thread throughout the discussion, is that the three enterprises of technical analysis, historical narrative and the critical hermeneutics of Haydn's rhetorical (that is, 'comic') strategies cannot be rigidly separated from each other. Narmour has written speculatively about a possible continuum between the neurological and aesthetic domains of perception, between the minute surprises of 'tiny cognitive "jolts" to the neuronal electrical system governing our subconscious cognitive expectations',[16] and the more conscious forms of surprise, such as the aesthetic pleasure we take in having our expectations disconfirmed. With perhaps a little indulgence, I extend this continuum to embrace the 'cognitive jolt' of style change. My pivot for this continuum is a technical procedure Narmour terms 'reversal'. By connecting the principle of melodic reversal to dramatic *peripeteia* and compositional evolution, I reveal how Haydn's 'reversals' engage style change, gesture and the implication-realization model.

---

[13] *Haydn's 'Farewell' Symphony*, pp. 359–66.   [14] *Ibid.*, p. 362.
[15] *Ibid.*, p. 365.   [16] *The Implication-Realization Model*, p. 138.

1 Stormy style shapes

James Webster's work on the 'Farewell' Symphony has at last put to rest the old shibboleth that Haydn's style only came of age in the early 1780s with the 'new and special way' of the Op. 33 quartets. Webster directs his fire towards evolutionist historiographical narratives which conflate Haydn's personal growth as a composer with the historical development of the Classical style itself. A consequence of this narrative, says Webster, is that pre-1780 periods such as the *Sturm und Drang* are falsely portrayed as 'immature', whereas Haydn achieved maturity at all periods of his life.[17] It is my contention, however, that the master-narrative Webster installs in the place of 'evolution' misrepresents the turning-points of Haydn's style, in particular the change from *Sturm und Drang* to *galant* in 1773. According to Webster's new explanatory framework, Haydn is the 'inventor of a rhetoric of through-composition',[18] and works such as the 'Farewell' Symphony create a paradigm of cyclic integration and progressive form which Beethoven, Haydn's disciple, was to follow more than thirty years later. Yet Webster's argument is still possessed by a paradigm that *Beethoven reception* has constructed, and simply reversing the priority, making Haydn originator rather than precursor, leaves this narrative scheme basically untouched. Not only does it miss characteristic traits of Haydn's style which are expressly *anti*-integrative and *non*-processive, it also heightens the perceived discontinuity across 1772–3. What other narratives are possible?

The historiographer Hayden White would call Webster's 'master/disciple' story an 'organicist mode of argument' (evolutionist narratives are the crudest versions of this mode).[19] The organicist 'insists on the necessity of relating the various "contexts" that can be perceived to exist in the historical record as parts to the whole which is history in general'.[20] I will suggest that Haydn's style-change is more suited to a 'mechanist' narrative, which represents the elements of the historical field as being related not in terms of

---

[17] *Haydn's 'Farewell' Symphony*, p. 366.   [18] *Ibid.*, p. 367.

[19] See Hayden White, *Metahistory: The Historical Imagination in Nineteenth-Century Europe* (Baltimore: The Johns Hopkins University Press, 1973). Building on Northrop Frye's theory of generic plots, White identifies four 'modes of emplotment' by which historians narrate their story (romantic, tragic, comic, satirical) and four 'modes of argument' (formist, mechanist, organicist, contextualist) which describe how these stories are structured. See especially pp. 7–29.   [20] *Ibid.*, p. 65.

part–whole relationships, but rather 'in terms of part–part relationships and in the modality of causality'.[21] Instead of regarding change as something new or revolutionary, mechanist narratives understand it as a shift of emphasis within an ongoing interaction of forces.[22] With its precise differentiation of psychological (personal) and conventional (social) factors, Narmour's implication-realization model is an ideal tool for tracking an incremental change of style. Narmour's theory is useful in a further way. Hayden White concludes his solitary yet perspicuous incursion into musicology with a provocative challenge for music theorists to draw their narratives from *music* rather than borrowing them from literary criticism.[23] Just as (his)story-telling is grounded in the linguistic field of tropes, music history should emerge naturally from the musical medium itself. In brief, we are in need of a 'listener-orientated' music historiography, where historical 'consequences' flow from musical 'implications'. Music historians should attend more to scores and less to contemporary rhetorical treatises. In this regard, it will do to begin with a well-known analysis which purports to be orientated to listeners, but in reality is addressed to readers.

Mark Evan Bonds, who has done so much to reveal the cultural background to Haydn's irony,[24] concludes his *Wordless Rhetoric* with a 'listener-orientated' analysis of the first movement of Haydn's Symphony No. 46 in B major.[25] Dispensing entirely with modern analytical techniques, Bonds interprets the work as he thinks eighteenth-century audiences would have

---

[21] *Ibid.*, p. 66.

[22] The prototypical 'mechanist' nineteenth-century narrative relates the origins and aftermath of the French Revolution. See White's discussion of Alexis de Tocqueville's *The Old Regime and the French Revolution*, in *Metahistory*, pp. 191–229.

[23] '*Commentary*: Form, Reference, and Ideology in Musical Discourse', in Steven Scher, ed., *Music and Text: Critical Inquiries* (Cambridge: Cambridge University Press, 1992) pp. 288–319. 'It would follow that musicology could profit from this exchange [with literary theory] only insofar as music could be considered as a form of discourse. And in that case, the exchange would run both ways, for if music were a form or mode of discourse, then literary theory would have as much to learn from musicology as music criticism has to learn from literary studies' (p. 319).

[24] Mark Evan Bonds, 'Haydn, Laurence Sterne, and the Origins of Musical Irony', *Journal of the American Musicological Society* 44 (1991), 57–91.

[25] *Wordless Rhetoric: Musical Form and the Metaphor of the Oration* (Cambridge, Mass.: Harvard University Press, 1991), see especially pp. 192–204.

heard it, namely as a 'metaphor of the oration'. The movement is analysed as a narrative of contrasts, a 'strategy of interruption and interpolation'.[26] Although Bonds couches his narrative in the terminology of eighteenth-century rhetoricians such as Mattheson and Sulzer, the translation of these literary conceits into hard musical facts is inevitably an act of intuition. And these intuitions are extremely vulnerable to countervailing evidence. So why does Bonds distance himself from modern theory? There are two reasons for this. First, despite avowing much common ground with the work of Meyer, Narmour and Gjerdingen, especially in its dealings with conventional signs and schemata, Bonds notes an unwillingness 'to extend these principles to movement-length form'.[27] At the level of the movement, Bonds finds it more useful to gauge listeners' expectations according to Ratner's I–V :|: X–I sonata-form schema rather than the melody-orientated theories of the Meyer school.[28] Bonds' prototypical narrative therefore engages directly with this schema: the false reprise – 'true' reprise model. Bonds adduces this model in his interpretation of Haydn's Symphony No. 41 in C major, as well as Symphony No. 46 (Haydn's false reprise was also the subject of the author's doctoral thesis). The second reason for Bonds' ambivalence towards theory is historical. He endorses Meyerian analysis only to the extent that it is directed towards learned, in other words 'cultural', conventions; he is silent about the theory's appeals to invariant (and thus cross-historical) psychological principles of perception. At the highest level Bonds grounds his interpretations not in a theoretical precept but in a venerable literary trope: Aristotle's principle of *peripeteia*. In the words of Frank Kermode, which Bonds cites at length:

> Peripeteia . . . is present in every story of the least structural sophistication. [It] depends on our confidence of the end; it is a disconfirmation followed by a consonance; the interest of having our expectation falsified is obviously related to our wish to reach the discovery or recognition by an unexpected and instructive route.[29]

At the level of the movement Bonds' operative principle is Kermode's 'disconfirmation followed by a consonance'. This is epitomized by the inter-

---

26 *Ibid.*, p. 202.   27 *Ibid.*, p. 183.
28 Leonard Ratner, *Classic Music: Expression, Form, and Style* (New York: Schirmer, 1980), p. 218.   29 *Wordless Rhetoric*, p. 190.

Example 6.1 Symphony No. 46 in B major, first movement, bars 1–8

ruption of the development by a false reprise (bar 70), the disconfirmation of this false reprise when the development resumes (bar 76) and the consonance of the 'true' reprise (bar 105). On a bar-to-bar level, Bonds analyses the music in terms of a workaday (and curiously Schoenbergian) musical logic based on simple oppositions. The elements which are played out throughout the discourse are four sets of contrasts presented in the opening eight bars (see Ex. 6.1).

The first set comprises a disjunct/conjunct contrast of contour. According to Bonds, '[t]he antecedent moves down a minor sixth (B–D♯) and up a major third (E–G♯), with a half-step (D♯–E) in between (mm. 1–2). The consequent moves principally in stepwise motion down a fifth (F♯–B, mm. 3–4).'[30] The phrase also reveals contrasts of rhythm (slow and even vs. fast and uneven), dynamics (loud vs. soft) and texture (unison vs. polyphony). Having presented these oppositions, Bonds then shows how Haydn reconciles them in a general *Zusammenhang*, or state of 'interconnectedness'.[31] For example, the sixths and thirds of the opening pervade virtually every bar; the intervallic profile of bars 1–2 is combined with the quaver rhythms of bars 3–4, and so forth.

---

[30] *Ibid.*, p. 196.   [31] *Ibid.*, p. 197.

MICHAEL SPITZER

Its engaging pragmatism aside, Bonds' *faux naïf* methodology begs more questions than it can possibly answer within the theoretical constraints it has set itself. Take the opening four bars: we may well ask whether the descent of bars 3–4 in fact balances or resolves the contour of the opening, with its rising third, E–G♯, or whether the opposition between them is a generative one which must be composed out later. Implicative and logical contrast are not the same, but Bonds' narrative conflates them. Does the rising third of bar 2 fully settle the preceding falling sixth, or is there some tension left over? Would a rising second resolve the sixth more fully? What are the precise implications of the crotchet rest? These are the kinds of question that only Narmour's theory can answer. These questions, when they are properly addressed, will turn Bonds' interpretation upside down. It will emerge, in due course, that the symphony begins with a cadence; this cadence is radically flawed; the reprise, rather than establishing a 'consonance', actually exacerbates the problem; the *peripeteia* is resolved later than Bonds thinks, at the end of a secondary development section. To understand why this is the case, we must first consider Narmour's concept of 'reversal'.

Narmour's concept of reversal is, in the first instance, remarkably broad:

> I believe that a case can be made for a concept of reversal in dance, painting, and film and perhaps even in speech perception. Certainly, Aristotle's notion of it in drama (*mimesis peripeteias*) is tantalizing and suggests that the perception of reversal operations may exist at a very deep, innate perceptual level.[32]

In the context of his theory of melodic structure, however, 'reversal' plays an extremely specific role. The two corner-stones of Narmour's theory are the principles of 'reversal' and 'process'. A pattern which is allowed to continue is a 'process'. When the pattern is broken, 'reversal' occurs. Although it sounds like a subversive principle, reversal actually creates closure and stability ('realization of an implication of a reversal creates a closed structure').[33] The process-plus-reversal sequence originated in Meyer's well-known 'gap-fill' pattern, as when a leap is filled by a stepwise progression in the opposite direction. Nevertheless, Narmour's reversals differ from 'fill'

[32] *The Implication-Realization Model*, p. 150.   [33] *Ibid.*, p. 152.

progressions in several vital respects. Reversal is accomplished with the first step, that is, the first onset of difference, without the need to continue with a full scale. Reversal can take the form of an interval larger than a step, such as a third or a fourth, as long as this interval is new. For example, a fifth followed by a third is still a reversal (two successive fifths would be a process). Most importantly, Narmour measures reversal in the parameters of interval and register separately. It is possible to conceive, therefore, of a structure which changes interval but continues in the same direction ('intervallic reversal'), or, conversely, of one which changes direction but repeats the same interval ('registral reversal'). The strongest, most stable kind of reversal, however, occurs when both pitch and register are changed. Narmour terms this 'reversal' pure and simple.

We see, therefore, that Narmour's separate treatment of pitch and register endows his system with tremendous flexibility. The process-reversal opposition generates eight possible permutations, which Narmour calls 'basic structures' (see Table 6.1).

Table 6.1 Narmour's eight basic structures

P = Full process.
IP = Intervallic process. Same interval, different register (that is, change of direction).
VP = Registral process. Moves in same registral direction, but different interval.
R = Full reversal.
IR = Intervallic reversal. Change of interval.
VR = Registral reversal. Change of register.
D = Duplication. Repeated note.
ID = Intervallic duplication. 'Zigzagged' intervallic pattern.

It is important to stress that these 'basic structures' are not melodies; they are the principles whose interaction produces melodies. They refer to the properties of individual parameters, and Narmour's name for these is 'style shapes'. In contrast, a 'style structure' is 'a highly specific amalgam of melodic, harmonic and durational patterning positioned metrically, texturally, timbrally and dynamically in a musical context characteristic of one particular style'.[34] In fact, as we shall presently see, Narmour's 'style struc-

---

[34] *Ibid.*, p. 34.

ture' is very like what Meyer terms an 'archetype' and Gjerdingen calls a 'schema'. The most far-reaching and, it must be admitted, contentious, aspect of Narmour's theory is his rigid separation between 'style shapes' and 'style structures'. The two are processed in different ways. Style shapes are innate, invariant, and are processed automatically from the 'bottom up'. Style structures comprise a learned lexicon of conventional figures and progressions, engage knowledge and experience, are subject to conscious control and are processed from the 'top down'. Naturally, music results from the complex and multi-layered interaction of both types of processing.

Narmour's implication-realization model is essentially a theory of melody, and it has no pretensions to being a theory of form. It can only be adapted for the purposes of movement-length analysis in combination with higher-level frameworks, such as Ratner's I–V :|: X–I sonata-form schema. Since sonata form operates far to the right of melody in the innate-learned spectrum, it is much less susceptible to bottom-up, perceptual processing. Even so, we can assess the 'form-contextual' qualities of melodic structures in so far as their level of closure or openness 'fits' within the sonata's junctures. This mode of analysis is actually already practised in Haydn studies. It takes the form of the common observation that Haydn often begins a piece with a cadence. Thus Meyer has stated that 'the use of an unmistakable cadential formula at the beginning of a movement is a strategy of which Haydn was especially fond'.[35] The listener comprehends the cadential opening against the template of the more conventional opening. Starting with a cadence creates a 'contextual dissonance' which is only resolved when the cadence is put in its proper place at the end. Before this point, however, the composer has several attempts to 'get it right', and the ensuing narrative bears all the hallmarks of 'disconfirmation followed by consonance'; that is, a *peripeteia*.

Haydn's cadential openings fall into three types. The prototypical variety comprises a plain V–I progression (see Exx. 6.2 and 6.3). A second, more complex, gambit is to stabilize the cadence by preceding or grounding it with a tonic. The second movement of the 'Military Symphony' (Meyer's example) outlines a I–V-I progression (see Ex. 6.4). In Op. 50 No. 1 Haydn

---

[35] Leonard B. Meyer, *Style and Music* (Philadelphia: University of Pennsylvania Press, 1989), p. 26. For Haydn's practice of starting a movement with 'a gesture of destabilization', see Webster, *Haydn's 'Farewell' Symphony*, pp. 127–33.

Example 6.2 String Quartet in G major, Op. 33 No. 5, first movement, bars 1–4

Example 6.3 String Quartet in C major, Op. 74 No. 1, first movement, bars 1–4

Example 6.4 Symphony No. 100 in G major, 'Military', second movement, bars 1–2

189

Example 6.5 String Quartet in B flat major, Op. 50 No. 1, first movement, bars 1–6

Example 6.6 Symphony No. 46 in B major, first movement, bars 1–2

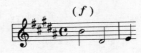

places a cadential progression on top of a tonic pedal (see Ex. 6.5).[36] Thirdly, the type that will concern us here is so subtle that I term it a 'bifocal cadence', because it works equally well in opening and end positions.[37] The B major symphony begins with such a bifocal cadence (see Ex. 6.6).

It enters on the tonic and does not look like a cadence at all. In fact, Bonds, for whom the opening phrase is 'relatively straightforward',[38] misses it altogether. So why might we hear it as a cadence?

According to Narmour's law of reversal, by means of which a large interval proceeds to a small interval in the opposite direction, a descending sixth followed by a rising minor second constitutes one of the most effective ways to close a phrase. Narmour cites examples from Haydn, Mozart, even

[36] See Janet Levy's insightful discussion in 'Gesture, Form, and Syntax in Haydn's Music', in Jens Peter Larsen, Howard Serwer and James Webster, eds., *Haydn Studies: Proceedings of the International Haydn Conference, Washington, D. C., 1975* (New York: Norton, 1981), pp. 355–62.

[37] I borrow this term from Jan LaRue, in 'Bifocal Tonality: An Explanation for Ambiguous Baroque Cadences', in *Essays on Music in Honor of Archibald Thompson Davison by his Associates* (Cambridge, Mass.: Harvard University Press, 1957), pp. 173–84.   [38] *Wordless Rhetoric*, p. 196.

190

Example 6.7 Narmour's 'reversal' cadences:
(a) Haydn, Symphony No. 97 in C major, finale, bars 12–16;
(b) Mozart, String Quartet in E flat major, K. 428, first movement, bars 6–8;
(c) cadences from Wagner, *Lohengrin*

(a)

(b)

(c)

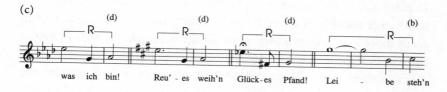

Wagner (see Ex. 6.7).[39] These cadences became particularly stylized in the earlier nineteenth century, to the extent that 'Wagner seems rarely to think of any other melodic closural gesture in his early operas'.[40] We find this gesture, in its regular terminal position, in the tonic group of the B major symphony (bar 12), and at the end of the exposition (bar 57, oboes – see Ex. 6.8).

Having established, *pace* Bonds, that Haydn's opening is more unsettling than it appears, I will proceed in two stages, first discussing the factors which conspire to make the gesture so effective, then looking at how Haydn exploits these principles to shape his movement.

Haydn's opening cadence demonstrates complete reversal, in that

---

[39] *The Implication-Realization Model*, p. 173.   [40] *Ibid.*

Example 6.8 Symphony No. 46 in B major, first movement, bars 12–13, 57–9

both interval size and registral direction are changed. According to Narmour's 'syntactic-intervallic parametric scale',[41] the sixth is the optimum interval to precede reversal. In Narmour's spectrum, intervals are arranged with small intervals on the left and large ones on the right. The wider, or more 'differentiated', the interval, the more it implies reversal. By contrast, the relative proximity of the smaller intervals (unison, minor second, major second, minor third, major third) implies continuation in a 'process'. The minor sixth occupies a liminal status in this spectrum, since 'all melodic intervals equal to or larger than a minor sixth imply reversal'.[42] In particular, 'a major sixth is implicatively strong because . . . it has a relatively large number of realizational possibilities'.[43] A sixth can resolve in many more ways than to a minor second, for example. Narmour evaluates the closural properties of an interval by measuring the arithmetic difference between the larger and smaller interval. As a rule, 'the greater the differentiation between the two intervals, the greater the closure'.[44] Furthermore, closure is stronger when the terminal interval is small, such as a minor second. In Haydn's cadence the differentiation between the minor sixth (F#–A#) and the minor second (A#–B) is a perfect fifth. Had the sixth been followed by, say, a minor third (D#–F#), the differentiation would have been lower (a minor sixth minus a minor third equals a perfect fourth).

Faced with this gesture's closural properties, Haydn has the option of either reinforcing them or attenuating them. By transforming his material in these ways, he can project regions of stability and tension on to his movement. The most direct way of fortifying a cadence is through metrical and durational factors. In bar 12 the note of resolution, the B, is reinforced by lengthening (see Ex. 6.9). Haydn exploits the stabilizing property of 'dura-

[41] *Ibid.*, p. 78.   [42] *Ibid.*, p. 77.   [43] *Ibid.*, p. 155.   [44] *Ibid.*, p. 157.

Example 6.9 Symphony No. 46 in B major, first movement, bars 12–13

Example 6.10 Symphony No. 46 in B major, first movement, bars 58–9

tional cumulation',[45] as when a short note goes to a longer one. In bar 58 the note of resolution is repeated, creating 'iterative closure' (see Ex. 6.10). It observes 'the closural effect of an additive pattern followed by a rest'.[46] These two examples can be compared with the extremely implicative effect at bar 2. Here the cadence is followed by a further leap of a third to G♯, stressing the second beat of a bar with a syncopation effect. We shall have occasion to explore this later.

The articulative function of reversal can also be strengthened through enchaining. Narmour draws attention, in the Mozart example above (Ex. 6.7b), to the fact that 'both penultimate and final usages of reversal are found'.[47] The interlocking leaps make the resolution sound even more final. There is a remarkable instance of this at the end of the secondary development section of Symphony No. 46, bars 121–3 (see Ex. 6.11). The first violin's D♯–E♯ at bar 121 interlocks with the cello's F♯–A♯–B. It makes greater sense to connect the violin's E♯ with the bass's F♯ rather than with its own C♯ in bar 122. This is because, by Narmour's lights, a small terminal interval (the E♯-F♯ minor second) promotes greater closure than a large interval (E♯-C♯).

Haydn can, of course, also weaken the effect of his cadence. Though our 'bifocal' cadence of bars 1–2 is contextually dissonant, it is not the

---

[45] *Ibid.*, p. 105.   [46] *Ibid.*, p. 115.   [47] *Ibid.*, p. 172.

Example 6.11 Symphony No. 46 in B major, first movement, bars 121–3

weakest statement in the movement. The opening cadence is partially saved by its ambiguity. Clearly, it suggests a resolution to E, in other words a V–I progression in E major. But Haydn could easily have chosen to make the subdominant bias explicit by flattening the seventh (A), as he actually does in the consequent statement, bars 5–6 (see Ex. 6.12). The latter, complete with tonic pedal (second violins and horn), points to a conventional I^7–IV–V–I opening gambit. Haydn's late Sonata No. 62 in E flat major begins this way (see Ex. 6.13).

But Haydn deliberately presents his cadence in octaves, and, as Janet Levy has shown, octave textures often signify openings.[48] The reprise (bar 105), rather than providing a 'consonance' after the development's 'discon-

---

[48] See Janet Levy, 'Texture as a Sign in Classic and Early Romantic Music', *Journal of the American Musicological Society* 35 (1982), 482–531, especially 490.

Example 6.12 Symphony No. 46 in B major, first movement, bars 5–6

Example 6.13 Sonata No. 62 in E flat major, bars 1–2

firmation', in fact realizes the gesture's subdominant implications (see Ex. 6.14). The change lies not in the reprise itself (the notes are identical, apart from a fuller horn and an adjusted viola part) but in the way it is approached. The bass's scalar descent to the B via C♯ (bars 104–5) denies the reprise sufficient dominant preparation. Since it is not approached by a strong root-position dominant in the bass, the B of bar 105 is interpreted, by default, as a cadential dominant to an E major tonic resolution at bar 106.

195

Example 6.14 Symphony No. 46 in B major, first movement, bars 103–6

The tonicization of E is confirmed at bars 109–10. The effect of the retransition, therefore, is to fortify subdominant leanings inherent in the material of bar 1. In summary, we can conclude that the implications of the falling sixth *interval* at bar 1 are reinforced at bar 105 but, paradoxically, at the expense of weakening the closure of the *cadence*. This produces 'disconfirmation' of the B's stability as a tonic. The same process of reinterpretation works to B's advantage when the gesture is transposed to F♯–A♯ at bar 122. This produces the narrative's 'consonance'.

At the highest level, therefore, Haydn's structure is staked out by the presentation (bar 1), disconfirmation (bar 105) and resolution (bar 122) of a three-note *gestalt*. Within this framework Haydn shades his regions of stability and tension by splitting the cadence into its constituent intervals and transforming their significance. As before, Haydn has the option of either reinforcing or attenuating their closural quality.

The opening sixth interval, which is presented in the tonic group implicatively within a three-note *gestalt*, that is, leading to reversal, is in due

196

Example 6.15 Symphony No. 46 in B major, first movement, bars 13–14

3 = third

Example 6.16 Symphony No. 46 in B major, first movement, bars 31–3

ID = Intervallic Duplication

course transformed into a closed dyad. 'Dyads', says Narmour, 'are formal structures. They consist of implications that have been denied'.[49] An example of a 'dyad' is the rising tenth, B–D♯, of bars 13–14 (see Ex. 6.15). Although the dyad is filled in with processive leaps and steps, these are encompassed on a structural level by a closed interval. Even more static is the patterning in bars 31–2 (see Ex. 6.16). The processive steps are here encompassed by a repeated rising and falling sixth. The alternation of sixths outlines what Narmour calls 'intervallic duplication',[50] a form of 'exact registral return'. The latter (symbolized as 'aba') is a pattern in itself, but a static, poorly implicative one. It is appropriate for regions of structural stability or arrival, such as bar 31, where the dominant key is first established. For aba patterns based on the interval of a second, see the neighbour-note oscillations of bars 45–8 (Ex. 6.17).

Haydn can also make his intervals sound more implicative, in regions of desired instability. The intervallic cycle of bars 42–4 employs reversal with minimal closure (see Ex. 6.18). The 'intervallic differentiation' between the falling major sixth (diminished seventh) and rising tritone of

---

[49] *The Implication-Realization Model*, p. 406.   [50] *Ibid.*, p. 133.

Example 6.17 Symphony No. 46 in B major, first movement, bars 45–8

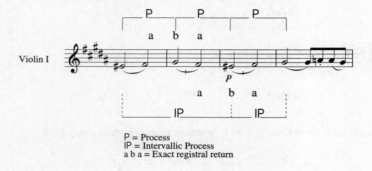

P = Process
IP = Intervallic Process
a b a = Exact registral return

Example 6.18 Symphony No. 46 in B major, first movement, bars 42–5

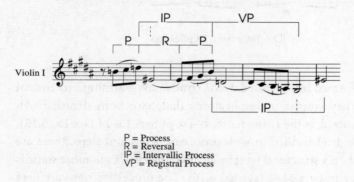

P = Process
R = Reversal
IP = Intervallic Process
VP = Registral Process

bars 42–3 (D♮–E♯–B) is a mere minor third, as compared with the differentiation of a perfect fifth at bars 1–2. The B–D♮ skip then generates a process of intervallic 'similarity': D♮–G♯, G♯–E♯. Narmour's understanding of similarity is that 'the difference between any two adjacent intervals could equal a plus/minus minor third'.[51] The difference between the sixth and tritone of bars 43–6 falls within this boundary. The intervallic process ('IP') has freed the opening gesture from its cadential strait-jacket and given it a dynamic trajectory. This trajectory carries through to the stretto entries at the start of the development section.

For a final demonstration of what can be achieved with Narmour's

---

[51] *Ibid.*, p. 129.

Example 6.19 Symphony No. 46 in B major, first movement, bars 1–4

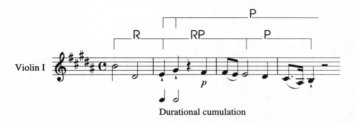

Durational cumulation

RP = Gap-Fill [Reverse Process]
P = Process

techniques, let us take a more extensive look at Haydn's opening. As we have already observed, the event which denies the E of bar 2 its stability as a goal note is the further leap of a third to G♯. The crotchet rest which follows emphasizes the G♯ through 'durational cumulation': it endows the E–G♯ leap with a short–long pattern. That the long note falls on a metrically weak beat further heightens the G♯'s unstable or 'open' quality. The implications generated by this event are handled by Haydn with consummate subtlety. The leap of a third is 'Janus-faced', implying both reversal and process, though the latter implication is in fact stronger (see Ex. 6.19). The reversal is realized directly, with the fall to F♯ and E in bars 2–3. The processive intervallic pattern, implying a further leap of a third from G♯ to B, is deferred until bars 6–8, where it is realized on several levels (see Ex. 6.20). On the lowest level the process is continued only in terms of register (VP = 'registral process'), in the quaver leap from G♯ to E in bar 6, since the actual interval of continuation has changed from a third to a sixth. On the next level the intervallic pattern is realized by the arrival of the B at bar 7. However, what Narmour terms 'the influence of harmony', symbolized as '(h)', relegates the B to being an accented passing note to A♯. At this level the third G♯–B is filled in as another process, consisting of rising seconds. Another aspect of the E–G♯ leap with generative potential is the 'durational cumulation' effected by the crotchet rest. Narmour states that 'the pattern ♩ ♩ 𝄾 is a closed, additive exemplar of an ostensibly archetypal ♩ ♩ set'.[52] Although a two-crotchet

---

[52] *Ibid.*, p. 115.

Example 6.20 Symphony No. 46 in B major, first movement, bars 6–8

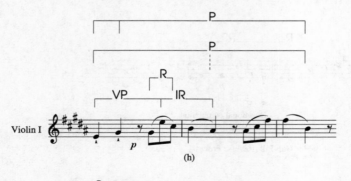

(h)

P = Process
VP = Registral Process
R = Reversal
IR = Intervallic Reversal
(h) = Influence of harmony

interval separates the inception of the G♯ from the F♯ in bar 2, the G♯ lacks the stability which a full minim duration would provide: 'the durational pattern ♩ ♩ is more closed than ♩ ♩ 𝄽'. Nevertheless, it is clear that the G♯-plus-rest initiates the syncopated figures which permeate this movement, beginning at bar 3. What, therefore, is the function of the crotchet rest? One of the effects of 'closure by cumulation', a short–long pattern, is 'suppression of melodic implication',[53] the conversion of the second note of an interval from an open pitch to a closed one. A minim G♯ would have sounded too stable and would have thereby inhibited a further leap from G♯ to B. The crotchet rest keeps this long-term implication open, while creating the same metrical effect. Strikingly, the figure is reinterpreted with a full minim at the very end of the movement in the horns (Ex. 6.21). Now that it has been transposed to the tonic, there is no further need for a rising intervallic process.

Narmour's cognitive model has thrown up a wealth of detail about Haydn's 'listener-orientated' approach which Bonds' historical model has failed to account for or even identify. Nevertheless, it must be said that the major weakness of Narmour's theory is its drastic reduction of the role historical-stylistic knowledge is deemed to play in our perception of music. Moreover, Narmour's rigid separation between bottom-up and top-down

---

[53] *Ibid.*, p. 105.

Example 6.21 Symphony No. 46 in B major, first movement, bars 149–51

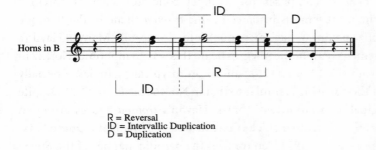

R = Reversal
ID = Intervallic Duplication
D = Duplication

factors understates the extent to which seemingly invariant, 'natural', principles are actually learnt through musical experience. For example, the 'fit' between the B–D♯–E gesture's implicative and conventional dimensions is so perfect that it is reasonable to conclude that it is recognized and processed just as automatically and unreflectively as any of Narmour's 'basic structures'. In this light, I would like to end my discussion of Haydn's symphony by proposing how Narmour's model might be improved. Figure 6.1 presents Narmour's model, his interaction between bottom-up style shapes and top-down style structures, together with a revised model. The latter conceives of an interaction between two style structures, each of which enshrines style-shape principles.

Figure 6.1

Narmour's model	Improved model	
Style shape vs. style structure	*style structure* vs. *style structure*	
	style shape	style shape

In basic terms, we hear bars 1–2 of the symphony not as an interaction between a cultural unit, a cadence and a perceptual unit, a style shape, but rather as an interaction of two psychologically motivated cultural units alone, that is, two 'style structures'. If the first style structure is a cadence, what is the second?

One of the commonest ways to begin a symphonic or concerto movement in the eighteenth century was with a rising tonic arpeggio, suggestive of a brass fanfare. Indeed, this gesture was largely associated with the 'Bologna School', composers of trumpet concertos such as Torelli.[54] Perhaps the most famous instance of this *tromba* cliché in the Baroque period is the opening of Bach's E major Violin Concerto.[55] Many of Haydn's first-movement symphonic Allegros begin this way. Symphonies Nos. 27 in G (1760) and No. 17 in F (1762) afford prototypical examples, especially given that their scoring is similar to that in No. 46 (see Ex. 6.22).[56] Despite their original association with brass, Haydn's *tromba* figures are often carried by other instruments. The first movement of his String Quartet in C minor, Op. 17 No. 4 (1771), epitomizes the parodic manner of the *Sturm und Drang*, with its reliance on octave or solo textures to promote ambiguity (see Ex. 6.23).[57] Without any harmony to guide us, we tend to hear the solo E♭–G opening in E flat major, and the following C (now tonicized) as an interruption of an expected B♭. The piece's games with this ambiguity come to a head at the end of the development section (bar 86) with a false reprise in E flat major, in which the E♭–G–B♭ *tromba* is realized (see Ex. 6.24).

Given its date of composition (1771), the quartet is arguably the model for Haydn's manipulation of the *tromba* figure in the B major symphony. Turning to the opening of the symphony, we notice that the horns are silenced after their first minim, the B of bar 1. It is significant, in this regard, that the reprise of bar 105 completes the rest of the B–D♯–E figure, so that the horns play in unison with the orchestra (this also occurs at the repeat of the theme at bar 5; see Ex. 6.25).

Despite their unison, the horns approach the D♯ *from below*, thus contradicting the orchestra's descending sixth with a rising third. The

---

54 See Arthur Hutchings, *The Baroque Concerto* (London: Faber, 1978), pp. 64–88. What I term 'tromba' is a member of Ratner's 'military' family of stylistic topics (see Ratner, *Classic Music*, pp. 18–19).

55 Another example of this 1̂–3̂–5̂ opening is the finale of Beethoven's Fifth Symphony.

56 Other examples of the *tromba* figure from this period include Symphonies No. 19 in D (1760) and No. 23 in G (1764). Sometimes, as in No. 38 in C (1768), the *tromba* figure is relegated to the oboes, whilst the horns or trumpets sustain a pedal.

57 My thanks to William Drabkin for drawing my attention to this example. Webster briefly refers to the major/minor ambiguity of this opening, *Haydn's 'Farewell' Symphony*, p. 130.

Example 6.22

(a) Symphony No. 27 in G major, first movement, bars 1–2

(b) Symphony No. 17 in F major, first movement, bars 1–2

(a)

(b)

Example 6.23 String Quartet in C minor, Op. 17 No. 4, first movement, bars 1–5

Example 6.24 String Quartet in C minor, Op. 17 No. 4, first movement, bars 79–88

Example 6.25 Symphony No. 46 in B major, first movement, bars 1–2 and 105–6

204

Example 6.26 Symphony No. 46 in B major, first movement, bars 5–7

Example 6.27 Symphony No. 46 in B major, first movement, bars 105–18

implications (in Narmour's sense) of this registral inversion are far-reaching. As Narmour's theory has stated, a falling sixth is far more likely to reverse to a small interval, such as a minor second (E) than a to a larger one, such as a minor third (F♯). By contrast, the rising third B–D♯ generates an intervallic process of rising thirds, which must be realized by a further leap to F♯. From a stylistic viewpoint, hardly any *trombas* begin with a falling sixth; the norm is a rising third. The orchestra and horns at bar 105 therefore pull in opposite directions: the orchestra's falling sixth is a terminal sign; the horn's rising third is an opening sign. The reversal to E at bar 106, which completes the cadence, simultaneously frustrates the *tromba*. The wonder is that Haydn achieves this with the minimum of means: the pitches and rhythms are the same. Haydn's strategy at the beginning of the movement is even more subtle. By truncating the incipient *tromba* of bar 1 after its first note, the horns' B pairs off with the D♯ of the orchestra. This timbral disjunction masks the identity of the *tromba*. The figure can thereby participate in the same game of *peripeteia* as the cadence. It is implicit at bar 1; explicit at the reprise of bar 105, but only to be overtly disconfirmed by the E♮ of bar 106. The resolution of this narrative, the *tromba*'s 'consonance', can only be effected by completing the B♯–D♯ pair with an F♯. In the exposition, this happens after the second statement of the theme, at bar 7. Here, the F♯ pedal-point is separated from the D♯ by a single bar (bar 6; see Ex. 6.26). In the recapitulation the elision of the theme's second statement means that the interval between the D♯ and F♯ is stretched to eleven bars (see Ex. 6.27).

The F♯ of bars 117–21 forms the longest dominant pedal of the movement and the element which sets up the end of the secondary development, bar 123, as the definitive tonic resolution. Paradoxically, the realization of the F♯, the note which completes the *tromba* opening figure, thus takes the form of a dominant pedal, a closing gesture. The subsequent entrance of the B–D♯–E cadential figure on an F♯ (F♯–A♯–B) in the cellos at bar 122 compounds the joke: this is of course the point when the cadence achieves its own moment of 'consonance', after the subdominant 'disconfirmation' of bars 105–6. That the two *peripeteias* coincide does not indicate that learned archetypes behave in the same way as implicative interval patterns. It does suggest, however, that Haydn composed with the consciousness that bottom-up and top-down realms of experience are entangled at a much lower level than Narmour would admit. Haydn's musical discourse is driven by the interaction of two schemata associated, respectively, with openings and closes.

One of the ironies which emerges from close analysis of the *Sturm und Drang* style is that the famed turbulence of its expressive surface is actually effected by processes of finely calibrated synchrony. The miraculous efficiency of Haydn's style in 1772 is borne out by its ability to compress so much musical content into the most meagre material, in this case a bare pitch cell, B–D♯. As we have seen, the B–D♯ cell forms the pivot for two sets of puns. Registrally, it outlines a $\hat{1}$–$\hat{3}$ opening gesture (*tromba*) at the same time as an $\hat{8}$–$\hat{3}$ closing gesture (cadence). Tonally, it can be interpreted either as $\hat{1}$–$\hat{3}$ in B major (tonic) or $\hat{5}$–$\hat{7}$ in E major (dominant). What makes this fourfold multivalence possible is the octave texture. As the locus for these concordances, Haydn's octave can hardly be regarded, in the words of Rosen's critique of the *Sturm und Drang*, as a token of 'harsh simplicity'.[58] On the contrary, it is a trace of an extraordinary density of argument. Nevertheless, in its *ne plus ultra* of reductionism and compression, the octave also marks the 'limit of fertile land', as Boulez would say of his own *Sturm und Drang* two centuries later.[59] Having coordinated style shapes and style structures

[58] Charles Rosen, *The Classical Style* (New York: Norton, 1972), p. 147. See also Rosen's cursory remarks on the B major symphony's opening: 'these are striking effects with little power to range beyond their immediate context' (p. 148).

[59] Boulez intended to use the title of Paul Klee's painting, 'An der Grenze des Fruchtlandes', as the title of his two-piano work *Structures 1a* (1951), a piece

at the vanishing point of a singularity, Haydn's only remaining option was to come out the other side and disperse them. The other side was *galant*.

2   *Galant* schemata

Haydn's 'retreat' in the mid- to late 1770s to a more conventional, *galant* style has been enshrined in reception history as a betrayal of the *Sturm und Drang's* radical experimentation. Thus Landon writes that 'in 1773 Haydn abandons the [*Sturm und Drang*] style for the formally clear, musically fresh and uncomplicated Piano Sonatas dedicated to Prince Nicolaus. Here the end of *Sturm und Drang* is announced with a vengeance'.[60] Similarly, A. Peter Brown maintains that 'the six Esterházy Sonatas Hob. XVI: 21–26 are the most conservative' works Haydn composed in that era, and some of their movements 'recall Haydn's pre-1765 style if not syntax'.[61] The operative distinction here is 'style if not syntax'. What I think Brown means is that Haydn's *galant* works of this period evince a disparity between form and content, or, returning to the technical language of Narmour, style shapes and style structures. This disparity, I argue, results from the displacement of the congruence we saw in the *Sturm und Drang* between style shapes and structures. Style shapes and structures now 'fight' each other. This would seem to lead to the paradoxical conclusion that the *galant* style is more dissonant than the *Sturm und Drang*, a claim which is belied by the *galant's* fuller and more triadic textures. For all their plenitude, these textures are nevertheless more heterogeneous. Haydn's Sonata No. 40 in E flat major begins with the octave texture so typical of the *Sturm und Drang*, but quickly bifurcates into left-hand octaves and right-hand melody (see Ex. 6.28).

The reason we find the octave accompaniment so troubling is that it jars against another vestige from the B major symphony, the descending-sixth cadential opening. Like the symphony, the sonata begins with a rever-

---

which brings to a climax (and draws to a close) the earlier, integralist, phase of his career. See *Pierre Boulez: Conversations with Célestin Delière* (London: Eulenburg, 1976), p. 55.

60 See H. C. Robbins Landon, *Haydn: Chronicle and Works II: Haydn at Eszterháza, 1766–1790* (London: Thames and Hudson, 1978), p. 341.

61 A. Peter Brown, *Joseph Haydn's Keyboard Music: Sources and Style* (Bloomington: Indiana University Press, 1986), p. 303.

Example 6.28 Sonata No. 40 in E flat major, first movement, bars 1–4

sal pattern based on a falling sixth followed by a rise. As in the earlier work, this also effects a cadential gesture. But the sonata's sixth is resolved much more weakly, not with a rising minor second (G–A♭) but with a processive pattern staking out a rising minor third (G–A♮–B♭). By choosing to tonicize the B♭ rather than the more normative A♭, Haydn overrides both the parametric, style-shape expectation of a rising minor second and a stylistic, style-structural cue for a conventional cadence type, as occurred at the equivalent point in Symphony No. 46. The falling sixth itself parodies the common practice of beginning a sonata with a *rising* arpeggio – a pianistic version of the *tromba* figure.[62] If the sixth is regularized into a rising third (and the A♮ removed), then Haydn's theme becomes remarkably like that of a more conformant sonata of the period, the Sonata No. 42 in G major (1776, see Ex. 6.29).

The tonicization of B♭ actively grates against the surrounding E♭ arpeggiation. This E♭/B♭ clash, which crystallizes with the laboured suspension of bar 2, generates the movement's piquantly discordant *tinta*. Another aspect of this quasi-bitonal gambit is the implicit, though suppressed, E♭–D voice-leading at bar 1. The E♭, converted by the A♮ into the seventh of the secondary dominant, needs to resolve down to a putative D above the B♭. Of course, a resolution to D in this register is out of the question, because of the octave D's in the bass. We now see why the octave accompaniment is so disruptive. Though octave textures are typical of openings, it is rare to

---

[62] See the openings of the Sonatas No. 36 in C major and No. 48 in C major.

Example 6.29

(a) Sonata No. 42 in G major, first movement, bars 1–4

(b) Sonata No. 40 in E flat major, first movement, bars 1–2 (regularized)

(a)

(b)

combine them with free textures in the upper voices. This is because of the danger of confusing the textural 'code', where parallel octaves are tolerated, with the contrapuntal 'code' of good voice-leading, in which parallels are strictly forbidden. The left-hand octaves render the implicit E♭–D voice-leading at bar 1 especially effective, hinting at a deliciously subtle parallel-octave solecism, a sort of 'double parallel'.

This comprehensive non-congruence between texture, style shape and style structure is, paradoxically, a function of the sonata's more conventional style. It is a mark of the *galant*'s schematicism that conformance obtains on a much broader scale than in the *Sturm und Drang*, on the level of the phrase. We can see this instantly by comparing the sonata's theme with that of two other contemporary works, the theme of Haydn's Twelve Variations in E flat major, Hob. XVII/3, and the first subject of Mozart's Sonata in E flat major, K. 282 (see Ex. 6.30).

All three phrases share the same package of features. B♭ is tonicized by means of a rising third-progression (an inner-voice progression in Hob. XVII/3 and K. 282) above a descending tetrachord bass-progression, E♭–D–C–B♭. After tonicizing the B♭, each phrase returns to the tonic via a descending scale, C–B♭–A♭–G, in the melody, harmonized with a circle-of-fifths sequence based on C–F, B♭–E♭. Given such extensive parallels, we can

209

Example 6.30

(a) Haydn: Twelve Variations in E flat major, Hob. XVII/3, bars 1–10

(b) Mozart: Sonata in E flat major, K. 282, first movement, bars 1–4

(a)

(b)

interpret the phrases as three instantiations of a single stereotypical pattern. In other words, they outline a style structure, but one of considerably larger dimensions than found in Narmour's theory. If so, then the 'form/content' disparity we have imputed to Haydn's *galant* style is manifest on two levels. On the first level, discussed above, the constituent features 'fight' each other. On a second level, these non-congruent features are framed by a conformant, stereotypical pattern. Since Narmour's theory does not address such block-like relationships, we must turn to a younger member of the Meyer school, Robert O. Gjerdingen, and his theory of stylistic schemata.

Gjerdingen's schema theory, first articulated in his *A Classic Turn of Phrase* of 1988,[63] emerged from Meyer's notion of stylistic 'archetype'.

---

[63] *A Classic Turn of Phrase: Music and the Psychology of Convention* (Philadelphia: University of Pennsylvania Press, 1988).

According to Meyer, archetypes 'establish fundamental frameworks in terms of which culturally competent audiences ... perceive, comprehend, and respond to works of art'.[64] Similarly, Gjerdingen's 'schema' is a stereotypical musical pattern, 'a set of features combined to form a specific structural complex'.[65] Schematas are therefore kindred with Narmour's 'style structures'. Nevertheless, the difference between a style structure and a schema entails an important change of emphasis. As a complex of melodic, harmonic and metrical features, a schema can be both larger and more multi-dimensional than a style structure. Moreover, it is inclusive not only of formal 'features' but also of the syntactic relationships which regulate them. For example, a schema typically comprehends the antecedent–consequent logic of an entire phrase. Such a schema, in the shape of Meyer's 'changing-note' figure, was the subject of Gjerdingen's A Classic Turn of Phrase.[66] Schema theory therefore stresses co-occurrence of features and coordination of movement, whereas Narmour emphasized the tensional interaction between the conventional surface of melodies and its psychological substrate. In schema theory these psychological principles are still operative, but they are interwoven with cultural factors in a much less conflicting, more harmonious, way. Most of all, Gjerdingen places the accent on the plasticity of our perceptual categories, given that prior experience shapes present cognition.

To analyse Haydn through schema theory is, in some ways, to look at him through Mozartian lenses. The stereotypical instantiation of Gjerdingen's 'Classic turn of phrase' was the first subject of Mozart's Sonata in G major, K. 283, of 1774. The subject of Gjerdingen's later study[67] is the theme from a work written in that same year, Mozart's Sonata in E flat major, K. 282, the theme we earlier compared with Haydn's. Since Haydn's sonata was published a year before Mozart's, one could even infer that the influence flowed from Haydn to the younger composer. It is all the more surprising, therefore, that Gjerdingen does not consider Haydn in his

---

[64] Cited in Gjerdingen, ibid., p. 47.   [65] Ibid., p. 45.

[66] See Leonard B. Meyer, Explaining Music (Chicago: University of Chicago Press, 1973), pp. 191–5. Changing-note melodies 'begin and end on the same pitch, which is "surrounded" by upper and lower neighbor-notes'. They 'involve motion away from and back to stability' (p. 191).

[67] 'Courtly Behaviors', Music Perception 13/3 (1996), 365–82.

Example 6.31 Gjerdingen's 'Romanesca' schema

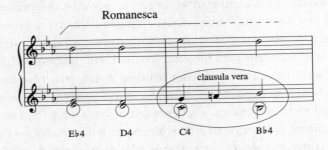

survey. One reason for this oversight might be that Haydn's phrase, even though it demonstrably belongs to the same family as Mozart's, is fraught with unresolved tensions. In short, although his schema contains and regulates its constituent features, it fails to *assimilate* them. The resultant antagonism between the two levels of the schema is not a characteristic of Mozart's style, nor is it typical of *galant* phrases in general. It is, rather, an idiosyncratic hallmark of Haydn's style in 1773. To understand exactly why Haydn's schema is different, we must first review Gjerdingen's analysis of Mozart's phrase from his Sonata in E flat major, K. 282.

Gjerdingen conceives of a schema as a clustering of several sub-schemas, or stereotypical features. Although these features are often found apart, they occur together in statistically significant quantities, so that the schema achieves a measure of stability. According to Gjerdingen, what holds these patterns together in Mozart's sonata is the courtly logic of 'Opening Gambit' followed by 'Prinner Riposte'. As a reflection in musical terms of the behavioural etiquette of court life, an assertive, ascending opening was typically answered by a 'concessive, descending pattern', the 'Prinner Riposte'.[68] Gjerdingen shows how each half of this ritual was expressed by a set of sub-patterns. While an opening gambit's melody tends to rise up the triad, its bass often employs a pattern dating from the Renaissance, the 'Romanesca' (see Ex. 6.31).[69]

In its traditional form, the Romanesca bass leaps downwards from the sixth of the scale to the third (Eb–D–C–G). Mozart assimilates it, by con-

---

[68] *Ibid.*, 368.   [69] *Ibid.*, 372.

Example 6.32 Gjerdingen's analysis of Mozart: Sonata in E flat major, K. 282, bars 1–4

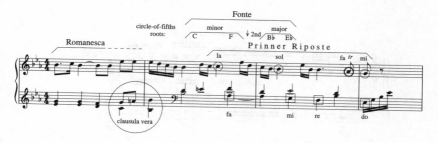

trast, into the descending-fourth tetrachord, E♭–D–C–B♭, as does Haydn. This descent to the B♭ is supported by a further pattern, the ancient *clausula vera* ('true cadence'), which rises from G to B♭ in an inner voice. The 'Prinner Riposte' answers the opening gambit with a melodic descent *la–sol–fa–mi* in parallel with the bass's tones *fa-mi-re-do*. Gjerdingen discovers in Mozart's Prinner yet another pattern, a progression that Riepel termed a *fonte*. A *fonte* is a 'closed descending sequence presented as a pairing of two similar gestures'.[70] It normally follows the double bar of a movement but composers can assimilate it to the *fa–mi–re–do* response. The result is a multi-layered complex of patterns, including a descent in parallel between melody and bass, a circle-of-fifths sequence, and a pairing of gestures, one in the minor (supertonic), one in the major (tonic; see Ex. 6.32).[71]

Haydn's phrase is, of course, just as multi-layered as Mozart's and the provenance of his patterns is equally conventional. For example, we now see that what we took to be a deflection of the descending-sixth reversal is really part of a traditional *clausula vera*. The latter provides an interpretative framework which should, ordinarily, comprehend the lower-order events, however problematic they might be. Alas, the layers of Haydn's complex overlap and interpenetrate in a way which 'short-circuits' the schema. Keeping with the opening gambit, we see that the tonic arpeggiation and the *clausula vera* are normally carried by separate voices; Sonata No. 40 conflates them within a single gesture, a falling sixth, which, furthermore,

[70] *Ibid.*, 374.   [71] *Ibid.*, 378.

Example 6.33 Sonata No. 40 in E flat major, first movement, bars 15–16

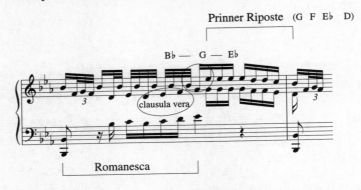

cues an antithetical implication of a resolution to A♭. More to the point, the falling sixth diverges from the norm of the rising fourth B♭–E♭ instantiated in the more conventional Hob. XVII/3 and K. 282.

Haydn's practice is remarkable on an architectonic level too. So far, schema theory has been preoccupied with issues of classification and has failed to account for processes across the length of single movements. In this respect, the Sonata in E flat major provides a striking instance of transformation and development applied not to a single generative event, as in the implication-realization model, but to a whole package of features – the schema. Astonishingly, the second group, bar 15, constitutes a retrograde, in compressed form, of bars 1–2 (see Ex. 6.33). The 'Romanesca' bass now *rises* from B♭ to E♭; the E♭–G–B♭ melodic progression now falls from B♭ to G and leaps to E♭. The *clausula vera* is given now in the inner-voice ascent, D–E♭–F. The E♭–D discordance, a consequence of the problematic octave texture of bars 1–2, is also brought out here in the disjunct voice-leading between bars 15 and 16. The left hand climbs to E♭; the right hand resolves the E♭ with a descending scale, but the bass's E♭ is cut off by a crotchet rest. This E♭ is left hanging in mid-air while the left hand dives down more than an octave to the B♭ at bar 16 (in strict voice-leading terms, of course, the E♭ is resolved by the inner voice of the right hand). Perhaps the most ingenious aspect of the bar 15 retrograde is the fact that it occurs at the same pitch as bars 1–2. That is to say, the E♭–D–C–B♭ and E♭–G–B♭ progressions have not been transposed into the dominant key, but recur

Example 6.34 Sonata No. 40 in E flat major, first movement, bars 57–9

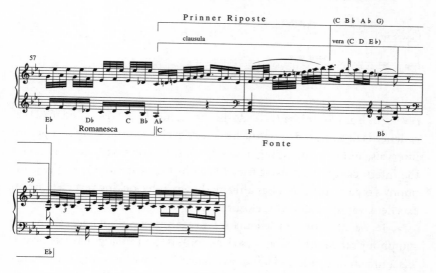

literally. This kind of block-like pitch invariance is associated with the 'monotonal' neo-Classical schemes of Schoenberg's piano works of the 1920s. In view of Webster's designation of Haydn's Classical school as 'The First Viennese Modern School',[72] this comparison may not be as outlandish as it sounds.

The second group comprises a transformation of a whole *complex* of features, rather than of a single element. As a retrograde of the tonic-group schema, it might be called a 'schematic reversal': a style-structural complement of Narmour's style-shape reversals. If so, then the resolution of Haydn's discourse is achieved by another kind of reversal in the retransition, bars 57–8 (see Ex. 6.34).

Haydn now cycles through the schema in its prime order rather than in retrograde. But he institutes even more dramatic changes. Firstly, the 'Romanesca' bass falls a full fifth, descending a further step to A♭ (E♭–D–C–B♭–A♭). The subdominant thus sets up the V–I of bars 58–9. Secondly, the E♭–G leap is assimilated (and neutralized) into a tremolo figure. Most importantly, the orientation of the *clausula vera* has been

---

[72] *Haydn's 'Farewell' Symphony*, p. 367.

215

Example 6.35 Sonata No. 40 in E flat major, first movement, bars 50–2

reversed from dominant (G–A♮–B♭) to tonic (C–D–E♭). The C–D–E♭ cadence is now unfolded on the broadest level, encompassing compound intervals, and correspondingly massive registral reversals (compare with the interlocking reversals at bars 121–3 of the symphony). As the symphony's own retransition has already shown, interlocking reversals are an excellent way to effect strong closure.

Just as the sonata's schema retains (and refashions) aspects of the symphony's thematic material, so it submits it to an analogous discourse of 'disconfirmation followed by a consonance'. We have just noted the sonata's consonance, the schematic reversal of the retransition. The 'disconfirmation' falls where we expect it, at the reprise of the first group in bar 51 (see Ex. 6.35). The sonata's development ends on the dominant of G minor and launches into the tonic reprise without any preparation at all. Hence the reprise's first proper resolutions fall on B♭, at bars 51 and 52.[73] It is notable that the harmonic *non sequitur* is much more drastic in the sonata than in the symphony. There it simply involved the weakening of a dominant. Here the dominant is withheld altogether.

In conclusion, we can say that both materially and formally Haydn's *galant* style of 1773, as it is evinced in his Sonata No. 40 in E flat major, continues to explore the same principles that had governed the *Sturm und Drang* symphonies of the previous years. It would be going too far, perhaps, to hear the sonata as a palimpsest on the B major Symphony, as stormy style shapes in *galant* fancy-dress. The deep-seated affinity between the first movements of the two works does, however, throw into question Webster's pat pairing of

---

[73] For general issues of tonal closure involving the retransition, see my 'The Retransition as Sign: Listener-Orientated Approaches to Tonal Closure in Haydn's Sonata-Form Movements', *Journal of the Royal Musicological Association* 121 (1996), 11–45.

Symphony No. 46 with the 'Farewell'[74] and his clean division between the 'personally expressive' style of 1772 and the 'light, theatrical' manner of 1773. The sonata might well be light in tone, but then again so is the symphony; *Sturm und Drang* works are by no means all in the minor mode. Regardless of superficial affective differences between the 'stormy' and the *galant*, I have shown that Haydn's alleged style-change is really a matter of a change of emphasis. Haydn's style both prior to and after the 1772–3 watershed is characterized by an interaction of style shapes and style structures, only the nature of this interaction is transformed. The earlier manner is marked by synchrony, congruence and general 'fit'. Afterwards, parametric and conventional patterns drift apart and the latter wax into full-blown schemata. Conflict and non-congruence reign between the schema and its contents, as well as between these contents themselves. And so historiography itself experiences a *peripeteia* of sorts. The *Sturm und Drang* is poised; the *galant* is stormy. That is Haydn's most dramatic reversal.

Such stylistic reversal is in fact the norm in the mid-career of our canonic composers. What makes Haydn's reversal unusual, perhaps unique, is its synergy with the fabric of his language, the 'micro-*peripeteias*' of his comic style. Haydn *ludens*, the master of mental play, may be accorded foundational status as the author of all our musical narratives. Wherefore, then, our Haydn blind-spot? We cannot see him because he is our eyes.

[74] *Haydn's 'Farewell' Symphony*: 'Both symphonies . . . are a "pair" musically and programmatically', p. 3.

7 Haydn's symphonies between *Sturm und Drang* and 'Classical style': art and entertainment

JAMES WEBSTER

The traditional narratives of Haydn's symphonic career view him as having developed gradually: from modest and to some extent conventional beginnings, through various phases of experimentation, to eventual mastery. In these accounts, two periods within his tenure at the Esterházy court stand out as high-points. Jens Peter Larsen finds that during the so-called *Sturm und Drang*, just before and after 1770, a 'remarkable expansion of expression and compositional technique' led to symphonies that 'still impress for their striking sincerity and directness [and] in their own time . . . must have come as a revelation' – led, indeed, to an already 'Classical' maturity.[1] Then, in some respects prefigured by the string quartets Op. 33 (1781), the mid- and late 1780s witnessed the triumph of 'Classical style' proper in Haydn's orchestral music, specifically the *Seven Last Words* and the 'Paris' Symphonies, both of 1785–6.[2]

By contrast, Haydn's symphonies that fall between the *Sturm und Drang* and the mid-1780s enjoy no comparably high reputation. Indeed, his stylistic 'turn' in the mid-1770s has been a distinct embarrassment for

---

[1] Jens Peter Larsen, 'Haydn, Joseph', *The New Grove Dictionary of Music and Musicians*, ed. Stanley Sadie (London: Macmillan, 1980), VIII, pp. 351, 352 (reprinted as *The New Grove Haydn* [London and New York: Macmillan, 1982], pp. 91, 93). For 'Classical' in this context see Larsen, 'Some Observations on the Development and Characteristics of Viennese Classical Instrumental Music', *Studia musicologica* 9 (1967), 130. Compare Landon, *Haydn: Chronicle and Works II: Haydn at Eszterháza, 1766–1790* (London: Thames and Hudson, 1978), pp. 271–84.

[2] For a critique of these accounts see James Webster, *Haydn's 'Farewell' Symphony and the Idea of Classical Style: Through-Composition and Cyclic Integration in his Instrumental Music* (Cambridge: Cambridge University Press, 1991), pp. 357–66; for a cultural-historically orientated treatment of artistic periodizations see Webster, 'The Concept of Beethoven's "Early" Period in the Context of Periodizations in General', *Beethoven Forum* 3 (1994), 1–27.

Haydn scholarship. Larsen regards it as a sort of let-down: 'Haydn may have felt a need ... to slow down after his years of intense exploration', although he also speculates (not entirely consistently) that 'a reaction on Prince [Esterházy's] part may have been the main cause of Haydn's moderating his progressive tendencies'.[3] The music

> does not reveal a conscious and continuous development of [genres] but rather isolated works or sets of works. Related to this discontinuity is the fact that the very personal style forged during Haydn's period of marked expansion gave way to a less consistent variety of style. . . . His development of the symphony [includes] pleasant, unpretentious works of the later 1770s.[4]

And H. C. Robbins Landon criticizes the works of this period in baldly negative fashion:

> The quality of the symphonies declines, partly because most were hastily written and some even *potpourris* of various earlier works, and partly because Haydn's search for the popular style led him to pander to the lowest common denominator.[5]

I cannot share these negative opinions. Haydn's symphonies from the mid-1770s through to the early 1780s seem to me as finely crafted, as interesting, indeed as original, as those from around 1770 – while admittedly very different in character. Even the critics acknowledge that they exhibit the highest level of compositional mastery; in Larsen's view the works of *c.*1773–4 'show a wealth of fine craftsmanship', with 'increasing individuality of the single movements, slow movements and finales in particular'.[6] Why, then, should they have posed a problem? Following a brief survey of the repertory, I will offer a critique of the traditional views and their cultural-historical presuppositions. I will then present two complementary rationales for these symphonies: first, an explanation of their 'popular' features in terms of an aesthetic of comedy and entertainment; secondly, an argument that in fact they stand on the same high artistic level as the rest of Haydn's music.

[3] *The New Grove*, p. 336 (reprint, pp. 33, 34).
[4] *The New Grove*, p. 354 (reprint, p. 101).
[5] Landon, *Chronicle and Works II*, p. 561. (In his earlier *The Symphonies of Joseph Haydn* [London: Barrie and Rockliff, 1955], pp. 341, 344, 353, 367, 383, the criticism is even harsher.)   [6] *The New Grove*, p. 353 (reprint, p. 95).

Table 7.1 Haydn's Symphonies, c. 1773–1784[a]

c. 1773–1774	Nos. 50, 54–7, 60, (51, 64?)	[≈3.5/yr]
1773	50 (C) /i,ii (as overture); perhaps also	
	Nos. 51 (B♭), 64 (A)	
1774	54 (G),[b] 55 (E♭; 'The Schoolmaster'), 56 (C), 57 (D),	
	60 (C; 'Il distratto'); 50/iii,iv (or early 1775)	
c. 1775–1776	Nos. 61, 66–9	[≈2.5/yr]
c. 1775?[c]	68 (B♭)	
c. 1775–6[c]	66 (B♭), 67 (F), 69 (C; 'Laudon')	
1776	61 (D), ?54 (G)[b]	
c. 1778–*c.* 1781	Nos. 53, 62, 63, 70, 71, 73–5	[≈2.0/yr]
c. 1778–1779?	53 (D; 'L'impériale'),[d] 70 (D), 71 (B♭)	
End 1779?	63 (C; 'Roxelane'),[e] 75 (D)	
c. 1780	62 (D), 74 (E♭)	
1781?	73 (D; 'La chasse')	
1782–4	Nos. 76–81	[≈2.0/yr]
1782	76 (E♭), 77 (B♭), 78 (c)	
1783–4	79 (F), 80 (d), 81 (G)	

Notes:

[a]Table 7.1 is based on data in the literature given in note 7.

[b]First version 1774 (without slow introduction; lacking flutes, second bassoon, trumpets, drums); final version *c.* 1776.

[c]According to Gerlach, No. 68 *c.* 1774–5, Nos. 66, 67, 69 *c.* 1775–6; according to Fisher, all four *c.* 1775–7.

[d]Two versions. According to Gerlach, Version 'B' *c.* 1778, version 'A' *c.* 1780; according to Fisher, both *c.* 1778.

[e]At various times Haydn employed several different movements in conjunction with this work; however, the sources document the existence of only one constellation *as a symphony* (= Landon's 'second' version).

1

These symphonies are listed in Table 7.1;[7] I will focus on those in the two middle groups, which together comprise thirteen works dating from *c.* 1775 to *c.* 1781 (Nos. 53, 61–3, 66–71, 73–5) and constitute the 'core' of the repertory, both chronologically and stylistically. (Many works in the 1773–4

7   The information in Table 7.1 is based primarily on Sonja Gerlach, 'Die chronologische Ordnung von Haydns Sinfonien zwischen 1774 und 1782', *Haydn-Studien* 2 (1969–70), 34–66; see also Stephen C. Fisher, 'Haydn's Overtures and their Adaptations as Concert Orchestral Works', Ph.D. diss., University of Pennsylvania (1985), and Webster, annotations to the complete

group still retain something of the *Sturm und Drang* manner. Conversely, Nos. 76–81 have a good deal in common with the 'Paris' Symphonies; in addition, they were the first symphonies that Haydn composed in the 'opus' format and marketed abroad.) Despite the slight imprecision, in what follows I will refer to the core group as Haydn's symphonies of the 'later 1770s'.

These works exhibit a mixture of styles: light, indeed 'popular' themes are as prominent as earnest ones, regular phrasing is as important as vast expansions. Notwithstanding the prevailing light tone, counterpoint is also present, most obviously in Symphony No. 70 in D, where it is associated with confrontations between major and minor and between learned and *galant* style.[8] In many of these symphonies the comic and the serious are not 'synthesized', as demanded by the ideology of 'Classical style', but juxtaposed in such a way as to give the impression of accepting, even courting, stylistic incongruity. In distinction to the *Sturm und Drang* symphonies, those of the later 1770s are set in major keys exclusively (until 1782) and favour variation, rondo and variation-rondo forms in the slow movements and finales. They also exhibit a gradual increase in independent and *concertante* orchestration, especially in the winds.

A key role in these stylistic changes appears to have been played by Haydn's compositions for the stage. Having composed three *opere buffe* between 1766 and 1769–70 (*La canterina, Lo speziale* and *Le Pescatrici*), between 1770 and 1772 (that is, at the height of the *Sturm und Drang*) he composed no major stage works. In 1773, however, he resumed operatic composition with *L'infedeltà delusa* and the marionette opera *Philomen und Baucis*, followed in 1775 by *L'incontro improvviso*; and with the inauguration of the new opera house at Eszterháza in 1776 he became virtually a full-time impresario, while continuing to compose Italian operas at the rate of almost one per year until 1783.

The most obvious sign of this orientation is that in a number of these symphonies Haydn 'recycled' overtures and other stage music; see Table

recordings of Haydn's symphonies by The Academy of Ancient Music, Christopher Hogwood, director (Decca/L'oiseau-lyre).

8   On this symphony see Landon, *Chronicle and Works II*, pp. 563–4; Elaine R. Sisman, *Haydn and the Classical Variation* (Cambridge, Mass.: Harvard University Press, 1993), pp. 161–2.

Table 7.2 Relations to vocal and stage Music[a]

No. 50 (C)	[i]–[ii] ≈ Overture to *Der Götterrat* (1773)
No. 53 (D)	Version 'B': [iv] ≈ Overture Hob. Ia:7 (1777)[b]
No. 60 (C)	Incidental music (1774)
No. 62 (D)	[i] ≈ Overture Hob. Ia:7 (1777)[b]
No. 63 (C)	[i] ≈ Overture to *Il mondo della luna* (1777)
	[ii]: Theme 'La Roxelane' probably composed in conjunction with Favart's stage-play *Soliman II*
No. 73 (D)	[ii]: Theme ≈ Haydn's lied 'Gegenliebe' (Hob. XXVIa:16)
	[iv] ≈ Overture to *La fedeltà premiata* (1780)

Notes

[a]Only securely documented relations are cited.

[b]That is, Haydn recycled this overture in two different symphonies, once as a finale, once as an opening movement. In addition, the first movement of No. 66 in B flat opens with a variant of the opening motif of this overture (to which, however, it is otherwise not related).

7.2. No. 60, 'Il distratto', comprises in its entirety the overture and four *entr'actes* composed as incidental music to Regnard's comic French play *Le distrait* (1774),[9] while Nos. 50, 53 (in one version), 62, 63 and 73 all begin or end with adapted overtures. Several additional symphonies from this period exhibit unusual or bizarre features even beyond Haydn's customary range which suggest the possibility of association with the stage; the most extensive case is perhaps No. 67 in F major.[10]

2

The criticism of Haydn's symphonies of the later 1770s is primarily ideological in origin. It is based not so much on expert or detailed study of the music as on the composer's apparent failure to conform to deep-seated

[9] Rudolph Angermüller, 'Haydns Der Zerstreute in Salzburg (1776)', *Haydn-Studien* 4 (1976–80), 85–93; Robert A. Green, '"Il Distratto" of Haydn and Regnard: A Re-examination', *The Haydn Yearbook* 11 (1980), 183–95; Fisher, 'Haydn's Overtures', pp. 181–3, 306–7; Sisman, 'Haydn's Theater Symphonies', *Journal of the American Musicological Society* 43 (1990), 311–20; Gretchen A. Wheelock, *Haydn's Ingenious Jesting with Art: Contexts of Musical Wit and Humor* (New York: Norton, 1992), pp. 154–70.

[10] See Landon, *Chronicle and Works II*, pp. 314–15; Fisher, 'Haydn's Overtures', pp. 183–4. Sisman, 'Haydn's Theater Symphonies', speculates that many *Sturm und Drang* symphonies may also have been drawn from stage music.

beliefs, more Romantic/modernist than characteristic of Haydn's own time, about the autonomy of art and the cultural-social role of the artist. Every artwork – so runs this old consensus – is a unique synthesis of form and content, necessity and independence. This ideal demands that the artwork be complete and intelligible in its own terms, that it exclude everything superfluous or contingent, that it be incapable of alteration without violating its essence and that it stake a claim to the realms of spirituality as opposed to materiality, transcendence as opposed to quotidian reality. Analogously, it demands that the artist create solely according to his muse and not for 'external' reasons. Hence to be great, an artwork must be psychologically and historically 'authentic' (in Adorno's sense): fully and in all details an autonomous expression of its maker's personality, yet reflecting the social-philosophical reality of its time and place of origin.

This ideology of the artwork lies at the heart of the concept of 'Classical style' in music.[11] One of the many difficulties with this concept is that it not only marginalizes all music dating from *c.* 1740 to *c.* 1780 (including Haydn's own early and 'occasional' works), as 'Rococo' or 'pre-Classical',[12] but also renders suspect any music that does not appear to fit its rather rigid notions regarding 'central' genres such as the symphony and the string quartet. The quartet in particular has been closely associated with the ideal of spirituality.[13] But this too has its darker side: the related notion of 'purity' is used to cast aspersions on heterogeneous genres, such as 'mixed' wind/string ensembles and the piano trio.[14] (The very term 'mixed' expresses a covert negative value-judgement.)[15] Similarly – and this

---

[11] For a historiographical critique of 'Classical style' see Webster, *Haydn's 'Farewell' Symphony*, pp. 341–57; the perspective here is more aesthetically and sociologically orientated.

[12] Webster, *Haydn's 'Farewell' Symphony*, pp. 357–66.

[13] Ludwig Finscher, *Studien zur Geschichte des Streichquartetts*, I, *Die Entstehung des klassischen Streichquartetts: Von den Vorformen zur Grundlegung durch Joseph Haydn* (Kassel: Bärenreiter, 1974), pp. 277–301.

[14] Sarah Jane Adams, 'Quartets and Quintets for Mixed Groups of Winds and Strings: Mozart and his Contemporaries in Vienna, *c.* 1780–*c.* 1800', Ph.D. diss., Cornell University (1994); Webster, 'Haydn's Piano Trios at the Crossroads', unpublished paper, symposium on eighteenth-century chamber music, Amherst College, 1995.

[15] On such judgements see Janet M. Levy, 'Covert and Casual Values in Recent Writings about Music', *Journal of Musicology* 5 (1987), 3–27.

is the key point here – any work that is seen to appeal to the 'wrong' audience, to adopt 'low' or 'inappropriate' stylistic modes or to be inconsistent in style will be denied admission to the canon.

According to these traditional views, in the later 1770s Haydn committed (at least) four violations of this aesthetic: he avoided emotional truth; composed pastiches; courted popularity ('pandered'); and focused on financial gain – all in distinction to producing genuine artworks. (These notions are interrelated and cannot be understood in isolation.) Regarding expression, Landon writes that

> in [1774–5] we can see how the *Sturm und Drang* evaporates. . . . It is if Haydn had drawn a curtain over the passionate daring of the past decade.
> . . .
>   Haydn's speciality was rapidly becoming these catchy . . . double variation movements . . . in the new style, which carefully eschewed any deeper emotions.[16]

Even the sober, ostensibly objective Larsen asserts that 'in perhaps no other period of his maturity are there so many works that seem to lack the distinctive stamp of Haydn's personality'.[17]

These views suffer from a double fallacy: they equate the personality 'in' the work with that of its creator – treating it as a notional utterance of the man Joseph Haydn – and they interpret a felt lack of expression as a lack of 'daring' or 'progressiveness' – of authenticity – and hence as a sign of lesser value. But on what basis can Larsen be sure that, say, Symphony No. 44 in E minor ('Mourning') authentically projects Haydn's personality, whereas No. 75 'lacks [its] distinctive stamp'? Even he didn't know Haydn *that* well. To reply that perhaps he only meant Haydn's 'artistic' personality would condemn his argument to circularity: if the personality 'in' the work is the only evidence we admit, there can be no basis for saying that No. 75 is less authentic than No. 44.

This fallacy derives from the complex and ideologically charged belief, in our culture, in the effective identity between artist and artwork,

---

[16] *Chronicle and Works II*, pp. 312, 561; compare p. 313 *et passim*. (For the identical stance regarding Haydn's earliest music, see *Chronicle and Works I: Haydn: The Early Years, 1732–1765* [London: Thames and Hudson, 1980], p. 82.)

[17] *The New Grove*, p. 354 (reprint, p. 101).

224

that which Donald Preziosi calls 'the-artist-and/as-his-work'.[18] By contrast, the dominant assumption in literary criticism today is that the narrator of a work of fiction, or even the speaker in a lyric poem, is not at all to be equated with the real person who created it. Conservative versions of these positions have recently become prominent in musicology as well, for example in Edward T. Cone's theory of the 'persona' and Carl Dahlhaus's theory of the 'artistic subject'.[19] It follows that a work that to a Romantically inclined critic seems 'cool' may be no less authentic (not to mention more coherent) than one that seems 'expressive'. (For example, it has become a truism that Adorno's valuation of Schoenberg as a 'more authentic' composer than Stravinsky is untenable.)

The aversion to pastiches (Landon's 'potpourris') is based on their apparent violation of the same notions of authenticity and consistency; absent those notions, and such a value-judgement has no inherent force.[20] Of course, the very fact of recycling is incompatible with the traditional ideal of autonomous artistic creation, especially when Haydn resorts to overtures, with their whiff of the morally suspect, artistically contingent world of the stage. But recent thinking about *opera buffa* in particular makes it clear that a work of multiple origins (or even multiple authors) need be no less successful, either intrinsically or in reception, than a unitary one.[21] Another aspect of these symphonies related to their status as pastiches is their stylistic mixture; as adumbrated above, this has traditionally been considered aesthetically suspect, and indeed was so viewed by Haydn's

---

[18] *Rethinking Art History: Meditations on a Coy Science* (New Haven: Yale University Press, 1989), chapter 2.

[19] Edward T. Cone, *The Composer's Voice* (Berkeley: University of California Press, 1974); Dahlhaus, *Ludwig van Beethoven: Approaches to his Music*, trans. Mary Whittall (Oxford: Clarendon Press, 1991), chapter 1, especially pp. 7–9, 30–42.

[20] Admittedly, there is as yet apparently no aesthetic of musical pastiche. A first step is found in Jennifer Williams Brown, '"Con nuove arie aggiunte": Aria Borrowing in the Venetian Opera Repertory 1672–1685', Ph.D. diss., Cornell University (1992). See also John Winemiller, 'Handel's Borrowing and Swift's Bee: Handel's "Curious" Practice and the Theory of Transformative Imitation', Ph.D. diss., University of Chicago (1996).

[21] Mary Hunter, *The Poetics of Entertainment: Opera Buffa in Vienna, 1770–1790* (Princeton University Press, forthcoming); see also Hunter and James Webster, eds., *Opera Buffa in Mozart's Vienna* (Cambridge: Cambridge University Press, 1997), pp. 1–21.

contemporaries.[22] In fact, however, even his late sacred vocal music was censured for its inclusion of popular, pastoral, and even dance topics;[23] no serious student criticizes them for this today. There seems even less reason to dislike such mixture in a symphony.

Moreover, an appeal to Haydn's 'haste' and declining productivity (owing to his duties as Esterházy's opera impresario) as a criterion of lesser value is a red herring. It is true that his rate of symphonic composition declined beginning around 1775 (see Table 7.1); indeed, it seems possible that between April 1776 and 1778 he did not compose a single symphony.[24] But the logic is faulty. Even if Haydn composed fewer symphonies, some of them in a hurry, it does not follow that he cared less about those he did compose. And many works composed in haste give no reason to posit a lack either of serious intent or of artistic achievement; an obvious example is the *Missa Sancti Nicolai*.[25]

What galls the critics seems to be not so much any intrinsic popularity of Haydn's 1770s style as his apparent desire to please – to present his music as entertainment for a non-connoisseur audience. Landon crudely interprets this intention as 'pandering' to the 'lowest common denominator'. But one must ask: *what* audience(s) precisely does Landon have in mind? As far as we know, Haydn composed no symphonies for direct sale and publication before Nos. 76–8 (although he certainly knew of their wide, unauthorized dissemination and had already sold No. 73). Until then, the presumption must be that his symphonies were still destined in the first instance for the Esterházy court (as Landon himself acknowledges for Nos. 53('A'), 62, 63, 70 and 75).[26] Even if the Prince's taste in symphonic music

22 Wheelock, *Haydn's Ingenious Jesting with Art*, pp. 33–51.

23 This was deliberate on Haydn's part; see Georg August Griesinger, *Biographische Notizen über Joseph Haydn* (Leipzig: Breitkopf & Härtel, 1810), p. 118 (trans. Gotwals, *Joseph Haydn: Eighteenth-Century Gentleman and Genius* [Madison: University of Madison Press, 1963], pp. 62–3). Compare Albert Christoph Dies, *Biographische Nachrichten von Joseph Haydn* (1810), ed. Horst Seeger, 2nd edn (Berlin: Henschelverlag, 1962), pp. 100–6, 108–9 (Gotwals, *Joseph Haydn*, pp. 135–8, 139–40); Seeger, 'Zur musikhistorischen Bedeutung der Haydn-Biographie von Albert Christoph Dies (1810)', *Beiträge zur Musikwissenschaft* 1/3 (1959), 30.   24 Gerlach, 'Die chronologische Ordnung', 59.

25 Landon, *Chronicle and Works II*, pp. 181, 251–2.

26 Gerlach assumes that they all were, since she employs detailed information about the instrumentalists available there as a primary basis for her datings ('Die Chronologische Ordnung', 49–58).

had become as resolutely comedic as it was in the realm of opera, this hardly constitutes 'pandering'. Nor were the tastes of Haydn's other audiences during these years of which we have knowledge 'common', still less 'low'; they included the nobility in the 'best houses' to whom he sang his lieder,[27] and the connoisseurs whom he solicited as purchasers of Op. 33.

The most devastating fallacy in this argument, however, is that it ignores the fact that Haydn, like almost all eighteenth-century composers, always strove to please his audiences, of all stripes.[28] With evident ambivalence, Landon calls the Haydn of the later 1770s (and even 1784) the 'Great Entertainer'.[29] The ambivalence is misplaced. The eighteenth-century concert venue (like the theatre, only less so) was a place of pleasure and display, devoted to social interaction and public self-representation. Most audiences for orchestral music were doubtless inattentive at times, by modern concert standards; the music's functions comprised not only stylistic innovation and expressive depth but also, precisely, entertainment (see note 35).

The leads to the issue of 'popular' style. Although popular music is increasingly seen as a legitimate subject of critical and scholarly study, the concept of popularity remains contested within traditional high-art contexts. The point, however, is that the concept of popular style is inherently unstable. Numerous different aspects of a composition can be called 'popular': the intention to appeal to a mass or lay audience; use as 'functional' music; the fact of being much loved; actual features of style. Not only can these attributes function more or less independently, but a work's later reception and significance often differ from the original ones.[30] (Beethoven's Fifth is 'popular' in many respects; the Beatles are widely

---

[27] Letter of 20 July 1781; *Joseph Haydn: Gesammelte Briefe and Aufzeichnungen. Unter Benützung der Quellensammlung von H. C. Robbins Landon*, ed. Dénes Bartha (Kassel: Bärenreiter, 1965), p. 101 (Landon, *Chronicle and Works II*, p. 449).

[28] David P. Schroeder, *Haydn and the Enlightenment: The Late Symphonies and their Audience* (Oxford: Clarendon Press, 1990); Mark Evan Bonds, *Wordless Rhetoric: Musical Form and the Rhetoric of the Oration* (Cambridge, Mass.: Harvard University Press, 1991), pp. 54–61; Wheelock, *Haydn's Ingenious Jesting with Art*, pp. 37–40, 90–117, 195–206; Webster, *Haydn's 'Farewell' Symphony*, pp. 189–91.   [29] *Chronicle and Works II*, p. 567.

[30] Gregory D. Booth and Terry Lee Kuhn, 'Economic and Transmission Factors as Essential Elements in the Definition of Folk, Art, and Pop Music', *Musical Quarterly* 74 (1990), 414; David Brackett, *Interpreting Popular Music* (Cambridge: Cambridge University Press, 1995), introduction.

treated as 'art'.) Moreover, many eighteenth-century works successfully addressed themselves to mixed or multiple audiences ('für Kenner und Liebhaber'); dances and marches – functional music – were a fundamental basis of meaning in eighteenth-century opera and, as 'topics', vitally important in instrumental music as well.[31] In eighteenth-century instrumental music, too, the issue of what constitutes 'popular' style is ultimately indefinable. Hence even if we did know that Haydn composed a given work for 'Liebhaber' (which is rarely the case), we could not legitimately use this knowledge as the basis for a negative value-judgement.

Haydn's success in selling his music, and especially his recourse to techniques that today would be called 'marketing', are another sticking-point. He offered symphonies Nos. 76–78 to the Parisian publisher Boyer in seductive terms: 'Last year I composed three beautiful, impressive, and above all not very long symphonies ... and in particular everything very easy'.[32] And with respect to Artaria's forthcoming piano arrangement of Symphony No. 69, 'Laudon', he rather cynically advised omitting the finale: 'The last or fourth movement ... is not practicable for the keyboard, nor do I find it necessary to include it; the word "Laudon" will aid the sale more than any ten finales'.[33] As far as I can see, however, one can criticize such practices only on specious grounds: the puritanical belief that artists become corrupted if they worry overmuch about making a living, or ignorance of the struggles necessary for eighteenth-century artists to ensure their interests in a society lacking any effective concept of copyright protection. In addition, from the mid-1780s on, when Haydn (according to the traditional view) attained 'Classical' heights, he remained no less vigilant regarding his financial interests.

Finally, in Haydn's case all these binary oppositions between authenticity and its opposites are embedded in the master narrative (adumbrated in my initial paragraph) that he achieved 'maturity' or 'Classical style' only after a long period of struggle and 'experimentation'.

---

[31] Leonard G. Ratner, *Classic Music: Expression, Form, and Style* (New York: Norton, 1980), parts I-II; Wye J. Allanbrook, *Rhythmic Gesture in Mozart: 'Le nozze di Figaro' and 'Don Giovanni'* (Chicago: University of Chicago Press, 1983), introduction and part I.

[32] *Briefe*, p. 130 (Landon, *Chronicle and Works II*, p. 477).

[33] 8 April 1783; *Briefe*, p. 127 (Landon, *Chronicle and Works II*, p. 474).

Larsen claims that in the later 1770s 'Haydn went through a period of experimentation … trying to find new ways in *response* to a *variety* of *external* stimuli'.[34] I have refuted this position elsewhere; suffice it to say that experimentation was always fundamental to Haydn, in all contexts, and cannot be used to distinguish between 'antecedent' or 'transitional' periods and those that represent 'goals' or 'maturity'. The stylistic variety of his music is far more constructively understood as displaying different facets of his musical persona, and as embodying his responses to differing conditions and audiences.

3

To justify Haydn's symphonies of the later 1770s (an enterprise that would be supererogatory, absent this tradition of criticism), two complementary tasks must be undertaken: first, to develop an aesthetic in which their 'popular' features, far from being explained away, are understood in social-cultural-historical terms, focusing on Haydn's milieu and the beliefs and practices of his audiences;[35] secondly, to show that they can be appreciated 'in their own right' in ways that satisfy us today. In both cases I can offer only brief and tentative sketches here, which I hope will at least stimulate further thinking on this topic.

The governing concepts for a positive reading of those features that have excited criticism would appear to be those of *comedy* (with respect to genre) and *entertainment* (with respect to reception).[36] In invoking comedy, I refer not so much to Haydn's famous wit and 'besondere Laune' as to something more pervasive and more deeply explanatory. Like 'popular' in comparison to 'serious' music, comedy in comparison to tragedy has

---

[34] Larsen, *The New Grove*, p. 354 (reprint, p. 102); the added emphases reflect the covert value entailed.

[35] See William Weber, 'Did People Listen in the Eighteenth Century?', *Early Music* 25 (1997), 678–91.

[36] I depend in this section primarily on recent writings on *opera buffa*, especially Mary Hunter's forthcoming *The Poetics of Entertainment*. I thank Prof. Hunter not only for sharing this work long before publication and for permission to paraphrase it here, but for many years of productive collaboration (including her careful reading of a preliminary version of this study) from which I have learned immensely. She is of course not responsible for any errors or oversights in what follows.

more often than not been treated as a 'low' art-form by theorists and scholars: as 'conventional', as 'mere' entertainment. In this century, however, comedy has received three new theoretical justifications: as carnival; as irony; and as a genre orientated towards entertainment, which celebrates its own conventions. (An essential point is that these aspects are not mutually dependent and may not all be present in any given comedic work.)

The earliest of these is the well-known interpretation of Mikhail Bakhtin that comedy incorporates the principle of carnival: the paradoxical reinforcement of social norms by a diverting and cathartic representation of their reversal or destruction. More recently, primarily in England and America, comedy has been interpreted (by analogy to irony) as a peculiarly self-reflexive art. A comedy can assert from within, as a tragedy generally cannot, the pleasurable nature of the occasion on which it is performed: whether as an escape or diversion from the struggles of daily existence, or an implicit celebration of the pleasures of a life of ease. The most relevant example is the *lieto fine*, the final tutti with which virtually every *opera buffa* ends, and which appeals to the audience, often overtly, to join in the celebration.[37] In the field of instrumental music, Wye Jamison Allanbrook has recently made the same point about Mozart's piano concertos, especially the rollicking codas in their finales, such as K. 459 in F and K. 453 in G.[38]

Regarding the final justification, that of entertainment, one thinks first of mass-media genres such as TV sitcoms or Hollywood musicals, in which precisely the pervasiveness of convention is the basis for artistic effects. Indeed, no form of entertainment can succeed without a strong conventional component. Audiences cannot follow such works (or know when they want to pay attention) without a well-understood set of clues and cues. Beyond that, in any artistic context, including the 'highest', it is precisely convention that enables the sort of multi-layered play with expectations and generic meanings that is a hallmark of Haydn's style, most

---

[37] Wye J. Allanbrook, 'Mozart's Happy Endings: A New Look at the "Convention" of the "lieto fine"', *Mozart-Jahrbuch* (1984–5), 1–5; Zvi Jagendorf, *The Happy End of Comedy* (Newark: University of Delaware Press, 1984), p. 34.

[38] 'Comic Issues in Mozart's Piano Concertos', in Neal Zaslaw, ed., *Mozart's Concertos: Text, Context, Interpretation* (Ann Arbor: University of Michigan Press, 1996), pp. 75–106.

famously in Op. 33.[39] There is no reason why an approach to composition as entertainment should be considered either morally suspect or inherently incompatible with the production of great art.

*

The notion of 'entertainment' is of great value in the appreciation of Haydn's music. The codas of many symphonic finales are no less 'comedic' than those in Mozart's concertos, except that the humour is often broader. (It is perhaps not supererogatory to mention that this comment and those that follow are not intended as negative criticism, in any sense.) Even in the London symphonies: in No. 93 in D major, the coda – ostentatiously announced as such by the G. P. 'hammerstroke' for full orchestra and timpani roll (bars 266ff.) – leads to a final wind-up in which the orchestra almost laughs with us. In the 'Military' Symphony finale the *batterie de bataille* from the slow movement unexpectedly returns, leading to a 'grand but very noisy' conclusion (in the words of a contemporary listener); contemporary notices vividly recount how this work 'excited agitation throughout the room' and describe its effect as 'truly electrical'.[40] One may doubt that 'high art' was much on the audience's mind. It was no different in principle in the 1770s. In No. 66 in B flat major the final variant of the theme (bars 208ff.) is less than subtle (to put it mildly), with its *fortissimo* stamping-about, crude hocketing and concluding horse-laugh. In No. 68, again in B flat major, everything is repeated to excess: the high dominant (bars 228–37); the 'echo solo' entries on the one-bar head-motif (wittily resolving that dominant) for all the instruments in turn, leading to a tremolo wind-up and 'too many' shouting chords at the close.

Symphonies like No. 63 in C ('Roxelane') and No. 69 in C ('Laudon') confirm Haydn's orientation towards 'easy', interesting, varied pleasure. They are in the major mode throughout, instantly apprehensible, lightly textured; they move within familiar styles and conventions and include few moments of expressive intensity. In the beginning of the 'Roxelane', for example, the contrast of dynamics, instrumentation and texture between

---

[39] The most interesting recent discussion is in Wheelock, *Haydn's Ingenious Jesting with Art*, chapter 5; compare Webster, *Haydn's 'Farewell' Symphony*, on Op. 54 ·No. 2.

[40] Landon, *Chronicle and Works III: Haydn in England, 1791–1795* (London: Thames and Hudson, 1976), pp. 307, 248.

the opening theme and its counterstatement (bars 1–8 and 9–16) is crystal-clear, such that the more rapid and complex contrasts in bars 17ff. are intelligible as well. The second group, which enters without transition, falls into a series of block-like, again contrasting phrases (bars 44–9, 50–6, 57–64, 65–8 and 69–77); the development restricts itself to closely related keys and avoids remote or 'difficult' modulations. The Allegretto, a double-variation movement on a familiar and well-loved tune, is 'easy' in this sense almost by definition.[41] As for the finale (of Landon's 'second' version – see Table 7.1), its disruptions and stylistic mixture – see the flat-submediant outbursts late in the second group (bars 56ff., 181ff.), the four-part counterpoint in the development (98ff.) and the indirect return to the tonic via III♯ and iii (133–8) – would almost have violated Haydn's 'stylistic contract' with his putative audience (if I am right about the intended function of the 'Roxelane' as entertainment), were they not merely inserted into the prevailing 'easy' context as manifestations of comic plurality, rather than integrated into a 'high-art' symphony, as they would have been a decade later.[42]

Symphony No. 61 in D major is one of Larsen's examples of Haydn's 'pleasant, unpretentious' symphonies of these years. That it is pleasant, nobody will deny. Its opening theme, like several others among those *not* actually recycled from overtures (notably that in No. 66), evinces a combination of surface activity and slow-moving harmony that may seem reminiscent of overture style; as the movement proceeds we find that a slowly moving, block-like phrase organization is characteristic. But these, along with the genuinely entertaining rondo finale on a ⁶₈ 'hornpipe' topic, are virtually its only features that can be called unpretentious, and even so only in the sense of 'unassuming', not that of being conventional or lacking artistic merit. In the first movement many of the block-like passages are memorable: the wind-band progression in quavers (bars 41–4) and its suddenly melodic repetitions, which lead to the even more striking closing theme (bar 71), whose quavers in bar 76 become four octaves deep in oboes

---

[41] See Sisman, *Haydn and the Classical Variation*, pp. 160–1.
[42] I make here an obvious analogy to the well-known 'generic contract'; see Jeffrey Kallberg, 'The Rhetoric of Genre: Chopin's Nocturne in G Minor', *19th-Century Music* 11 (1988), 238–61.

and horns and thus 'surround' the strange, chromatically rising semibreve melody. (The two immediately preceding symphonies in D major, No. 42 [1771] and No. 57 [1774], also have unusually long, repetitive second groups.) In the Adagio we hear the earliest example of an important thematic type in late Haydn slow movements, the 'beautiful', hymn-like melody in $\frac{3}{4}$.[43] The epithet 'unpretentious' applied to this gorgeous movement, with its expressive extension in the transition (bars 26–34) and positively Schubertian second theme (bars 36ff., especially 40–4 and the like), is simply inappropriate.

4

Some readers will have noticed that my comments on Symphony No. 61 (just above) were no longer restricted to an aesthetic of 'mere' entertainment. In fact, very few Haydn symphonies (or even single movements) of the later 1770s can be adequately understood within this framework alone. The vast majority are characterized by the highest art; as Charles Rosen insisted, their apparent unpretentiousness is rather 'selfconsciously unlearned' – a matter of the persona Haydn chooses to adopt, no less than in the 'Surprise' Symphony.[44] The point is related to Ernst Ludwig Gerber's famous comment that 'Haydn possesses the great art of appearing familiar [*die große Kunst, öfters bekannt zu scheinen*] in his ideas':[45] his emphasis on 'art' and on 'appearing' familiar is a striking adumbration of persona-theory. Similarly, it is not merely that Haydn 'was forced to *become* original', as he even more famously said,[46] but that he could not help composing in an original manner, whatever the context.

Before turning to individual examples, it may be useful to survey a single movement-type, to see to what extent it bears out the image of Haydn's 'superficiality' in this period. Of the thirteen slow movements in

[43] Webster, 'When Did Haydn Begin to Compose "Beautiful" Melodies?', in Jens Peter Larsen, Howard Serwer and James Webster, eds., *Haydn Studies: Proceedings of the International Haydn Conference, Washington, D. C., 1975* (New York: Norton, 1981), pp. 385–8.

[44] Charles Rosen, *The Classical Style: Haydn, Mozart, Beethoven* (New York: Viking, 1971), pp. 162–3.

[45] *Neues Lexikon der Tonkünstler* (Leipzig: J. G. I. Breitkopf, 1790), I, col. 610.

[46] Griesinger, *Biographische Notizen*, p. 25 (Gotwals, *Joseph Haydn*, p. 17); emphasis mine.

the core group, only those in Nos. 53, 63 and 73 are based on unambiguously 'popular' melodies: Andante rather than Adagio, regular short
phrases, simple textures. Of the others, Nos. 66–8 are Adagios with muted
violins, featuring filigree work that even today appeals more to connoisseurs than to amateurs; Nos. 61 and 75 feature the new $\frac{3}{4}$ hymn melodies;
the themes of the variation movements in Nos. 71 and 74 exhibit Haydn's
characteristic 'sprightly profundity'. No. 62 (discussed below) is a delicate,
somewhat enigmatic, pseudo-contrapuntal affair; No. 69, although not
difficult, is decidedly eccentric; and No. 70, a double-variation movement,
is based on a severe D minor theme in invertible counterpoint. Taken as a
group, these movements give the impression not of a composer who has
'sold out' or is 'experimenting', in the sense of seeking (while not yet having
found) his way, but of immense stylistic and typological variety.

*

A simple and hence illuminating example of Haydn's use of art to conceal
art is the theme of the double-variation Andante of Symphony No. 53 (see
Ex. 7.1). The theme is a straightforward double period, 8 + 8; each strain is
divided into 4 + 4 by the half-cadences in bars 4 and 12, and further into 2 +
2 + 2 + 2 by the constant two-bar subphrases, which are thus heard eight
times in succession (sixteen, counting the repeats). Yet each of these eight
phrases is different from all the others. In the diatonic and homophonic
first strain the dotted motif introducing bars 1–2 skips up to C♯, from which
we descend by step; in bars 3–4 it skips higher, to E, from which we first step
up to F♯ and then *skip* down to B; in bars 5–6 it skips to D and then descends
as in bars 1–2, except that the harmonies now lie athwart the motif, turning
the local goal into II⁶; finally in bars 7–8 it moves *down* to A, and the quavers
move *up* to the medial cadence on $\overset{\wedge}{3}$.

The second strain, while continuing the ongoing variation of these
motifs, introduces two new elements: chromaticism and syncopation. In its
first subphrase (bars 9–10) the lower strings remain silent on the downbeat,
in order to enter on the second beat on an unexpected G♯⁶ chord, which the
ensuing bass A♯ clarifies as related to the supertonic B minor. At the same
time, they have suddenly become legato; indeed, the second violins suspend
G♮ over the bar-line, creating a 5–4–5 suspension-resolution figure with the
firsts, which barely disguises the latent parallel fifths D/G♮–C♯/F♯. (If one
imagines the lower strings entering on the downbeat, as Haydn must ini-

Example 7.1 Symphony No. 53 in D major, second movement, bars 1–16

tially have done, the seconds would probably have played A, creating overt fifths E/A–D/G♮.) The unexpected chromaticism, change of texture and latent fifths create a slightly *unheimlich* air. Then bars 13–14 actually bring a climax of sorts: the crotchet–quaver motif of the subphrase endings is transformed (bar 14) into an augmentation of the dotted upbeat motif and rises by skip all the way to c♯³, the highest note of the theme.[47] Meanwhile, all three lower parts adopt the syncopation from bars 9–10, producing a highly dissonant triple suspension-resolution into the I⁶ chord. Finally, the legato ductus and harmonic rhythm bind the second strain into two *four*-bar phrases: V⁶/II resolves to II across the motivic divide in bars 10–11, as does VII⁶₄ to I⁶ across bars 13–14. In short, the theme *develops*, from some-

---

[47] A subtle point (see Ex. 7.1) is that this motif is also a variant of what would have been the normal leap *down*, from a crotchet e² to c♯², and this 'missing' interval is supplied in the short-note upbeat to the final motif.

thing whose art is indeed largely concealed to something overtly sophisticated.

*

Haydn's 'mixed' style in this period is splendidly exemplified by the
sonata-form Adagio cantabile of Symphony No. 68 in B flat major. The
muted violins alone perform almost the entirety of the main theme and
transition (bars 1–16 and 17–24). The melody (see Ex. 7.2), after rising
through the triad in plain long notes (bars 1–2), spins out a series of delicate
filigree-motifs; each of its three phrases (bars 3–6, 7^2–11^1, 12–16) ends on
the tonic without strong cadential motion, yet each is constructed
differently and is slightly different in length. The overall effect is one of
non-goal-directed rumination. Bars 3–6 comprise four (2 + 2) detached,
one-bar diatonic motifs, but bars 7^2–11^1 are continuous, legato, chromatic
and in part syncopated (though still constructed as 2 + 2), while the third
phrase reverts (bars 13–14) to the rising long notes from bars 1–2 – now a
thematic constituent rather than an introductory figure – preceded by a
downward arpeggiation, and followed by more filigree-work.

Meanwhile, the accompaniment proceeds in an unbroken, almost
mechanical semiquaver ostinato, seemingly dissociated from the freely
developing melody above – except for the *forte* interjections by the full
band, on the same semiquaver motif.[48] They are certainly amusing. The
first interjection (bar 6) is totally unexpected, although we immediately
grasp it as filling the otherwise 'empty' afterbeat (which in turn makes the
violins' ticking-on in the first half of bar 7, as if nothing had happened, even
more hilarious). Hence we almost expect its return at the end of the second
phrase (although we may notice that the dysfunctional bar 7^1 has delayed it
to a position five bars after the first one). But the third interjection (bar 14)
rudely interrupts the bland rising long notes of the third phrase; this dis-
orientates us sufficiently that we do not expect the following one, even
though it enters when it 'should' at the end of the phrase. (On the other

[48] Even the 'ticking' accompaniment in the 'Clock' Symphony, No. 101, is more
varied and more flexibly related to the melody; see Rosen, *Sonata Forms* (New
York: Norton, 1980), p. 178. Rosen discusses this exposition insightfully as an
example of reciprocal relations between melody and accompaniment (that is, as
an example of *thematische Arbeit*, not named as such in this context), without
unpacking as many levels of meaning as I attempt here.

Example 7.2 Symphony No. 68 in B flat major, third movement, bars 1–22 and 34–8

Example 7.2 (*cont.*)

hand it comes one half-bar 'too soon', overriding the cadence rather than waiting for it to round off.)

As the movement proceeds, the heretofore rigid distinction between self-absorbed melody and mechanical accompaniment becomes more complex. In the first transitional phrase (bars 17–20) the melody begins and ends with the ticking motif itself, in parallel tenths with the seconds, such that the interjection (bar 20^2) is more a 'completion' than an interruption. And in the second group the full band finally gets to play 'real' music. Although at first the ticking motif is largely absent, it returns with a vengeance at bars 34–47, now in the lower instruments underneath a new, long-note theme derived from bar 1, before comically dying away in all the instruments (bar 38). In the final cadences it returns to the inner strings where it 'belongs'. And there it stays, through the widely modulating development, until a dominant pedal in the horns (bars 63–6) signals the retransition. But this is a deception; the oboes resume the long-note motif in imitation, the demisemiquavers return, also in imitation, and we are off on a long, harmonically complex sequence all the way to bar 77, where the dominant is finally articulated as a proper retransition. Bars 63–6 thus function as an unusual 'false retransition'.

This movement is not easy to interpret. What is the import of the *forte* interjections – playful wit? A guffaw? A *buffa* character stamping his feet in frustration? (Could this movement also have been recycled from stage music? The suggestion perhaps explains less than it explains away.) Does the eventual absorption of the mechanical accompaniment motif into the musical discourse create a synthesis of disparate elements, or merely a complex juxtaposition of incommensurables; or is it perhaps to be understood as *Verfremdung* of the comic in the Brechtian sense, in which popular or 'routine' material is isolated, even disembodied, as if it were inherently significant? As a whole, the movement is not primarily comic-stagey: the initial notes and delicate filigree of the main theme convey refined sentiment, the long-note theme at bar 34 is 'comic' only at the end and the complexly modulating development and rich sequential retransition are as expressive as one could wish. Do these changes relativize, or even overcome, the grotesqueries of the exposition, or do the latter win out after all when they return in the recapitulation?

*

As even Haydn's critics acknowledge, the 1770s symphonies brought many innovations in form, style and instrumentation.[49] I have space here to mention only one feature: the use of thematic and gestural links between the slow introduction and the following Allegro.[50] Whereas previously slow introductions were rare and bore no obvious relation to the fast movement, they now begin to become more common, and to exhibit such relations in increasingly prominent and important ways. In Symphony No. 57 these relations are largely subliminal, whereas in No. 71 they are obvious (see Ex. 7.3).[51] The brief introduction strikingly contrasts the topics of stern majesty and tenderness or pleading, which, however, project the identical structural motif, $\hat{1}$–$\hat{2}$–$\hat{3}$. These paired motifs are then repeated a step higher in the supertonic, $\hat{2}$–$\hat{3}$–$\hat{4}$. A third *forte* on IV soon leads to the pause on the dominant; the Allegro con brio begins *piano* in $\frac{3}{4}$ with a cantabile theme. After it cadences on $\hat{3}$ (bar 13), the unison *forte* texture from the introduction breaks in, rising $\hat{1}$–$\hat{2}$–$\hat{3}$ as before; also as in the introduction, it is immediately sequenced a step higher. (The turn can be heard as derived from the *piano* motif in bar 2.) The next phrase continues to follow the introduction by beginning on IV, except *piano*, so as to capture the 'other' mood as well; the cadence on to $\hat{3}$ subliminally recomposes that in bars 10–13 (see the broken lines in Ex. 7.3). A varied repetition of bars 14–21 (not shown) brings the entire paragraph to closure on $\hat{1}$, following which the vigorous transition paragraph further develops the turn motif. Thus the Allegro cogently recomposes every element from the introduction.

∗

As a final example of the complexity of tone in Haydn's symphonies from the later 1770s, I choose the slow movement from No. 62. The movement is

49 On these innovations see Gerlach, 'Eine chronologische Ordnung', 49–64; Landon, *Chronicle and Works II*, pp. 312–15, 560–7; Sisman, *Haydn and the Classical Variation*, pp. 150–1, 180–3; Wheelock, *Haydn's Ingenious Jesting with Art*, pp. 68–9, 77–82, 117–24, 132–9, 177–9.

50 On this subject generally in Haydn, see Webster, *Haydn's 'Farewell' Symphony*, pp. 162–5, 167–73, 321–6, 330–1.

51 On No. 57, see the stimulating (if over-enthusiastic) account in Daniel Heartz, *Haydn, Mozart, and the Viennese School 1740–1780* (New York: Norton, 1995), pp. 368–71. (I do not mean to imply that 'subliminal' relations are either more or less meaningful than 'obvious' ones.)

Example 7.3 Symphony No. 71 in B flat major, first movement, bars 1–21

unconventional even by his standards. Not only is it in the unusually fast tempo of Allegretto, but it is set in the overall tonic, D major. That is, all four movements are in this key, something found in no other Haydn symphony (other than those beginning with a slow movement). Predictably, scholars have seen this as a problem, which they 'explain' by appealing to the work's status as a pastiche, or by invoking the 'Baroque suite',[52] or by imagining that Haydn originally considered this Allegretto as a 'first' movement.[53] Nobody has considered that, as in all cases where Haydn does something unexpected, this may have been a deliberate choice, made for artistic reasons. Rosen perspicaciously notes that the off-tonic beginning of the finale makes good sense, given that all three previous movements have been in the tonic, but one can also argue this point in reverse: since the finale is the weightiest and tonally most adventuresome movement in the sym-phony, the Allegretto participates in a process of understated tonal action, to set it up.

The mood of the delicate opening, *piano*, for high strings, violins muted, basses silent, does not seem to conform to the material, which Rosen characterizes as the 'least possible – two notes and a banal accompaniment' (see Ex. 7.4). At the same time (what Rosen does not mention) these scraps are presented in a kind of rudimentary counterpoint, with bar 2 (cellos) imitated by the violins in bar 3, melodically inverted in bar 4 and contra-puntally inverted with the quaver motif in bar 6. It is almost dream-like, ethereal.[54] As the exposition continues, the winds enter one by one: flute in bar 13, at the turn to the dominant; oboes and bassoon[55] in bar 22, to enrich the repetition of the chromatic cadential phrase; horns in bar 28, at the entry of a loud, tremolo theme; after this climax, the exposition dies away as quietly as it began. The development, organized around D minor, is notated with a change of key-signature, as if it were the 'B' of an ABA; it moves from the pseudo-counterpoint of the beginning to the loud theme in F, before

---

52 Rosen, *The Classical Style*, p. 153.

53 Landon, in his miniature-score edition of the symphonies (Philharmonia), VI, pp. xv–xvi.

54 Rosen, in *The Classical Style*, suggests vaguely that it seems derived from stage music; this is worth about as much as my comment in parentheses above regarding the slow movement of No. 68.

55 One bassoon, not two as in Landon's miniature score edition; see Gerlach, 'Eine chronologische Ordnung', 57–8.

quickly reverting to the home dominant and the reprise. The latter is deco-rated by an attractive high descant in the first violins, after which the recapitulation proceeds normally (by Haydn's standards), with a big expansion of the cross-rhythmed staccato hemiola in bars 82–91 (from 25–7), and a brief six-bar coda.

5

The Allegretto of Symphony No. 62 is beautiful, not superficial, well wrought, with sufficient variety – a delicate dream or reverie. It is neither more nor less revelatory of Joseph Haydn's personality than the stately opening movement of No. 61, or the finale of the 'Surprise' Symphony, or for that matter the stormy opening movement of the 'Farewell' Symphony (which in fact culminates in one of his very few movements that is even more ethereal). That the 'Farewell' is based on a programme is no objec-tion; programmatic symphonies make no less a claim on our attention 'as music' than any others.[56] The same is true of Haydn's 'entertainment' sym-phonies.

Even those who interpret Haydn's high comic style in a more general way than mere 'besondere Laune' have tended (since his own day) to make an analogy with the ironic novels of Laurence Sterne and the fantastic ones of Jean Paul. This is certainly not inappropriate; but a better analogy seems to me to be the staged comedies of the eighteenth century, particularly those of Goldoni and Beaumarchais – or, since, after all, we are in the world of music, the *opere buffe* of the time, including, or perhaps especially, Haydn's own. This notion might encourage us to appreciate the dramatic quality of these symphonies; their continual parade of witty, ironic, sur-prising musical 'agents'.[57] In the 1770s Haydn the symphonist was Europe's greatest master of comedy, in any art-form. He *was* a great enter-tainer. But he was also, always, a great artist. My two justifications for this

---

[56] Webster, *Haydn's 'Farewell' Symphony*, chapters 4 and 7; Richard James Will, 'Programmatic Symphonies of the Classical Period', Ph.D. diss., Cornell University (1994).

[57] On musical agency see Cone, *The Composer's Voice*, pp. 112, 122–3, 134–5; Fred Everett Maus, 'Music as Drama', *Music Theory Spectrum* 10 (1988), 56–73; and the articles by Marion A. Guck, Maus and myself in the symposium on Cone's volume printed in *College Music Symposium* 29 (1989).

Example 7.4 Symphony No. 62 in D major, second movement, bars 1–42

music – one praising entertainment as if independent of artistic value, the other interpreting it as high art after all – cannot be brought into a stable relationship, either logical or experiential; our responses to these works will doubtless continue to move fluidly within the field defined (somewhat arbitrarily) by these two poles. Indeed, allowing for different combinations of weight and emphasis, all of Haydn's instrumental music can

Example 7.4 (*cont.*)

profitably be understood as reflecting the same balance, or tension, between art and entertainment. If it should be objected that I am thereby trying to have my cake and eat it too, my response would be: that was precisely Haydn's achievement.

8   The Haydn piano trio: textual facts and textural principles[1]

W. DEAN SUTCLIFFE

In a survey of the piano trios in her *Master Musicians* volume, Rosemary Hughes grants exceptional status to the opening movement of Trio No. 22 in A major (see Ex. 8.24 later in the chapter), as representing 'for once a real interplay between keyboard and strings'.[2] While this vote of approval implies a rather limited conception of the possibilities of the form, one based on the opposition of its two constituent instrumental forces, the vote is at least registered, whereas both H. C. Robbins Landon and Charles Rosen, for example, surprisingly make no comment on this Adagio. Certainly in no other Haydn trio movement is the duel between keyboard and strings so explicitly waged, in the form of a large-scale melodic dialogue that Haydn normally shunned in favour of a more closely contained exchange of ideas. The opposing melodic contributions remain mostly separate and successive until the coda (bars 55ff.). Here the violin and piano (and ultimately the cello, at bar 57) engage in a stretto whose purpose is to reconcile the previously sectional melodic interests at the point of climax. Somewhat ironically, given the prevalent textural image of the Haydn trios, this governing principle of alternation was to become the most common means of progress in later piano trios (to take just one example from many, see the opening of Ravel's Piano Trio in A minor), whereas Haydn, having hit upon a new timbral effect, as with the all-pizzicato ending to the String Quartet Op. 33 No. 4, or the *col legno* conclusion to the Adagio of his Symphony No. 67, characteristically leaves the discovery behind to move on to fresher fields. When Haydn does return to this principle in later trios, it is within a seemingly more limited context, as in the

---

[1] This article is based on chapters 2 and 3 of my doctoral work: 'The Piano Trios of Haydn', Ph.D. diss., University of Cambridge (1988).

[2] *Haydn*, rev. edn (London: Dent, 1970), p. 147.

development section of the first movement of Trio No. 23 (bars 52–98). It is not altogether clear why the present Adagio's texture should be regarded as being inherently more just as chamber music than that heard at the opening of Trio No. 23, where the overlapping imitative entries of the head-motif also allow equality of interest between the parts. Unless this equality is specifically a long-range melodic one, however, it is as if it does not count for most ears; hence the somewhat exaggerated claim to uniqueness that Hughes makes for this Adagio.

Of course, a little further on in the history of the genre the two stringed instruments became more compelled to act as a team against the piano, due to the increased strength of the keyboard's sound. Simultaneously this became the most common solution to the problematic nature of the medium, which is one of inevitable textural compromise, given the forces it assembles. For this reason it is perhaps surprising that the piano quartet never established itself as a superior alternative: the addition of a viola ought to allow greater textural subtlety, the strings would have less need to band together *en masse* against the keyboard, and the piano would be relieved of some of the note-spinning duties required by the thinness of its support in the trio. While Haydn's solutions to the trio 'problem' are generally held to be inadequate because of the supposedly soloistic role of the piano part, it is an interesting reflection that, in the performance of duo sonatas, the string or wind player is invariably regarded as the 'soloist', a principle that is conventionally viewed as foreign to the spirit of chamber music.

Indeed, the assessment of chamber-music textures first and foremost in melodic terms is precisely what has given rise to the marginal life led by the Haydn piano trios both on the concert platform and in the literature. They would appear to have, to use the term of a recent writer on the subject, a 'crippled'[3] textural image, one that is incompatible with generally agreed principles of good chamber-music behaviour. In current parlance, their disposition of material is not texturally correct, although this seeming lack of democracy (subliminally reinforced perhaps by a traditional picture of Haydn as a faithful servant of the *ancien régime*) can be rescued by an appeal

---

[3] Basil Smallman, *The Piano Trio: Its History, Technique, and Repertoire* (Oxford: Clarendon Press, 1990), p. 18.

to a feminist historiography. Thus Peter Brown writes in a recent programme note on Trio No. 42:

> Haydn's chamber music is gender[-]specialized: the keyboard sonatas were
> dedicated to or intended for women players, while the string quartets were all
> dedicated to men. Though Haydn's piano trios, known during the time as
> sonatas for the fortepiano or harpsichord with an accompaniment of a violin
> and cello, are all dedicated to women, who played the principal keyboard
> part, the accompaniments were performed by men. Thus, the piano trio
> represented a musical meeting ground of the sexes. Intended mainly to be
> heard in the drawing room or chamber, their textures partially reflect the time
> available to women and men in eighteenth-century society; the women, who
> stayed in the home, had the time to improve their musical accomplishments
> while men were occupied with business. Thus, the keyboard takes the leading
> role while the violin often plays together with the right hand of the keyboard,
> and the cello almost always follows the bass line of the left hand.[4]

While such a reading of the sexual politics of Haydn trio textures
intriguingly suggests an eighteenth-century equivalent of the recent strain
of '100 Things to Do with a Useless Man' in popular literature, the interpretation of textural evidence on which it is based is hardly new.[5] Indeed,
the reception of the trios from this point of view rather encapsulates, if in

---

[4] 'Haydn, Piano Trio, Hoboken XV:30', programme notes for *The Collection in
Concert*, a series of concerts presented by the Pierpont Morgan Library, New
York, based on manuscripts held in the Library's music collection, 15 April
1993.

[5] A few instances of 'received opinion': 'With one or two exceptions the piano
trios are in fact piano sonatas with accompaniment by the strings. They were so
published, and many can be played as piano solos' (Cornelius G. Burke, *The
Collector's Haydn* [Philadelphia: Lippincott, 1959], p. 95); 'the prevailing
conception, in the latter half of the eighteenth century, was that of a kind of
piano sonata with accompanying parts for violin and cello, essentially intimate
and domestic in character, as the piano was predominantly a woman's
instrument. This is the conception represented by Haydn, in whose piano trios
violin and cello rarely gain more than a fleeting independence of the keyboard'
(Rosemary Hughes, 'Joseph Haydn (1732–1809)', in Alec Robertson, ed.,
Chamber Music [Harmondsworth, Middlesex: Penguin, 1957], p. 42);
'Nevertheless Haydn continued, in his marvellous late trios, to compose what
are essentially keyboard works with accompaniment' (Julian Rushton, *Classical
Music* [London: Thames and Hudson, 1986], p. 96); 'he was perfectly content to
carry on his "continuo" technique long after Mozart and Beethoven had shown
him a better way' (Marion Scott, 'Haydn's Chamber Music', *Musical Times*

extreme form, the composer's fate in so much of the critical literature. The significance in Haydn so often lies around the edges of his work, whether we think formally, aesthetically or even texturally; so often all that has been grasped is the potentially misleading 'big picture', with such notions as his monothematicism, his 'wit and humour' or his use of popular musical imagery. Haydn does not yet enjoy the luxury of having his individual works routinely regarded as constituting self-sufficient worlds, as being worthy of detailed exegesis in their own right. For this reason in particular Webster's recent voracious treatment of the 'Farewell' Symphony has had such a liberating effect.[6] Correspondingly, a certain carelessness of detail has enabled the same comfortable conclusions to be drawn time and again, nowhere more so than with the piano trios.

In an article of 1987, 'Haydn's Piano Trio Textures', I suggested that the common textural understanding of the composer's work in the genre needed a radical reassessment.[7] The usual line was, and has continued to be, that these were essentially piano sonatas with the string parts tacked on as creative afterthoughts to satisfy a hungry amateur market. In denying this, I was concerned to evoke the far more idiomatic chamber-music qualities evoked by the trios. The understanding of Haydn's trio textures outlined there can be reinforced and fleshed out by reference to a number of very specific textual clues in the body of the works. These again raise the question: 'who is doubling whom?'[8] Some of these are only too obvious in their implications for the projected balance of sound – none more so than the

---

73/1069 [1932], 215). More favourably disposed towards the trio textures are, for instance, Karl Geiringer, who says with reference to the finale of Trio No. 42: 'A new type of piano trio in which all three members share responsibility is breaking through, a type that was to gain increasing importance in the future' (*Haydn: A Creative Life in Music*, 2nd edn, revised and enlarged in collaboration with Irene Geiringer [London: G. Allen and Unwin, 1964], p. 343); and Giorgio Pestelli: 'The fifteen or so trios for piano, violin and cello written in 1794 and 1795 are also no longer piano sonatas "doubled" by the other instruments, but real chamber music in the sense already indicated by Mozart' (*The Age of Mozart and Beethoven*, trans. Eric Cross [Cambridge: Cambridge University Press, 1984], p. 124).

6   *Haydn's 'Farewell' Symphony and the Idea of Classical Style: Through-Composition and Cyclic Integration in his Instrumental Music* (Cambridge: Cambridge University Press, 1991).   7   *Music Analysis* 6/3 (1987), 319–32.

8   *Ibid.*, 321.

Example 8.1 Piano Trio No. 45 in E flat major, first movement, bars 1–15

'Solo' uniquely marked over the violin part at the opening of Trio No. 45, where the piano right hand plays exactly the same material (see Ex. 8.1). This annotation merely clarifies what should be apparent from a reading of the score of the first fifteen-bar section: after a typical outer-voice dialogue at bars 2–7, that should be understood as primarily the responsibility of the strings[9] (note the greater registral continuity of the cello part compared

---

[9] *Ibid.*, 321–3.

Example 8.2 Piano Trio No. 45 in E flat major, third movement, bars 264–86

with the piano left hand), the piano only assumes a dominant role from bar 8. The two lower voices that accompany the piano's ornamented descending line are just as clearly designated for the strings by the greater detail of their notation (as evidenced by the eb[1] in the cello at 9[2]). Bar 12 represents a textural transition point; by bar 13, assuming a crescendo up to this point, the violin has once more taken over the melodic leadership, to complete a textural ternary form. At the other end of this trio occurs an equally telling piece of evidence. At bars 273–85 of the finale the piano's Bb octave is tied over for the thirteen-bar duration of this transitional passage (see Ex. 8.2).

The concept of 'doubling' is at its least meaningful here: the cello, with its tied B♭ over the same section, is rather more capable of sustaining its sound until the fermata at bar 285, not least since the pedal notes of both parts are marked *piano*.[10] If this piece of writing indubitably issues from the capacities of the cello, what does this tell us about the textural conception of the surrounding movement? Is it really conceivable that the cello should simply melt back into an anonymous 'doubling of the piano left hand'?

In addition to the sort of textual clues found in Trio No. 45, the following list also accounts for some of the favoured ways in which the composer deploys his three instruments, to give some sense of his 'common practice' in the genre.

(1)   Greater precision in the notation of the string parts where they are purportedly 'doubling' the piano is a strong indicator of aural priorities. Aside from the allocation of sharper detail as in bars 8–11 of the first movement of Trio No. 45 (henceforward references will take the form of 45/i/8–11), where the strings reproduce in a definitive form that which appears in the keyboard part in a skeletal and supportive version, there are many instances simply of greater exactitude in duration and articulation. For instance, in bars 91–2 of the first movement of Trio No. 19 (Ex. 8.3) the rhythmic form of the string parts, with their final crotchet rests, provides a stronger sense of punctuation in the approach to the climactic diminished seventh of bar 93[1]. On the other hand, it is equally appropriate for the keyboard to retain its longer note-values in the bass, since they will of course lend greater resonance to the upper voice through overtone support. This differentiation of roles is also applicable to the scoring of bars 95–6.

Another aspect of the string parts at bars 91–2 which suggests that they took precedence in the conception of the passage is their thematic relevance. Their second-shape recurs at the next and final climactic point of the development, in bar 104 (Ex. 8.4). The cello part in the preceding bar is

---

10   Compare Misha Donat's comments on the movement: 'Its conclusion is marked by a sudden diminished chord played *fortissimo*, after which a long-held pedal note (for the greater part of its duration the cello will find itself on its own, as the piano sound will long since have disappeared) signals the start of the coda.' In 'Haydn: Late Chamber Works', programme notes for the 'Haydn Festival', Wigmore Hall, London, 3–10 September 1988, p. 23.

Example 8.3 Piano Trio No. 19 in F major, first movement, bars 89–96

Example 8.4 Piano Trio No. 19 in F major, first movement, bars 102–7

doubly significant: by again achieving a more precise rhythmic form than the equivalent piano left hand, it is in turn thematically relevant as an augmentation of the previous intensely treated cell. (The same process is evident in the piano's augmentation at bar 109.) In addition, the cello's two detached crotchets match and support those of the violin, a function enhanced by its registral separation from the piano. Thus, apart from its implications for Haydn's calculation of balance with the instruments of his

253

Example 8.5 Piano Trio No. 25 in E minor, first movement, bars 68–76

time, this notational refinement, far from being a minor disagreement of detail, is of timbral, thematic and articulative significance.

Other comparable examples of such refinements, among many, can be seen in the first two bars of 34/iii and in 23/i, bars 3 and 7 in both strings and bars 15, 18–23, 26, 30, 47 and 49–50 in the cello. On occasion the strings are also provided with independent dynamic markings which are absent from the piano part, as with the cello's *fz–p* succession at 37/i/30–1 and the *fz* apportioned to violin and cello at 32/i/167 and 36/i/206. The significance of the latter marking lies particularly in the cello part, as it re-enters the texture after the exotic prolongation of the ♭VI neighbour-note chord from bar 199. The cello now recalls its c♭ pitch from that bar and thus by a process of registral reactivation signifies the impending resolution back to a bass V.

(2)   A related, but much rarer phenomenon is the presence of ornaments in the string parts that find no parallel in the equivalent piano line. The most striking of these launches the development section of 25/i (Ex. 8.5). The cello's across-the-strings grace-noted figure (bar 71) represents an idiomatic reworking of the piano's close-position arpeggio of bar 1. It also

Example 8.6 Piano Trio No. 33 in G minor, first movement, bars 49–54

illustrates an application of the dialogue principle, replying as it does to the piano's figures of the second-time bars 69–70 and, with its exclusive *piano* dynamic, implies once more the assumption of melodic leadership for the intensively thematic bars that ensue. Another piece of seemingly spontaneous elaboration with structural-articulative importance is heard in the cello in the recapitulation of Trio 40/i, at bar 65. The unexpected turn on f♯[1], cutting through the rest of the texture with its high-register position on the instrument, constitutes an echo of the piano's written-out turn figure in the previous bar. Both lead to a C♯. Several bars earlier, just before the reprise, the violin displays another example of independent ornamentation with its melodramatic implied trill at bar 61[4]. Without it, however, the passage lacks shape and direction. A similar use of a trill is heard at 33/i/52, all the more effective for the violin's sudden emergence from an inner voice (see Ex. 8.6): Other examples of this important textual clue can be seen in the cello's additions at 19/i/34–5, 24/ii/85, 27/iii/173–9, 43/ii/11 and at 29/iii/80, as well as 44/i/14 and 45 in the violin.

(3)   There are many passages in which idiomatic string figures are duplicated by the piano. These have remained unnoticed because of the insensitivity to keyboard idiom discussed in my earlier article.[11] This is defensible to the extent that the versatility of the instrument often precludes a straightforward definition as to what is or is not suitable pianistic material. Nevertheless, in the case of the doubling shown in Example 8.7, the finale of Trio No. 32, there can be no doubt that the accompanying

---

[11]   See the discussion in 'Haydn's Piano Trio Textures', 320.

Example 8.7 Piano Trio No. 32 in A major, third movement, bars 36–40

figuration is much more characteristic of a stringed than a keyboard instrument, with its alternation between strings, the pitch on one remaining constant. (Compare, for example, the accompanying second-violin parts in Symphonies 93/i/76–82 and 95/i/33–4.) The 'wedged' staccato markings given exclusively to the violin only reinforce its prior claims on the more effective execution of the figure.

This combination of piano right-hand melody plus staccato violin 'bass' is also employed at 26/ii/3–6; in both cases the texture is enlivened far beyond what could be imagined simply by looking at the piano part (this particular texture never occurs in the piano sonatas). Indeed, this string figure is much favoured by Haydn for accompanimental purposes; for instances where the piano left hand in effect doubles the cello, see 21/i/113–16, 26/ii/24–9 and 28/i/46–52.

There are, however, other types of figure with which the stringed instrument seems more at home than the keyboard, for instance the rather feverish stretches of bass repeated notes that are heard at all important structural points in the exposition of 19/i (opening theme, bars 1–5 – note the cello's double-stopping; transition, bars 13–18; dominant version of theme, bars 26–8; codetta, bars 55–6). The very opening bars of this trio bear a strong resemblance to the start of Sonata No. 44 of 1774 (compare also the loud, emphatic dominant-minor beginnings to the respective development sections). On the other hand, the textural differences between these two F major movements are also telling – the repeated-note motif is far more consistently employed in the trio movement, due, of course, to the presence of the cello. Whereas the texture of Sonata 44/i is individualistic and unpredictable, in the trio movement texture is used to articulate large-scale structural areas. Another instance of a pair of same-key works pro-

Example 8.8 Sonata No. 62 in E flat major, first movement, bars 1–7

Example 8.9 Piano Trio No. 36 in E flat major, first movement, bars 1–10

ceeding from a similar gestural type offers a more pointed comparison. The first movements of Sonata No. 62 and Trio No. 36 (Ex. 8.8 and 8.9) not only feature the same initial opening-up of 'tonal space' from $e\flat^1$, but both follow this with a descending scalic passage in thirds from $c^3/a\flat^2$. However, whereas in the sonata the shape develops into a virtuoso passage for the right hand, the trio shape is answered immediately by the bass.

Example 8.10 Piano Trio No. 23 in E flat major, second movement, bars 96–100

Example 8.11
(a) Piano Trio No. 21 in B flat major, first movement, bars 164–7
(b) Sonata No. 59 in E flat major, first movement, bars 213–18

(a)

(b)

But perhaps the most convincing example of a string-inspired figure reinforced by the piano occurs at 23/ii/94–9 (Ex. 8.10) and 110–15. This is barely manageable for the piano left hand, unless one has the stretch of a Rakhmaninov. Of course, when it is transferred to the right hand at bars 100 and 116, there is no difficulty. On a different level, the concluding bars of 21/i (Ex. 8.11(a)) demonstrate a fundamental indebtedness to the capabilities of the strings. The *piano–forte* succession of bars 166–7 implies a crescendo over the penultimate bar up to the final chord that can, naturally, only be achieved by the strings. Even if one prefers the interpretative possibility of a sustained *piano* followed by a *subito forte*, the effect remains more dramatic when executed by violin and cello. Another instructive solo-sonata comparison may be drawn here. Note the very different realization of this same gesture at the end of another first movement, that of Sonata No. 59 (Ex. 8.11(b)). Here a whole scale is needed to create the same effect in intrinsic keyboard terms.

(4)   Textures that are based on the dialogue of outer voices were introduced in 'Haydn's Piano Trio Textures' (with reference to the opening theme of No. 39),[12] but there are many less obvious examples of this feature, which is central to the understanding of the works. The opening theme of the contemporaneous Trio No. 38 (Ex. 8.12) is also generated by various forms of parallelism between the outer parts, and once more the piano's supporting inner-voice line assumes thematic significance. Its d^1–$d\#^1$–e^1 cell at bars 4^2–6^1 returns with rhythm intact in the upper voice at 10^2–12^1, while the violin's line at the same earlier point is now transferred to the bass. This process of exchange continues beyond the confines of the first theme proper: the cello's ascending F♯–D cell of bars 13^4–15^1 is replicated by the violin at 20^4–22, accompanied by a transposition of the bass line from bars 8^4–9. Nothing resembling these procedures can be found in the solo works.

Trio No. 38 in fact maintains this procedure through its subsequent movements. The opening theme of the slow movement (see Ex. 8.13) is transferred to the bass in the consequent phrase beginning at bar 4^2. At the same point, a free reworking of the initial bass part is heard in the upper voice. The bass rhythm of bars 1–2 is now expressed in a heavily stressed chordal form; the piano's right-hand chords are given arpeggiation signs so as to correspond to the violin's naturally arpeggiated triple-stops and final quadruple-stop. The succeeding linear descent from a^2 to c^2 (with another significantly exclusive dynamic marking for the violin) is also directly derived from the antecedent's bass part, the foreground progression from a to c♯ at bars 2^2–3^2, moving from an inner voice to the true bass line. Finally,

---

12   *Ibid.*, 321–3.

Example 8.12 Piano Trio No. 38 in D major, first movement, bars 1–22

Example 8.13 Piano Trio No. 38 in D major, second movement, bars 1–9

the repeated-note rhythm of bar 4 is moved to the top of the texture at bar 8, while the corresponding earlier arpeggiation is reworked into a dominant-minor bass form. As usual, the piano mediates between these outer voices by filling in the harmonic sense in continuo fashion. The essentially two-part conception of this Andante is laid bare in the reprise at bars 19^2ff. The finale transmutes this principle to create a subtle and affecting two- and three-part invention texture.

The stratagem employed in the slow movement of Trio No. 38 is found in similar circumstances in the first movements of Nos. 26, 37 and 41, all involving andante tempos and dotted rhythms. Such a distribution of a variation-type theme occurs nowhere in the solo piano music until the F minor Variations, written in the same period as the three latter works. However, whether or not the issue of mutual influence can be sustained here, it is notable how much less exact the correspondence between right- and left-hand forms is in the Variations (see bars 1–12), just as the larger texture is more freely shaped than would be possible in a trio.

The two-voice dialogue is seen at its purest form in the first four bars of 28/iii (Ex. 8.14). Here the question of performing priorities is at its most

Example 8.14 Haydn: Piano Trio No. 28 in D major, third movement, bars 1–6

Example 8.15 Sonata No. 56 in D major, second movement, bars 1–6

basic: it is a case of doubling either by piano of the flute (or violin) and cello, or vice versa. Another D major finale, that of Piano Sonata No. 56 (Ex. 8.15), is the only immediately comparable solo work, and it suggests a fundamental means of distinguishing between the two genres. In the trio movement the gap between the hands is too wide, and the resulting texture too bare, to owe its form to an idiomatic solo conception (compare the initial closeness of the hands in the sonata movement). Still more importantly, the fact that the bass leads in the trio separates it still further from a piano sonata. This never happens at the start of a solo movement, and the independence of the two lines is once more confirmed by their interchanging in the reprise (bars 12^2–16^1). Thus the textual evidence again indicates that the opening bars were conceived in terms of the stringed instruments, and not the keyboard.

(5) One of the earliest twentieth-century enthusiasts for these trios, Donald Tovey, stated rather rashly in the Preface to his rescoring of two of

the works that 'for the violoncello independent bars are so rare that there are hardly a dozen distributed throughout the whole thirty-one extant trios'.[13] This assertion, quoted approvingly by Marion Scott in her bicentenary article on Haydn's chamber music,[14] was only too open to arithmetical correction, and one Arthur T. Froggatt, in a letter to the *Musical Times* a few months later, attempted a more accurate count:[15]

> In the thirty-one published trios there are seven hundred and forty-four bars in which the 'cello part differs from the pianoforte bass – an average of twenty-four bars to a trio. In this calculation I take no account of difference of octave, or of repeated notes, but only of a difference in the twelve notes of the scale. I have not counted the number of notes: possibly three hundred.
>
> . . . Mozart wrote seven trios with a 'cello part . . . there are nine hundred and ten bars in which the 'cello doubles the pianoforte bass. (In the adagio of the first Trio, K. 254, it does nothing else.) As for Beethoven, there is not one of his trios in which the 'cello does not occasionally double the pianoforte bass; in the last and finest, Op. 97, there are a hundred and seventy-seven bars in which the 'cello (according to Miss Scott's gospel) goes astray.[15]

While the calculation of 'stray' cello notes is a useful, if conservative, estimate, the mere counting of notes cannot do justice to the variety of roles fulfilled by the instrument, whether or not it is independent of the piano's bass line. Indeed, the transition from independent to 'subservient' passages is always accomplished so seamlessly as only to confirm the greater coherence of the cello line compared to its piano equivalent – and also suggests, once more, that the cello cannot be imagined as simply disappearing into what Tovey called the 'whitewash'.[16] As has already been stated, the cello parts are often more completely realized and registrally coherent – see, for example, 20/ii/19–22. Trio No. 23 demonstrates in both movements a

13 'Joseph Haydn: Pianoforte Trio in A major [No. 32]. Redistributed for the Benefit of the Violin and Violoncello' (London: Oxford University Press, 1939), ii.

14 'Haydn's Chamber Music', 215.

15 'Haydn's Trios', *Musical Times* 73/1074 (1932), 742.

16 'Joseph Haydn: Pianoforte Trio in A major. Redistributed for the Benefit of the Violin and Violoncello', ii. The full sentence reads: 'But the modern pianoforte either drowns Haydn's unisons or merges with them into a kind of musical whitewash that is none the better for diverging into flakiness'.

Example 8.16 Piano Trio No. 23 in E flat major, first movement, bars 52–7

conjunction of the two apparent roles which argues for a larger view of the cello as the dominant bass instrument. In the second movement at bars 71–72[1] and 218 (a figure answered by the piano at 224) the cello provides a continuity of movement that is still more important in Example 8.16, at bar 57 of the first movement. This shape, supporting the violin's imitation of the previous bar, provides an inversion of the piano's two triplet figures of bar 20[2], outlining the same falling minor third.

Another important role for the cello is to provide the true bass while the piano is otherwise engaged, although this procedure is far more common in the Mozart trios, where the bass line is rarely conceived in such a thematically vital manner. Examples can be found at 20/i/2–3, 26/ii/44 and 210–11, 29/iii/108–9, 30/i/14 and 32/ii/10–12. Example 8.17, at 19/ii/11, not only belongs to this group but also has registral and colouristic significance. The G in the cello maintains its consistent occupation of the lower octave throughout the first section, lending a particular registral breadth to a very broadly conceived melody in the piano right hand. The colouristic value of the G lies in its registral complementation of the keyboard's highest note, f[3], the most poignant moment of the section, all the more so since both strings enter *forte* after the piano's echoing solo comments of bars 8[3]–10[2].

The cello assumes a more overtly colouristic role with such features as the unexpected, solitary pizzicato that marks the recapitulation at 32/i/125, or the low D♭ that softly underpins the remote modulation at 30/i/54, which makes harmonic capital from the dissonant unison D♭ that initiates the development section. In the first movement of Trio No. 21, the cello shows

Example 8.17 Piano Trio No. 19 in F major, second movement, bars 6–18

the penetrating power of its A string in the two-note pairs of bars 46–9 and the corresponding f¹ reiterations at 64–7; the open G string is exploited in the sudden *forte* of 25/ii/19, a harmonic colouration which is recalled by the early outburst of the E major theme of the slow movement of the String Quartet Op. 74 No. 3. A more subtle form of timbral exploitation can be heard at 31/ii/147, which is doubled by the piano left hand; like the bass line of 42/ii, the rapid changing of registers is clearly more indebted to the properties of the cello than the piano. An especially frequent colouristic use of the cello is to emphasize the turn to minor through a more *cantabile* approach – see 26/ii/179–82, 36/iii/85–9¹ and 42/i/119–22¹. It can also perform an independent thematic role, as it does briefly at 25/iii/45 and in a more thorough fashion at 42/i/16–17¹, 51–3 and 57, while it contributes a clearly characteristic voice at such points as 27/iii/52–7 and 45/ii/13ff. In the latter instance, the two-note pairs at bars 13 and 14 provide an expressive interjection that inverts the initial b¹–a♯¹ shape, while its subsequent independent line at bars 17–18 is then imitated by the violin. At 21/ii/19ff. the cello maintains the minuet rhythm while the violin and piano imitate each other, so that the high-tessitura flowering of bars 24–7 is a natural outgrowth of the cello's previous rhythmic prominence.

Example 8.18 Piano Trio No. 18 in G major, third movement, bars 49–58

(6) The frequent instances of small-scale dialogue between the three instruments often prove a point about the composer's textural conception, as a thematic cell is explicitly passed from one part to another. In the final movement of Haydn's first 'mature' trio, No. 18, the first variation features a scalic form passed from cello to violin to piano in successively higher octaves at bars 52–4 (Ex. 8.18).

Similar threefold imitative structures are found at 42/ii/23–5 (piano–cello–violin) and 58–63 (piano–violin–cello), 33/i/42–4 (cello–violin–piano) and 42/i/105–12 (cello–piano–violin/cello–piano). More intimate instances occur at 29/i/162–3, where the violin immediately takes up the piano's altered form; 32/i/182–7, where the initially transitional figure is expanded in the coda so as to match its use at the outset of the development (arguing for the necessity of observing the second-half repeat); and 45/i/43, where the cello's *sforzando* $e\flat^1$–d^1 pair is immediately answered by the violin's $b\flat^2$–$a\flat^2$. In such interplay, the instruments often prompt each other to a new course of action rather than merely agreeing with what another has already said;[17] in the twelve-bar sentence that opens Trio No. 43, the violin's seem-

---

[17] Compare my discussion of Haydn's string quartet textures in *Haydn: String Quartets, Op. 50* (Cambridge: Cambridge University Press, 1992), pp. 94–5.

Example 8.19 Piano Trio No. 25 in E minor, first movement, bars 27–41

ingly ornamental triplet in bar 6[1] is what prompts the piano's sudden sextuplet burst on the following beat. The manner in which the violin subverts its
ostensible accompanimental function can also be seen at 24/i/38, where its
repeated crotchets turn out to signal an imitation of the piano's phrase at a
bar's distance. This kind of overlapping imitation between violin and piano
is most commonly associated with repeated cadential figures, as at bars 68–70
of the same movement or at 37/iii/38–41. It will not do to imagine that the
violin part is somehow tacked on in such instances, since the piano figuration
to which it responds is too 'raw' to stand alone in the finished product.

A more complex process of exchange is evident in 25/i/30–40 (see Ex.
8.19). The piano's semiquaver figure that supports the parallel-tenth

267

head-motif in the strings inspires the violin to take up the same motion at 31^3 (compare 20/ii/7), in quasi-inversion. Normal imitation is resumed at bars 33–4 and the procedure is expanded over the following bars, but with the piano providing an imitation of the imitation in its echoing comments at 37^3–38^2. However, the violin's answer to the piano at 38^3 reverses the earlier chromatic descent, thus in turn reversing the respective directions of the two units at bar 31. The level of the dialogue here, as in the earlier examples, undoubtedly inhabits the world of 'true chamber music' rather than that of the solo or *concertante* work.

(7)   One of the most important specialized textures in these trios is the use of sustained notes in the string parts to support a remote harmonic excursion articulated by the piano. The technique is a good example of the manner in which greater breadth is achieved in the works compared with a solo sonata. Typically, the piano reiterates a figure while the strings bind the texture together. It is also generally the case that the piano figuration would not stand up by itself, but, when no longer the sole focus for the listener, becomes acceptable when integrated into a larger web of sound.[18] These factors are all at play in the spectacular events of the development of Trio No. 36/iii. At bars 58–68 the violin and cello sustain while the piano has eleven consecutive bars of the same arpeggiated figuration (which is, however, thematic, deriving directly from the flourish which closes the exposition). By the end of the passage we have moved from the B flat major V, by enharmonic means in the bass voice, to A major.

The same technique is applied with quite different results at 23/ii/124–35. Here the strings enter after the piano has turned several harmonic corners by itself, and they reinforce the unexpected settling on to an E♭ pedal note. The sudden presence of the strings lends great warmth to this turn to the subdominant; this is one of the most finely calculated examples of scoring in all the trios. Other examples include 18/ii/109–14, 19/i/75–79^1, 21/i/100–3, 29/ii/29–30, 32/i/56–9 and 38/i/85–90^2.

The second and final movement of Trio No. 26 features a passage that is also relevant here, even though not involving the use of sustained string sonority. Nothing illustrates better the greater breadth of these trios than

---

[18]   See 'Haydn's Piano Trio Textures', 331.

Example 8.20 Piano Trio No. 26 in C minor, second movement, bars 29–44

the enormous phrase at bars 31^2–43^1 that acts as a transition to the establishment of the dominant (Ex. 8.20). At no stage of this passage can a structural downbeat be perceived; its tension is strengthened, rather than diminished, by the literal doubling of violin and piano right hand throughout. This tension is only relieved at bar 43, where both cello and violin strike out on new paths.

(8)   Another specialized technique, one that is virtually exclusive to Haydn in the trio repertory, is the employment of the violin to delineate an 'inner-voice' bass line. In such cases, it is generally doubled by the piano left hand, but, as has been said, this method of scoring lends an extra vitality to

Example 8.21 Piano Trio No. 23 in E flat major, second movement, bars 1–6

the texture. Few violinists would not relish the occasional opportunity to play at the bottom rather than the top of the texture, one would hope. The fact that it rarely represents the true bass line is often indicated by a subsequent cello entry that confirms the structural bass (see for instance 18/i/59–62 and 20/i/9–11). The outstanding instance of this feature is displayed throughout the finale of Trio No. 37 (note also 33/iii/5–8 and 30/i/45[4]–47[1]). In an equal number of cases, the violin takes charge of an inner voice without any bass implications, but the shapeliness of these lines is clearly calculated for the superior sustaining power of the stringed instrument. The violin part of 19/ii/1–4 is similarly conceived to that of 34/iii/20–23, both lying low on the G string, while at 44/iii/13–16 it provides a beautiful sense of poise with its repeated notes. Perhaps the best example of an inner voice conceived in terms of the violin occurs at the beginning of 23/ii (Ex. 8.21). The mercurial acceleration that takes place in the fourth bar of this opening unit is what gives the whole theme such a distinctive profile. On the other hand, at 35/iii/98–108[1], the violin is quite subordinate to the leading piano right-hand part, but the continuous pulse of its repeated-note quavers lends an urgency to this transitional passage far beyond that which is indicated by the look of the page.

(9)   The only point at which two of the three instruments become consistently subordinate is during those various sections when The Great Violin Tune is unveiled. In these sections, for instance 19/ii/32[3]–78[1], 39/ii/17–36 and 41/i/94[2]–114, the piano part becomes compliantly homophonic, while the cello has the equally important role of providing timbral support for the

Example 8.22 Piano Trio No. 27 in A flat major, third movement, bars 102–8

leading violin part. Thus another primarily two-part texture is held together in continuo-like fashion by the piano. In addition, its accompanimental figuration often gently reflects the violin, as in the voice-exchange patterns at 41/i/96 and 104.

(10) Occasionally the piano trio form is exploited as one complete unit. In such movements as 32/iii, 35/i, 41/ii and 45/iii the three instruments function as a small indoor band, where questions of textural dominance or subordination do not arise.[19] On a much smaller scale, the use of unisons indicates the superior punctuating ability of the form compared with the piano sonata. Example 8.22 (27/iii/104–8) could hardly find a place in a solo work: the disjunction between *piano* and *forte*, high and low register, solo and 'tutti', as well as the breadth of the gesture, represent intrinsic ensemble music. A very similar gesture is heard, for instance, in the finale of Symphony No. 93, where the repeated C's on solo cello at bars 165–8 are answered by a tutti account of the upbeat figure on D. (Beethoven later appropriated this technique for use at similar transitional points in the first movements of both his early piano concertos – see Op. 15/i/257–60 and Op. 19/i/39–42.) Haydn uses unisons elsewhere too for the purposes of structural demarcation, as at 29/i/90–93[1], 42/iii/195–200, and most strikingly in the wide-ranging transitional figures of 24/ii/67[2.]–73.

A more obvious means of punctuation is the use of pizzicato strings, employed by Haydn mostly in slow movements, for example 25/ii, 27/ii,

---

[19] *Ibid.*, 331–2.

31/i and 32/ii. One of the most dramatic timbral effects occurs in the recapitulation of 25/ii: as the consequent phrase turns unexpectedly to the minor, the strings exchange their pizzicato for close-position arco chords (bars 55–6). The slow movement of Trio No. 43 is unsurpassed in the imaginative detail of its scoring, finding many different ways to inflect and punctuate the basic material. The manner of the strings' entry at bar 5 is instructive of the subtlety Haydn expends, replacing the dual presentation of theme so heavily favoured by Mozart and most later trio composers with a process that emphasizes uninterrupted continuity. The cello enters with a seemingly subordinate pedal note, but responds to the violin's imitation of the piano by itself imitating the piano – at the distance of one semiquaver! By bar 6, the violin has gained melodic leadership. After a repetition of this process, the piano presents its phrase for the third time, at bar 9. The strings now team up to frame the piano line with contrary-motion staccato, while at bar 15 another method of inflection is introduced, legato parallel tenths. The A minor middle section presents a quite different form of 'punctuation', as the texture resolves itself into a series of layers. This form of stratification is even more notably employed at 34/ii and at 26/i, where in the final variation the violin has the melodic role, the cello plays staccato arpeggiation and the piano provides accompanimental continuity in its left hand while the right interposes brief comments in its highest register.

(11) Quite the opposite of the above 'split-level' texture is found in those passages where no one part can be claimed as the *Hauptstimme*, usually when harmonic elongation and prolongation are involved. This feature, introduced in my earlier article with reference to 29/i and 38/i,[20] can scarcely be classified as a technique or specialized procedure; rather, it represents a blending of subordinate voices into a whole that drives the music on to the next point of thematic articulation. Thus, it may be understood as being as much an agent of large-scale rhythmic as harmonic movement. This is the case in Example 8.23, bars 48ff. of the finale of Trio No. 22, to which work we shall shortly return. This passage leads to the establishment of the dominant at bar 54. Another representative instance occurs at 43/iii/149–59[1], where neither the piano's motivic fragments nor the strings'

[20] *Ibid.*, 329–31.

272

Example 8.23 Piano Trio No. 22 in A major, second movement, bars 47–52

arpeggiated figures could survive by themselves, but together they form an impressive harmonic climax to the development.

(12) The Flute Trios, Nos. 28–30, almost represent proof by inversion of Haydn's sensitivity to his assembled forces. Brown speaks of a 'retreat to a more conservative stance',[21] but more to the point is the fact that their structural, textural and stylistic differences arise directly from the implications of the presence of the new instrument, both in itself and in combination with the other two. Thus the character of much of the music is distinctly *aperto* (as Mozart marked the first movement of his Flute Concerto, K. 314) and the textures are more open and spacious. The scale of the action is less intimate than where two strings can work in combination, and indeed one must often speak more of alternation in the Mozartian manner than of true dialogue. Most of the movements begin with a dual presentation of the theme, the important exception being Flute Trio No. 30/i; here the structure of what is, as it were, a 'through-composed' theme is much more subtle. The flute enters with an echo of the piano's bar 4[1] before duplicating the line of the previous bar, and the melodic presentation is so rich and continuous that it is only at bar 13 that we hear any point of structural-harmonic articulation.

This very openness of sound and texture, even looseness, by Haydn's standards of argument, is exploited as such by the composer. Proceeding from the *aperto* character, he takes several opportunities to indulge in a

---

[21] *Joseph Haydn's Keyboard Music: Sources and Style* (Bloomington: Indiana University Press, 1986), p. 353.

273

marked laxity of structural thought. The finale of Trio No. 29, for example, contains the one of the biggest of all Haydn's upbeat jokes, carried to the limits of tolerance. The retransition at bars 59–65 already seems excessive enough, but it is easily outdone by that of 121–31, where the ruling upbeat motif literally disintegrates, becoming lower and slower until only its initial two-quaver impulse remains. The second note of the final pair looks as strange on the page as it sounds: enharmonically notated as an a♯¹ so as to act as a 'leading note' to the b♮¹ of the following bar, it is in fact heard as b♭¹, and sounds odd (like a question-mark) because it conflicts with the dominant harmony which is prolonged throughout the transition. (Beethoven must surely have had this finale in his head when he wrote the first movement of his Sonata Op. 14 No. 2, also in G major.)

There is nothing 'conservative' in the first movement of No. 28 except its opening theme, which is highly Mozartian (note particularly the grace notes of bar 6 which decorate the inversion of the fourth bar). Misha Donat notes: '[The] easy-going main theme is given to the piano, with minimal support from the cello – a simple texture of a kind that Haydn would scarcely have exploited at such length in his conventionally-scored piano trios of the period.'[22] However, this simplicity, tedious though it is for the cello, is just the point: Haydn could hardly have been so absent-minded as to write exactly the same cello rhythm four times in a row at bars 1–8, or six times in succession at 18–23. Indeed, reinforced by the bass arpeggiations at 9–10 and 16–17, the movement sits on the bass D for the first twenty-six bars. Even the following bars 27–30 only move on to, rather than into, the dominant. This is, in its way, a sensational event (or non-event), particularly for Haydn, who normally cannot wait to initiate the tensing move away from the tonic.

It is this initial refusal to budge which enforces the remote modulations of the development and coda sections. The development, indeed, achieves the rare feat of being longer than the exposition (sixty-five to sixty-one bars). Bars 87–113 seem to be suspended in time, representing a very large expansion of the first transition at bars 18–23. The series of pedal points turns to account, indeed 'develops', the initial 26-bar pedal, on a more dramatic level. The development is so long and harmonically far-

22 'Haydn: Late Chamber Works', p. 32.

ranging that a separate and lengthy coda is needed to balance it, beginning with a foreground E flat major!

After this attempt to see beyond the too-frequently painted 'big picture' we may now return to the supposedly ideal 'textural correctness' of the first movement of Trio No. 22 (given as Ex. 8.24). Rather than simply leaving it as an honourable exception in Hughes' global terms, perhaps we might investigate what it does within its own frame of reference, as an individually significant work. The construction of the trio as a whole suggests an echo of the Baroque French overture, both in style and in spirit, with the slow, dotted and double-dotted rhythmic material of the opening and the frequent rapid flourishes that ensue in the Adagio succeeded by a quick concluding movement. However, any intimations of a Baroque grandeur in the piano's opening phrases are quickly mitigated by the 'singing style' of the strings' interjections at bars 2 and 4, and when violin and cello expand their comments into a full reply from bar 8, singing their way through the undulating accompaniment of the piano, the tone becomes more lyrical, and the style plainly Romantic. There are few moments in Haydn that originate so strikingly in the future, as it were, since the music here could quite plausibly have been conceived at least fifty years after it was, in 1785. This is due not just to the layout of the string parts, but also to the undifferentiated sextuplet rhythms in the piano part, a marked contrast to the previous metrical complexity. This accompanimental figure is reminiscent of the use of a solo cello soon after the opening of the slow movement of Symphony No. 102, paradoxically introduced to fulfil a similar secondary role by means of the same sort of sextuplet figure. This remarkable use of a solo (and especially stringed) instrument to play an accompaniment in an orchestral texture gets to the heart of Haydn's very individual and versatile textural ethos, the spirit of which the foregoing discussions have attempted to evoke.

When first hearing the present Adagio, one is tempted to say that it sounds like nothing else in Haydn's oeuvre, quite apart from the unusual textural treatment of the medium. In fact, there are at least three comparable slow movements in triple time that feature the same initial combination of arpeggio, dotted rhythms and a turn. The first is the same slow movement of Symphony No. 102, and also the slow movement of Trio No. 40, where it is transposed up a semitone (Ex. 8.25). Here the similarities, not

Example 8.24 Piano Trio No. 22 in A major, first movement

Example 8.24 (*cont.*)

Example 8.24 (*cont.*)

*) Autograph ♩ ♩

Example 8.24 (*cont.*)

Example 8.24 (*cont.*)

Example 8.25 Piano Trio No. 40 in F sharp minor, second movement, bars 1–5

just in the first bar, but even more strikingly in the melodic curve of the second (compare the last two beats of Trio No. 22's first bar), are even more suggestive for being followed by the same sort of accompanimental figure in the middle of the texture. The kinship with the opening phrase of Trio No. 22 is most marked in the case of the slow movement of the 'English' Sonata, No. 60 (Ex. 8.26), written, like the previous example, in 1794–5. Not only are the melodic diminutions of the opening two bars very much alike, but the initial grace-note arpeggiated figure in the sonata version represents the same lower chordal constituents that are present in the piano part of the trio. To push this parallel further, one could equate the sonata's arpeggiation with the violin's efforts in executing its close-position triple-stopped chord in the opening bar of the trio, which will produce much the same rhythmic effect. The last two bars of the sonata's opening eight-bar phrase produce another parallel with the trio's initial unit, as a scalic ascent over II^6 (note the equivalence of the F♯–G successions and the a♯^{1}–b^1 of the trio, bar 5) is answered by a falling scale. The comparison between the two passages indicates once more the essential difference between keyboard

Example 8.26 Sonata No. 60 in C major, second movement, bars 1–9

writing in solo and trio contexts. The solo sonata version is much more individually shaped – the solidly expressive ascent in bar 5 of the trio is replaced in bar 7 of the sonata by a whimsical rise in a grace-note conformation to the second beat, while the corresponding descent is also made more personal by the detailed articulation and *sforzando* markings.

The same element of greater rhapsodical freedom in a solo context is also clear in the third companion to the opening of our Adagio movement, the Andante con espressione that is the first movement of two in the Piano Sonata No. 58 (Ex. 8.27), written in 1789. This example furnishes the least direct comparison with the opening shape of the trio, but, in the larger context of its first ten-bar sentence, suggests that Haydn returned again and again to this initial gesture as an 'ideal type' of slow-movement opening, a particular expressive *gestalt*. The similarities between these two opening sentences become stronger as they both progress. While the third and fourth bars of each passage present a generously embellished version of their respective opening pairs of bars, the correspondences become more

Example 8.27 Sonata No. 58 in C major, first movement, bars 1–14

Example 8.28 Comparison of melodic lines, Piano Trio No. 22, first movement, bars 5–8, and Sonata No. 58, first movement, bars 6–10

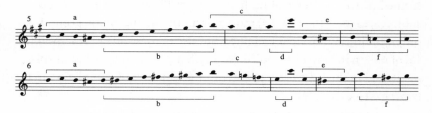

exact when one compares bars 5–7 of the trio and bars 6–10 of the sonata (see Ex. 8.28). The differences in the realization of these two versions of an 'ideal type' reinforce once more the distinction between genres that Haydn always recognized (unlike Mozart, who tends to mix generic suggestions more freely), which, even within this brief context of a trio conspicuously free from such sins, undermines any understanding of the Haydn trios as 'accompanied piano sonatas'.

The string interjections which 'qualify' this opening piano phrase

Example 8.29 Linear intervallic patterns in Piano Trio No. 22, first movement

become a sort of chorus-like motif within the movement, occurring at the ends of phrases and generally having a connective function. After their initial appearances at bars 2 and 4, echoing the piano's material at 1^3–2^1 and 3^3–4^2 respectively, the basis of scalic tenths is maintained in their form at bars 19, 24 and 25. However, their direction and rhythmic form are altered under the influence of the piano's right-hand figure at bars 18–19, which itself derives from a fusion of the ascending semiquaver scale of bar 5 with its surrounding demisemiquaver rhythmic units. Only in the bass figure of bars 16^3–17^1 is their original shape overtly recalled. Nevertheless, the influence of the initial second-bar form exerts itself on a higher level of the structure at precisely the point where its foreground version is transformed, since the descending linear intervallic patterns of the second-subject area (6–6, then 10–10) move this motif into the middleground. Not only is the linear movement retained, but also the descent by the same interval of a sixth in both outer voices, somewhat disguised by octave displacement, and in the first instance also by different rates of completion in the two parts (see Ex. 8.29).

Of course the demisemiquaver rising scale is not just employed in a connective context in this part of the movement, but represents its most prominent motivic cell. It reaches its full expressive potential in the coda, which is in fact a large cadenza for the whole ensemble. The cadenza is prepared by a full bar's rest on a V$^6_4$ chord, and its tension is guaranteed by the fact that the expected continuation of bar 52 is reached only at bar 63, after the cadential flourish has been completed. The new link which the violin supplies at bar 53 to the $^6_4$ chord represents a contracted form of part of its e^2–b^1 fourth-progression at bars 42–6. What makes the recollection of this shape at this point particularly logical is the fact that both perform a linking function, whereas the structural equivalent of bars 42–46[1] in the exposition plays a quite different role. Bars 8ff. sound more like a natural blossoming of the previous string comments on the piano's theme, even if their function is ultimately to be understood as a transitional one, whereas bars 42–6 in the recapitulation are clearly moving towards a new section rather than being a new section in themselves. This effect is secured by the dominant pedal, as well as by the fact that the violin's descending fourth-progression is itself an echo of the piano's melodic bridge back to the recapitulation, at bar 34. The most expressive role in the transition of bars 42–6, however, is given to the cello, whose wide-spanning arpeggios offer a remarkable equivalent to the same figuration in the Adagio finale of the String Quartet Op. 54 No. 2, written several years later. The effect here, though, has none of the freakish quality that attends the cello's part in the quartet texture.

Just as the original string-part motif underwent a transformation in the second-subject area, so in the cadenza the demisemiquaver scale itself moves into the middleground, as the piano and violin enter on successively higher scale-degrees from bar 55 until the octave ascent is completed (from a^1 at 55 to a^2 at 57^2, allowing for the octave displacement). Once more, the cello's presence is only too obviously required, since without its ability to sustain the E through two long bars of a slow $^3_4$, the idea of this rather rapturous cadenza would never have entered Haydn's head. Just at the point of climax, the cello itself joins in the stretto. In performance, this entry must be heard to belong to the stringed instrument rather than the piano left hand, since this 'rush of blood' is a consequence of the tension of its preceding long-held pedal-note, to which a crescendo will quite naturally have been applied. The dialogue between on-beat bass and off-beat upper-voice contours which this figure introduces can be understood as a heightened form, in diminution, of the earlier bars 21–3 and 51–3. This agitated moment leads to a significant point in the structure, the only time at which the demisemiquaver scalic motif descends, first in piano, then in both strings (bars 58–9), in a neat illustration of the relationship between motif and function: the change of direction enacts the 'falling' role of this stage of the dramatic action.

The very fact that Haydn provides a textural resolution through this unexpected cadenza shows that for him what was later to become a standard distribution of piano trio texture was not self-evidently acceptable in

Example 8.30 Piano Trio No. 22 in A major
(a) first movement, bars 57–62
(b) second movement, bars 195–210

(a)

chamber-music terms. He thus provides an exceptional outcome to an exceptional textural situation, one which is not any sort of ideal solution but an object of scrutiny. Just as the composer is ceaselessly fascinated by the possibilities of structure, such that we can never speak of settled formal procedures, so he places texture under the same omniscient gaze.

A larger-scale equivalent to the central part of this cadenza can in fact be found in the concluding movement of Trio No. 22, which itself features a large, unexpected cadential passage near its conclusion (an expansion of the exposition's bars 60–4 – see Ex. 8.30). Typically, the faster movement reorders the Adagio shapes into a more concise form. In the finale the chromatic fall of a third (motif (a), recalling I/34, 42–5, 53–4) is followed by the same ascent of a fourth (b), but this is then elided with the diminished-seventh harmony heard at I/59³, followed by the same scalic ascent from e¹ (motif (d)). Its more chromatic unfolding in the Adagio should not be

Example 8.30 (*cont.*)

(b)

understood or performed casually, since this amounts to an intensification of the previous chromatic strains, in particular the guiding inner-voice $d\sharp^1-e^1-e\sharp^1-f\sharp^1$ succession from the beginning of the development. In rhythmic terms, it represents the longest stretch of continuous demisemiquaver movement in the Adagio, and, taking its cue from the upbeat nature of the previous like figures, it initiates a long structural upbeat of four bars to the I of bar 64. The trill towards which this upward flourish leads represents a classic Haydn ambiguity: it is structurally comic, yet there is no overt humour in the 'text' of the piece at this point. This very long ornament is at once ridiculously overdrawn, like a parody of the feature that inevitably marks the end of a cadenza (made more eccentric by the dual efforts of violin and piano in this direction), yet also highly relevant as an answer to the earlier long bass pedal on E. (Haydn later attempted a similar effect in the coda to the slow movement of Symphony No. 96, with its cadenza leading to a prolonged trill for the woodwind principals. Indeed, this combination of parody and affectionate 'sentimentality' also constitutes a classic Haydnesque ambiguity of tone – for another example see the slow movement of Symphony No. 93.)

The trill is also structurally logical as an ironing-out at length of the earlier trill-hemiola 'problem' that arises at bars 20 and 50; here, the repeated combination of the scale-plus-appoggiatura shape (as at bars 18ff.) seems to change the metre to $\frac{2}{4}$, a sense that is maintained through to the following trill, which therefore appears to last for a beat too long. The bass shape which slips in to accompany the final trill, at bar 62, again belongs to the cello, particularly since it represents a filled-in version of the memorable cello lines at bars 42 to 45. Its insertion and elaboration at this juncture is also particularly appropriate, since it means that the piano's meandering shape at bars 64^2–65^1 can now be grasped as an inverted outline of the same figure (d^2–b^1–$g\#^1$–e^1–d^1 [$-c\#^1$]), both lines thus unfolding under the influence of the initial dominant-seventh arpeggiated figure at 1^3. In addition, the final five notes of the cello line (b–$c\#^1$–d^1–$d\#^1$–e^1) are an exact retrograde of the violin's fourth-progression against which it played its related arpeggiated shapes at bars 42–6.

While the correspondence of their cadential patterns offers the most striking instance of thematic interplay between the movements of this Trio, there are other important similarities between the two, ranging from the recollection of the connective scale of I/16–17 at the same structural point of the Vivace, bar 53 (Ex. 8.31), to the reworking of the lyrical bars I/8–10 in a more perfunctory form in the Vivace (Ex. 8.32), to the dialogue of cello and violin at II/41–5, where the $e\#^1$–$f\#^1$/$g\#^1$–a^1 pairs recall the opening two-note successions of the Adagio's development.

On a different level, the very opening of the concluding movement

Example 8.31 Piano Trio No. 22 in A major, second movement, bars 53–9

Example 8.32 Piano Trio No. 22 in A major
(a) first movement, bars 8–10
(b) second movement, bars 16–22

(a)

(b)

recycles the Adagio's initial shapes, both in its melodic detail as well as in its arpeggiation from a^1 to a^2, while the start of its development section also moves from F sharp minor to a full statement of the theme in D major (at II/89ff. – compare I/27–30). What is most striking about these correspondences is that they all occur at the same formal juncture within each movement, suggesting that the composer has made the final movement a structural and thematic answer to, indeed a parody of, the earlier one. What was stylistically and texturally exceptional is transformed into the composer's best and most robust finale manner. It is as if, by 'dumbing down' the material of the Adagio, Haydn is offering us the opportunity to forget its textural novelty – or as if he is withdrawing it for the benefit of the many future Texture Inspectors who cannot include such rogue elements in their reports. And yet, as I have tried to suggest through the preceding examination of textual facts and textural principles, Haydn did of course carry forward his discoveries in this trio, not so much in the sustained reproduction of similar textures in his later works, but in the ability to apply the same principles of textural awareness in less exceptional contexts.

9 Papa Doc's recap caper: Haydn and temporal dyslexia

GEORGE EDWARDS

Discussions of sonata form, and especially analyses of movements in sonata form, routinely pay less attention to recapitulations than to expositions or developments, probably because of an assumption that a section whose main purpose is resolution should raise few new problems of its own. Such an assumption is not always unjustified: sparks might not often fly in a discussion of Schubert's (or even many of Mozart's) recapitulations.

But if some composers take a vacation during the recapitulation, Haydn is not among them. His recapitulations often involve the complete recomposition of their respective expositions, causing Tovey repeatedly – and misleadingly – to remark that they resembled Beethoven's biggest codas.[1] The means by which Haydn transforms the exposition into something completely new in the recapitulation (prefix, suffix, expansion, contraction, parenthetical insertion, reinterpretation of function, ellipsis, splice, overlap, elision) are the same ones he uses to turn simple sentences or periods into more complex or asymmetrical local groups.[2] In addition to putting the material of the exposition through a kaleidoscope, Haydn usually changes the position and harmonic orientation of its main cadences: he is equally inventive with respect to phrase design, harmonic structure, *and* to the relationship between the two.

Haydn's extreme wildness can provoke an unseemly haste to demonstrate the hidden lawfulness of his most delicious misdeeds. Just as performances often smooth over Haydn's rough edges, we run the risk of

---

[1] Donald Francis Tovey, *Essays in Musical Analysis,* I (London: Oxford University Press, 1931), p. 145.

[2] For an excellent account of Haydn's manipulation of phrase structure see William Rothstein, *Phrase Rhythm in Tonal Music* (New York: Schirmer, 1989), pp. 125–69.

291

attributing his compositional decisions to thought-processes as pedestrian as those of the analyst. Instead of attempting to provide a taxonomy of Haydn's recapitulations (an impossible task), I will explore his varied responses to several structural situations in symphonies and string quartets written after 1767: to the 'hinge' between development and recapitulation; to the omission or destabilization of the first part of the recapitulation; and to the consequences for the rest of a movement of introducing a tune of popular character late in the exposition. My emphasis will not be on Haydn the 'father of the symphony', or on the recipient of an honorary doctorate from Oxford, but on Haydn the subversive: on 'Papa Doc'.

If the beginning of the recapitulation is the 'central aesthetic event'[3] of a sonata movement, then the double return (of the main theme in the tonic) is critical precisely because its location and treatment are so free – including the possibility that it may never occur.[4] If it does, it is either the strongest possible indication the recapitulation has begun or the easiest way to fool us into thinking so. The nature and degree of the continuity or articulation at the beginning of the recapitulation are endlessly variable in Haydn (only slightly less so in Beethoven, still notable in Brahms). In a context where major formal issues may be at stake, this hinge between development and recapitulation is treated with the freedom and eccentricity typical of Haydn's handling of detail.

Most of the conceptions of sonata form we first encounter are persuasive only for a relatively small number of movements by Mozart and Beethoven, and for later composers who took these as models. Yet the non-specialist can hardly avoid applying these conceptions backwards on to music Haydn wrote before the sonata began to be understood as a relatively fixed form. Thus my earliest childish ideas about the hinge between development and recapitulation came from an annotated piano arrangement of the first movement of Mozart's Symphony No. 40 in G minor, K. 550. Mozart provides elaborate preparations for the double return: half-cadences on the dominant of the dominant and on the dominant, thematic liquidation, a long dominant pedal and smooth voice-leading back to the tonic chord – a retransition so mesmerizing we can almost forget that the

---

3 James Webster, 'Sonata Form', *The New Grove Dictionary of Music and Musicians*, ed. Stanley Sadie (London: Macmillan, 1980), XVII, 497–508.

4 Charles Rosen, *Sonata Forms*, rev. edn (New York: Norton, 1988), p. 161.

development ends with a half-cadence followed by a lead-in to the tonic (*not* with a full cadence). The tonic key returns at least nineteen bars before the thematic return, and at least twenty bars before the first tonic $^5_3$ chord: thematic and harmonic returns are closely coordinated but distinct. This incomparably gentle landing back at the beginning includes an almost literal repetition of bars 2–22, like them avoiding any full cadence in the tonic. The unstable expansion at bars 191–221 is both a secondary development and a necessary adjustment of the transition.

It would be foolish to claim that this hinge, or this movement, is typical of Mozart. But this is: (1) the kind of movement that defined sonata form for Czerny and Marx; (2) the kind of movement theorists examine in attempting to find paradigms for the deep structure of sonata movements; and (3) utterly atypical of Haydn. While Mozart often aims for a recapitulation which seems to arise organically, even inevitably, out of the development (as if without the need for human intervention), Haydn often forces us to confront the artificiality of recapitulation, to doubt its efficacy, or even to remain unsure where it began. In Haydn, unlike Mozart, we can hardly help being aware of the composer's interventions in the work (like Jane Austen's 'tell-tale compression of the pages' in *Northanger Abbey*), or of his extraordinary awareness of the listener's likely expectations. Haydn's discontinuities are intended to amaze us, and to remind us that we are encountering a work of art, not of nature. Thus Haydn will always seem deficient if we want works of art to masquerade as natural objects, if we imagine their creators as distant gods, active only behind the scenes, or if, as the Romantic aesthetics of absolute music did, we regard the listener as subordinate to the work.

Haydn has tremendous confidence in the willingness of the listener to supply mentally events which are not physically present. Many passages in Haydn put to a severe test the proposition that the resolving powers of the tonic and dominant depend little on their salience (duration, loudness, completeness, proximity to one another) – see, for example, Haydn's Symphony No. 75, fourth movement, bars 118–30,[5] or Symphony No. 64, second movement, bars 98–108.[6]

[5] Ethan Haimo, *Haydn's Symphonic Forms: Essays In Compositional Logic* (Oxford: Clarendon Press, 1995), pp. 140–2.

[6] James Webster, *Haydn's 'Farewell' Symphony and the Idea of Classical Style: Through-Composition and Cyclic Integration in his Instrumental Music* (Cambridge: Cambridge University Press, 1991), pp. 147–52.

At one extreme of Haydn's handling of the hinge between development and recapitulation lies the cosmically predictable beginning of the recapitulation of the first movement of Symphony No. 53, whose full cadence overlaps the development and recapitulation. Much more frequently, the dominant at the end of the development and the tonic at the beginning of the recapitulation are hardly on speaking terms. The cause is the juxtaposition of a backward-looking dominant and an inconsequent or forward-looking tonic; typical symptoms include disjunctions of dynamics, register, instrumentation, material and voice-leading. The two basic patterns are the 'big' dominant/'small' tonic (Mozart's preferred version) and the more disruptive and paradoxical 'small' dominant/'big' tonic (most frequent in Haydn before the mid-1780s). Examples of the big dominant/small tonic include the hinges of the first movements of Symphonies Nos. 101, 103 and 104 and of String Quartets Op. 50 No. 5, Op. 76 No. 2 and Op. 77 No. 2; small dominant/big tonic hinges appear in the first movements of Symphonies Nos. 45, 66 and 69 and String Quartets Op. 33 No. 1 and Op. 42.

In the cases we have just considered, the continuity at the hinge is comparable to that found between the end of a slow introduction and the beginning of the following Allegro (usually big dominant/small tonic). Similar discontinuities are frequent at hinges where any sense of cadence or new beginning is blurred by using inversions of the backward-looking dominant, the forward-looking tonic, or both. Examples include the first-movement hinges of String Quartets, Op. 20 No. 1 and Op. 33 No. 2 (both dominant $^4_2$; tonic $^5_3$) and the fourth-movement hinge of String Quartet Op. 20 No. 4 (dominant $^6_5$; tonic $^6_3$). At the hinge of the first movement of the String Quartet in G minor, Op. 20 No. 3, the tonic $^5_3$ begins one bar before the thematic return; two lead-ins (one to the tonic, the other to the thematic return) are spliced together (see Ex. 9.1).

Perhaps too much ink has been spilled on Haydn's premature and false recapitulations in the first movements of Symphonies Nos. 43 and 55.[7] We can initially be fooled by a false recapitulation, especially when (as in Symphony No. 55) it is followed by the kind of developmental material

---

[7] See Rosen, *Sonata Forms*, pp. 276–80; Haimo, *Haydn's Symphonic Forms*, pp. 105–13.

Example 9.1 String Quartet in G minor, Op. 20 No. 3, first movement, bars 160–66

which often follows real recapitulations. But it is quite atypical for a movement with a false recapitulation to approach the real recapitulation with a problematic or ambiguous hinge, or to follow it with an early move to secondary development (as in String Quartet Op. 77 No. 1, first movement). The first movements of String Quartet Op. 20 No. 4 and Symphony No. 91 are among the rare cases where premature or false recapitulations seem to cry 'Wolf!' rather than to whet our appetite for the real thing.[8] In the case of Symphony No. 91, we may remain in doubt as to where the real recapitulation begins.

The counterpart to the false recapitulation is the delayed recapitulation (or 'false end-of-development'). In last movements with rondo-influenced sonata forms, we often find repeated arrivals on suitable hinges, followed by digressions or delaying tactics before the recapitulation actually begins. In Symphony No. 66, fourth movement, we are ready at the end of bar 139 – after seven bars of dominant pedal – for the

---

[8] Charles Rosen's strictures on this quartet's opening in *The Classical Style* (New York: Viking, 1971), p. 150, seem the result of a poor (mental) performance. These six-bar groups are, at first, neither phrases nor independent (pp. 56–7).

recapitulation to begin. Instead we get four bars conventionally tonicizing the dominant; we're ready again. Next a two-bar lead-in takes us to the tonic, but with the wrong scale-degree in the top voice – we need to reach $\hat{5}$, the head-note of the theme. Another two-bar lead-in gets to the right scale-degree and register – but we're made to wait one more bar for the recapitulation to begin! This false end-of-development is pure Haydn in its ridiculous humour; a subtler variant is delicious in Symphony No. 88, fourth movement.

Symphony No. 81, first movement, is a more unusual case of false end-of-development. The opening material begins returning (away from the tonic) late – as we suppose – in the development; at each appearance (bar 94, bar 101) it edges closer to the tonic, so that by bar 106 a tonic $^5_3$ briefly appears, narrowly avoiding a quotation of bar 4. This tonic chord is on the way to what we initially take to be the concluding half-cadence of the development (110). But bars 108–15 keep recycling the material of bars 5–10 (over a dominant pedal from bar 110): while thematic return is well under way, we're still only flirting with harmonic return. In the eighth bar of the pedal a destabilizing shift to the tonic minor triggers a brief move to the flat submediant, and propels us towards an overlapped full cadence in the tonic in bar 124. The false end-of-development was the half-cadence in bar 110; the *real* end of the development got back to the dominant as part of the full cadence which also begins the long-delayed recapitulation. This is an amazing and exhilarating moment, and one of Haydn's great expansions.[9]

Major-mode movements by Haydn and Mozart often precede a recapitulation with a major chord built on the mediant, either as part of an arpeggiation in the bass from $\hat{5}$ to $\hat{3}$ to $\hat{1}$ (as is often the case with Mozart) or (as is much more frequent in Haydn) as a half-cadence in the submediant. Examples include the first movement of Symphony No. 85, the second movements of Symphonies Nos. 54, 98 and 99, and the last movements of Symphonies Nos. 80, 95 and 103 – this is a hinge which is increasingly frequent in the 1780s and 1790s. A recapitulation which follows such a hinge will rarely be in a hurry to raise new problems, *not* because a dominant-of-

---

[9] Rosen, *The Classical Style*, pp. 157–9, puts the recapitulation somewhere between bars 105 and 110.

Example 9.2 Symphony No. 49 in F minor, first movement, bars 58–69 (recomposition)

the-submediant hinge is strange or unconventional (it is a Baroque cliché), but because it makes the tonic feel so relaxed.[10]

Other non-dominant hinges to recapitulations which begin on the tonic triad are relatively uncommon. In the major mode, they include the supertonic (Symphony No. 56, fourth movement) and the dominant of the mediant (String Quartet Op. 33 No. 1, third movement). All these non-dominant hinges are higher than the tonic on the circle of fifths, and all contain either $\hat{2}$ or $\hat{7}$; all involve ellipsis – the omission of events which would normally intervene between the chord of the hinge and the tonic. In the minor mode, we can add the mediant $^6_3$ (another ellipsis) in the fourth movement of Symphony No. 52 and the dominant $^6_3$ of the minor (!) dominant in the first movement of Symphony No. 49 (1768).

This movement's hinge provides a bizarre reversal of the double lead-in of the first movement of String Quartet Op. 20 No. 3: a backward-looking half-cadence (bar 59) is followed by another backward-looking half-cadence in the minor dominant (bars 60–1). The interpolation of bars 60–1 separates the dominant of the 'real' hinge from the recapitulation (bar 62) – or does it? We notice that at bar 59 the semiquaver figure refers both back to bar 54 (F–E♮, B♭–C) and ahead to the next arrival on the dominant: the half-cadence at bar 67. We could imagine a splice from bar 59² to bar 67², bypassing the beginning of the recapitulation altogether (see Ex. 9.2)!

Since we could also imagine an insertion replacing the elliptical rest on the third beat of bar 61 to connect plausibly with the recapitulation

[10] Many Haydn hinges insert something to mitigate the ellipsis of a III♯/I hinge. See Symphony No. 66, first movement, bars 97–103, and Piano Trio No. 43, third movement, bars 159–63.

(even a slight elongation of the rest makes this transition seem almost reasonable), there are, if anything, too many ways to construct a more normal prototype for this eccentric hinge. Haydn has had to take drastic measures – even if we're not sure what they were – to avoid strong cadences in the tonic. Otherwise, this movement – with its slow tempo, highly unified material and extremely restricted harmonic range – would die on its feet.[11]

The fascination of the hinge in Symphony No. 49, first movement, is equivocal because the sources of disruption seem essentially local. Most strange or ambiguous returns in later Haydn are more clearly implied by the beginning and have greater consequences for what follows. The first movement of String Quartet Op. 50 No. 1, for example, begins with the confirmation of a full cadence that never happened (bars 1–6); bars 7–12 supply the missing full cadence and overlap with a second inappropriate beginning: sixteen bars of confirmation of *that* cadence. The instability of this beginning arises from its refusal to think about anything but ending. The dangers for the return inherent in beginning a movement with endings are avoided by placing the beginning of the recapitulation between two cadences. The retransition, preceded by a full cadence in the submediant (bar 103), treats the material of bars 3–4 sequentially, leading gradually to a varied repetition of bars 3–4 in the tonic (at 108–9), a varied repetition of bars 5–12 and a half-cadence in bar 117 (replacing the full cadence of bar 12). One recognizes the point where the recapitulation begins only after the fact.[12]

The instability of the beginning of this recapitulation is emphasized by its brevity (ten bars replace bars 1–27) and its single half-cadence (replacing full cadences in bars 12 and 27). This instability is maintained by eliminating the transition (which was grouped in the exposition with what followed it) and by completely recasting the second group. Table 9.1 shows the rather few points of correspondence between the exposition and recapitulation.

[11] See Haimo, *Haydn's Symphonic Forms*, pp. 72–84, and Webster, *Haydn's 'Farewell' Symphony*, pp. 262–5.

[12] Tovey, 'Haydn's Chamber Music', in *The Mainstream of Music and Other Essays* (Cleveland: Meridian, 1959), p. 55, denies that this movement has a recapitulation.

Table 9.1 Correspondence between exposition and recapitulation, String Quartet Op. 50 No. 1, first movement.

Exposition		Recapitulation
bars 3–12 (full cadence)	=	bars 108–17 (half-cadence)
bars 13–39		– – – – – –
bars 40–5 altered and transposed		bars 118–23
– – – – –		bars 123–33
bars 45–50		(see bars 142–50)
bars 50–6		bars 134–40 (deceptive cadence)
bars 57–60		(See coda, bars 152ff.)

The full cadence in bar 150 is followed by a coda which responds to the instability of the beginning of the recapitulation by returning to the material of the opening of the movement, now in its proper role of confirming an ending. This 'correction' of the opening gives this movement affinities with movements which, like the first movement of Symphony No. 81, return to the opening only at the end of the recapitulation: so-called mirror recapitulations.

No cliché of sonata form is so hoary that Haydn cannot find a new use for it. The first movement of the String Quartet in D major, Op. 33 No. 6, even plays on the premature recapitulation, in which a development begins with two statements of the opening phrase, the first in the dominant, the second in the tonic. But Haydn places his version of this idea at the *end* of a very short development (bars 59–77). The dominant statement (bars 71–4) is preceded by three bars of its dominant (as if this were the recapitulation). The real recapitulation (beginning at bar 78 with the equivalent of bar 5) is preceded by its own three-bar dominant lead-in. But a second development (which moves further afield harmonically than the first one did) makes us wonder if the recapitulation was really a false recapitulation. Only at bar 99 does it become clear that the 'second development' (85–98) was a secondary development inserted between the equivalents of bars 11 and 13 of the exposition.

Unless special circumstances intervene, an off-tonic beginning of the exposition (as in the first movements of Symphonies Nos. 86, 92 and 94) is appropriately answered by an off-tonic beginning of the recapitulation. As the first movement of Symphony No. 90 shows, Haydn is alert to every

Example 9.3 Hinge and beginning of the recapitulation, String Quartet in B flat major, Op. 55 No. 3, first movement, bars 125–32

opportunity to lead to repetitions of a non-tonic beginning from a variety of different hinges. The first movement of String Quartet Op. 33 No. 1 takes a different tack. Both Webster[13] and Rosen place the reprise at the thematic return beginning at bar 59, even though the opening material (originally on the mediant) is here an elaboration of the half-cadential dominant of 58 and leads to a strikingly ferocious, disjunct and increasingly fragmentary developmental passage (bars 65–71). I prefer to think of the recapitulation as beginning with the tonic $^5_3$ of bar 72 (the equivalent of bar 11); Rosen plausibly prefers to hear 'the climax of the movement not just before, but just after, the beginning of the recapitulation'.[14]

Even a movement whose exposition begins in and on the tonic can begin the recapitulation off the tonic as long as we can find a reasonable coordination between thematic and harmonic returns. Thus the first movement of String Quartet Op. 33 No. 3 ends the development with an elided full cadence in the mediant (weakened by the sudden absence of the root in the low register), which overlaps with the thematic return. Since the movement began with a tonic $^6_3$, it is easy for this hinge to begin an altered return of the first eighteen bars of the exposition.

In the first movement of String Quartet Op. 55 No. 3, the dominant at the end of the development is both dragged in at the last moment and allowed to bleed into the beginning of the recapitulation. The 8–$\hat{7}$ of the opening is reharmonized as $\hat{4}$–$\hat{3}$ in the dominant (see Ex. 9.3). The first phrase of this highly unstable recapitulation leads to a half-cadence in the dominant. We know the recapitulation has begun, but only feel securely in

13 See Webster, *Haydn's 'Farewell' Symphony*, pp. 127–30.
14 Rosen, *The Classical Style*, p. 118.

Table 9.2 Overall harmonic motion, String Quartet Op. 42, fourth movement.

Exposition		Development/Recapitulation					Coda
i	III	iv	v	(i)	V	i	(1̂–3̂–4̂–5̂–1̂)
(bars 1–11)	(bars 15–40)	(bars 41–58)	(bars 60 – – 71 – – 82)				

the tonic some twenty bars after the beginning of the thematic return. Meanwhile, we've had to weather strong references to the exposition's modulation to the dominant. This movement features a collision between Haydn's tendency to make each successive appearance of an opening idea more unstable than the last (compare bars 1ff., 27ff. and 129ff.) and the relative stability appropriate to beginning the recapitulation.[15]

It is relatively rare for the location of a recapitulation to remain ambiguous even in retrospect. But in the fourth movements of String Quartet Op. 42 and Symphony No. 87 the counterpoint between material, grouping and harmonic structure makes returns to the tonic feel relatively incidental and/or too late to articulate the beginning of a recapitulation.

The learned style and texture which appear to dominate the fourth movement of String Quartet Op. 42 are hard to square with sonata form, since the learned style tends to blur formal divisions. Evocations of the Baroque actually occupy less than a third of the movement – but they provide most of the essential harmonic information (except the final tonic), leaving homophonic or relatively popular material to provide the expansions (introductions, parenthetical insertions, confirmations of endings) which create most of the formal rhymes of material. The overall harmonic motion is quite normal for a sonata movement in the minor mode (see Table 9.2).

The subdominant arrival at bar 50 could perhaps be taken as a false recapitulation beginning from the equivalent of bar 11; but this material also recurs in the minor dominant, starting at 60. By bar 66 the leading-note has been raised, and the tonic returns in bar 68 with the equivalent of bar 15. This potential return is weakened by the earlier returns of material from the

---

[15] Rosen, *The Classical Style*, pp. 130–1, and Rothstein, *Phrase Rhythm*, p. 321n, emphasize the instability of this movement's exposition.

Example 9.4a String Quartet in D minor, Op. 42, fourth movement, bars 1–4

Example 9.4b Expansion of Example 4a in bars 76–84

exposition (beginning at bar 50), by adverting to material which was already in the mediant in the exposition, by providing the movement's climax of contrapuntal complexity, and by heading directly to the arrival at a half-cadence in bar 71, a dominant which is prolonged through to bar 81.[16]

The arrival at the movement's structural tonic at bar 82 is probably too late to seem like the beginning of a recapitulation. Even more telling is the fact that it forms the middle of an expansion of bars 23–30, themselves an expansion of bars 1–4 (see Ex. 9.4).

Neither tonic return (the tonic of bar 59 was utterly local and incidental to getting from the subdominant to the dominant) provides the coordination of harmony, grouping, material and location appropriate to beginning a recapitulation.

The mirror recapitulation of the fourth movement of Symphony No. 87 is the by-product of another overarching tonal scheme which subordinates all returns to the tonic before bar 156 to the elaboration of the structural dominant from bars 111 to 155. The final return in the tonic of the rondo-like opening theme completes a pattern in which every structural harmonic area has been associated with at least a partial statement of the theme (see Table 9.3).

---

[16] Hans Keller, *The Great Haydn String Quartets* (New York: Braziller, 1986), p. 86, suggests the recapitulation begins in bar 68.

Table 9.3 Harmonic structure of Symphony No. 87, fourth movement, as defined by returns to the opening theme.

I	V	vi	IV (ii)	V	I
bars 1–28	bars 41ff.	bars 84ff.	bars 99ff.	bars 111ff.	bars 194ff.

Any thematic returns before bar 156 are unsupported by the harmonic structure: the passing references to the tonic at bars 124–6 and 134–7 serve to prepare the expanded half-cadences of bars 130–3 and 144–55; the tonic at 152 is part of the continuation of a series of 7–6 suspensions (146–55) leading to the structural arrival at bar 156.[17] This arrival transposes the exposition's closing theme to the tonic, telling us the movement is coming to an end, while providing the only interruption of a pattern of retrogression in the order of returns in the tonic of material from the exposition (see Table 9.4).

Table 9.4 Retrogressive order of returns of material from the exposition in the tonic, Symphony No. 87, fourth movement.

bars 1–9	return as	bars 194–202
bars 52–5	return as	bars 152–5
bars 57–9	return as	bars 134–6

∗

From the moment it 'returns' to the beginning, even the most regular recapitulation enters a hall of mirrors. By beginning and ending in the tonic, a recapitulation becomes the only portion of the movement which we could imagine as a complete piece by itself; yet a recapitulation which raised no new tensions could no more be complete in itself than could a consequent phrase. The recapitulation corrects the exposition's preliminary – and necessarily defective – attempt at completion; yet it begs to be understood in relation to what came before. Haydn's recapitulations almost always listen to and incorporate the instability they mean to resolve – but they insist on a dynamic sense of closure in which rhyming symmetries often play a relatively minor role.

---

[17] Haimo, *Haydn's Symphonic Forms*, p. 155n.

The recapitulation's main structural responsibility is to ensure that important material which appeared away from the tonic in the exposition is resolved by reappearing in the tonic later in the movement.[18] Such resolution is occasionally supplied, in part, by the development. In the first movement of the String Quartet Op. 64 No. 3, the lyrical theme in the dominant which begins the second group (bar 33) never reappears in the recapitulation; it returns instead (beginning in the tonic minor) towards the middle of the development section (bars 86ff.). The first movement of the String Quartet Op. 77 No. 1 introduces a new theme in the dominant only after the second group is well underway (bar 39). This material returns in the tonic (bars 119–23) to prepare the half-cadence which precedes the recapitulation, but not in the recapitulation itself (we might have expected it at bar 149).[19] These are remarkable examples of Haydn's kaleidoscopic or temporally dyslexic sense of form.

Since the return of the opening material of the exposition in the tonic in the recapitulation is an optional feature (of greater rhetorical than structural importance), we should not be surprised to find at least one Haydn recapitulation which omits the whole first group. This is the case in the second movement of the String Quartet Op. 55 No. 2, and is justified both by the monothematic character of the movement and by the fact that the development is dominated by fugal treatment of the opening theme, including several returns to it in the tonic.

But instead of eliminating the return of the first part of the exposition, it is much more common for Haydn to prune and destabilize it[20] and to give the return of the material which first appeared outside the tonic the kind of emphasis we ordinarily expect to find at the hinge between development and recapitulation. In the first movement of Symphony No. 80 in D minor (1783–4) this makes for an ambiguous boundary between the two. The development ends (or does it?) with the saucy new tune introduced in

---

[18] The first movement of Trio No. 27 is perhaps the most serious challenge to the widely accepted sonata principle first formulated in Edward T. Cone, *Musical Form and Musical Performance* (New York: Norton, 1968), pp. 76–7.

[19] Rosen, *The Classical Style*, pp. 73–4.

[20] The simplest way to destabilize a recapitulation's first group is to substitute a half-cadence for the exposition's first significant full cadence (as in the first movement of Op. 50 No. 1).

the last eight bars of the exposition, heard again at its original transposition level (in the mediant). At the sixth bar of its reappearance, the tune loses its bearings, slides into a diminished-seventh chord and flutters vaguely towards the tonic. A condensed summation of the opening ensues, in the tonic but heavily orientated towards the dominant (bars 128–46). Since more than half of this recollection of the opening is taken up by a dominant pedal – extending a half-cadence reached in its ninth bar – we are unsure whether this is a very free and truncated recapitulation of bars 1–24 or a continuation of the development. What follows is a literal transposition to the tonic major of the material that was in the mediant in the exposition (plus two bars added to nail the cadence).[21]

This displacement of emphasis from the preparation for the recapitulation to that for the second group (or even the 'second theme') is characteristic of a cluster of works from 1787–8. In addition to String Quartet Op. 55 No. 2, second movement, these include the first movements of String Quartets Op. 50 No. 4, Op. 54 No. 2 and of Symphonies Nos. 89 and 90; the first movement of Symphony No. 95 is a later instance. We will find traces of the same idea in the String Quartet Op. 50 No. 2, first movement. These movements ring changes on three possibilities which have rarely joined forces before: (1) a destabilizing or perfunctory preparation for the recapitulation; (2) the return of the opening of the exposition in a much more unstable form; and (3) clear preparation for, and articulation of, a relatively stable second theme or group.

In the laconic first movement of the String Quartet in F sharp minor, Op. 50 No. 4, the preparation for the recapitulation (bars 111–15) is less disjunct and emphatic than that for the second group (bars 136–47), and the beginning of the recapitulation is condensed and features highly unstable developmental material from its fifteenth through to its thirtieth bars (from 130 to 146). But the most dramatic stroke of the whole movement is the sudden shift to the tonic major at bar 148. This is the first time that a version of the opening two-bar subphrase has provided essentially new information on the downbeat of its second bar. This is emphasized by Haydn's cunning control of hypermetre. In the exposition odd-numbered bars are strong until bar 44, where a weak bar is replaced with a strong bar by

---

[21] Webster, *Haydn's 'Farewell' Symphony*, p. 167.

elision. The same regular alternation (with even-numbered bars strong) reverses the hypermetrical status of 147–8 with respect to 27–8 (where the mediant was major as a matter of course). As in the second movement of Op. 55 No. 2 and the first movement of Symphony No. 80, the recapitulation of the second group is extremely literal except that bars 147–63 are interpreted differently from a hypermetrical standpoint than were bars 27–43: a substantial difference (see Ex. 9.5).

So far our examples of the promotion of the second group to an importance rivalling, exceeding or replacing the first have come from movements in the minor mode and have relied on a dramatic shift to the tonic major. Creating similar drama in a movement in the major mode will require the use of relatives of the tonic minor to facilitate the approach to the dominant $\hat{3}$–$\flat\hat{3}$–$\hat{2}$) before restoring the major to prepare for a notably stable arrival at the beginning of the second group.

In the first movement of the String Quartet in C major, Op. 54 No. 2, the exceptionally brief development and the abbreviated return of the first group help to place unusual emphasis on the recapitulation's drastically expanded second group. The preparation for the recapitulation is made as bland as possible except for the Haydnesque small dominant/big tonic hinge: the second group gets longer – and much more memorable – preparation than the recapitulation did. The flat submediant (a shock in bar 7 of the exposition) eases the approach to the arrival on the dominant in bar 152. Within four more bars all remnants of the minor have been dispelled, and a dominant pedal stretches like a rubber band towards the beginning of the second group at bar 163. But this recapitulation of the second group remains relatively stable for only about sixteen bars, and incorporates a huge interpolation of thirty-four bars between the equivalents of bars 70 and 72 of the exposition. This interpolation includes the climax of the main theme, and of the movement.

The first movement of the underrated Symphony No. 89 in F major provides a remarkable example of a recapitulation which postpones any stable arrival until that of the second group. The end of a development obsessed with the relationship between E♭ and D ($\flat\hat{7}$–$\hat{6}$) couples an attempt to cadence in the submediant (via its Neapolitan, E♭) with an elided full cadence in the tonic (bar 111). After only two bars of tonic harmony to begin the recapitulation, E♭ returns. It leads to a second version of the pro-

306

Example 9.5a String Quartet in F sharp minor, Op. 50 No. 4, first movement, bars 21–8

Example 9.5b Op. 50 No. 4, first movement, bars 140–8

gression which led to the recapitulation: a clear admission that the tonic of the recapitulation was not solidly grounded (see Ex. 9.6(a) and (b)).

Haydn then deftly avoids a cadence in the subdominant (bar 118) and interrupts a potential cadence in the tonic with a deceptive elision/insertion leading from an explosive flat submediant (bar 122) to a half-cadence in bar 127. The following music, unlike anything else since bars 111–12, is

307

Example 9.6a Symphony No. 89 in F major, first movement, bars 108–11

Example 9.6b The similar progression immediately after the recapitulation, bars 114–17, and the avoidance of a cadence in IV, bar 118

lifted directly from the exposition (31–42 are transposed as 127–38). Yet even this passage, with its feint towards the flat submediant, seems to respond to the instability of its new context before subsiding into another half-cadence (bars 136–8). Apart from its uncanny resemblance to the Beatles' 'A little help from my friends', the tune which begins the second group hardly seems worth all the trouble. But Haydn saves the day with a return to, and development of, the material of the first group.[22]

The first movement of the String Quartet in C major, Op. 50 No. 2, is a tantalizing counter-example: a movement whose refusal to follow its own suggestions that the beginning of the second group should be the main arrival of the recapitulation causes jagged discontinuities throughout. These occur at full cadences which are elided (replaced by new beginnings) at bars 58, 63 and 93 in the exposition and by phrases which threaten to

---

[22] See Rosen, *Sonata Forms*, p. 355n, and *The Classical Style*, p. 157.

Example 9.7 String Quartet in C major, Op. 50 No. 2, first movement, bars 171–7 (the end of the development and beginning of the recapitulation)

sotto voce

break off in the middle (bars 54, 95). On a larger scale, we note the extraordinary prominence of backward-looking half-cadences whose elaborations refuse to connect with what follows: bars 12–20, 187–95 and 214–24.

Only when approaching the beginning of the second group do prominent half-cadences lead smoothly into what follows. From the tonicization of the dominant of the dominant at bars 34–5, eight bars beautifully prepare the new theme in the dominant beginning in bar 43. Virtually the same eight-bar lead-in (on the dominant of the submediant) prepares the return of the second-theme material in the development, first in the submediant, then on the subdominant, and finally headed towards a hesitant and inconclusive half-cadence on a dominant $^4_3$. One feels that this material wants to continue and expand; instead, it serves as a disjunct hinge to a seemingly unmotivated recapitulation, beginning with the material of the opening of the exposition (see Ex. 9.7).

The return of the second group of the recapitulation is also not prepared smoothly (as it was in the exposition – and even in the development). Instead, a summary of the 'learned' first part of the development leads (by way of a rude dominant pedal) to a half-cadence whose upper voices have no particular affinity with the beginning of the *galant* theme of the second group (see Ex. 9.8).

With so many disjunctions between backward-looking half-cadences and the material they precede, we are tempted, as we were in first movement of Symphony No. 49, to look for a more natural order of events which the composer has manipulated or shuffled. When we do so, we notice immediately that the discontinuities we found at the beginnings of both the recapitulation and of its second group can easily be 'corrected' by using the end of the development to prepare the recapitulation's second group (Ex.

Example 9.8 String Quartet in C major, Op. 50 No. 2, first movement, bars 220–6; the hinge to the recapitulation's second group

Example 9.9a String Quartet in C major, Op. 50 No. 2, first movement; recomposition to connect the end of the development to the recapitulation's second group

Example 9.9b Op. 50 No. 2, first movement; recomposition of the hinge to the recapitulation

9.9(a)) and the transposed final bar of the exposition's preparation for the second group to attenuate the bluntness of the beginning of the recapitulation (Ex. 9.9(b)). Without eliminating the first group (as in Op. 55 No. 2, second movement) or deifying the second, Haydn has clearly suggested how easily he could have done so.

Starting a second group with a clearly articulated new theme is not a

Example 9.10 String Quartet in D major, Op. 20 No. 4, first movement; the basic eight-bar phrase expanded in bars 47–67

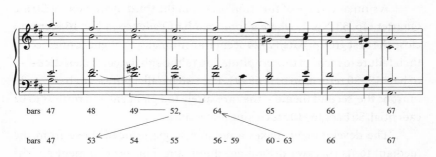

stereotype we should normally associate with Haydn. There may be no new theme. If there is, it may not be used to begin the second group, which frequently reverts to a version of the opening material (as in the first movements of Symphonies Nos. 98, 100 and 104 and the Sonatas Nos. 59, 60 and 62). Such 'monothematic' expositions naturally require major alterations in the recapitulation if they are to avoid redundancy, as we found in the first movement of String Quartet Op. 50 No. 1.

But many movements fail to conform to any of our stereotypes. The first movement of String Quartet Op. 20 No. 4 has a clear division (full cadence at bar 30) between the first group and the transition, but little or none between the transition and the beginning of the second group, which seems to begin at bar 47. If this is right, the second group can be understood as two drastically expanded eight-bar phrases (bars 47–67 and 71–99) separated by an inserted reference to the final cadence of the first group (bars 68–70) (see Ex. 9.10).

The recapitulation entirely eliminates the original transition (bars 31–46) and drastically cuts the exposition's first group, whose half-cadence (bar 233) leads directly to the equivalent of bar 49 (the third bar of the exposition's second group), now extending the half-cadential dominant. As a result of this splice the recapitulation's first solid full cadence in the tonic, its first answer to the half-cadence of bar 233, and the first tonic $^5_3$ on a strong beat since bar 232, are all delayed until bar 252. I therefore regard the material of the first part of the exposition's second group as transitional in the recapitulation. Bars 253–6 (the equivalent of 68–70) are now a prefix to the second group, rather than (as in the exposition) a parenthetical insertion within it.

A similar change of function occurs in the third movement of String Quartet Op. 33 No. 1, where a tonicized half-cadence in bar 16 seems to close the first group. Bars 17–24 seem transitional, a thought confirmed by their failure to recur in the recapitulation (although the characteristic $\hat{8}$–$\hat{7}$–$\hat{6}$ of bars 19–20 returns in bars 68–9). The two parallel phrases of bars 24–36 must be the 'second theme' – they are surely too plangent and restless to be cadential. So bars 36–40 are closing material.

The development makes a notably single-minded move from the mediant to its (backward-looking) dominant. This development revisits that of the first movement (especially its bars 44–9). The hinge of the third movement is remarkably colourful in the contrast between the major chord built on $\hat{7}$, bright and steely, and the velvety warmth (almost like a Neapolitan) of the tonic.

Haydn cuts the exposition's first sixteen bars to eight in the recapitulation; the recapitulation's eighth bar (bar 62) is a half-cadence which overlaps with a counter-statement on the dominant. Since we are solidly in the tonic thereafter, bars 62–7 must have replaced the original transition. Bars 68–75 might seem like an interpolation of new material – but 68–72 virtually quote bars 28–30 of the first movement, a passage whose function was clearly cadential (see Ex. 9.11(a) and (b)).

A full cadence in bar 76 replaces the exposition's half-cadence in the dominant (bar 24); preceded now by a full cadence and by interpolated cadential material from the first movement, the exposition's 'second theme' must be reinterpreted as cadential (a reinterpretation confirmed by the more tentative instrumentation of bars 76–82 in comparison with bars 24–30). If anything functions as 'second theme' in the recapitulation, it must be the material interpolated from the first movement!

We find a similar mutability of position or function almost anywhere we look in Haydn's music of the 1790s. Consider the tunes in a markedly popular style which appear at or near the ends of the expositions of the first movements of many late symphonies (Nos. 92, 94, 99, 100, 102, 103, 104) and of a few late quartets.[23] Few of these tunes appear early enough to help define

[23] See Rothstein, *Phrase Rhythm*, p. 182, for a justification of the inclusion of Symphony No. 102 in this list.

312

Example 9.11a String Quartet in B minor, Op. 33 No. 1, first movement; bars 28–9 as the source for:

Example 9.11b material interpolated in bars 68–72 of the third movement

the beginning of a second group (whose material is often a variant of the main theme); none is generic enough to function merely as cadential material.

The first movement of Symphony No. 80 in D minor (our old friend) is a marvellous earlier instance of such a popular tune, utterly unexpected in this grim and powerful exposition. The exposition is clearly tripartite – despite its tremendous forward thrust, there is a clear articulation (half-cadence in the mediant and lead-in) before bar 25, and another (full cadence in the mediant) to usher in the incongruously silly new tune at the very end of the exposition.

That this tune alters the whole course of the movement is undeniable: neither at the false recapitulation nor at its ambiguous last appearance can the opening material recapture its original ferocity. If we focus on the bizarre transpositions of the tune in the development (more appropriate to *Verklärte Nacht* than to a Haydn symphony), we will find that this movement has been 'hijacked by a Pythonesque tune'.[24] If we focus instead on how little this tune changes – despite its adventures, it seems to have learned and experienced little, except that it sheds its humble pizzicato accompaniment and gradually takes on richer orchestral garb – we may think its literal-mindedness mirrors that of the whole return of the exposition's

[24] W. Dean Sutcliffe, 'Haydn Seek', *Musical Times* 134/1806 (1993), 447.

Example 9.12a The glorification of the Ländler: Haydn: Symphony No. 103 in E flat major, first movement, bars 180–4

Example 9.12b Symphony No. 103, fourth movement, bars 1–4

non-tonic material in the recapitulation. From this point of view, the tune, while hardly god-like, is nevertheless an unmoved mover.

The lilting *Ländler* introduced at bar 80 of the first movement of Symphony No. 103 is unusual in sounding like a real 'second theme'; the preceding diminution of the theme of the Adagio introduction – whose beginning completes the exposition's first strong cadence in the dominant – sounds like a prefix. Our tune leads directly to closing material based on its third and fourth bars. The *Ländler* returns in the development (bars 144–50), where it undermines a sublime near-recapitulation (bars 138–40). It gets an enriched accompaniment, including imitative commentary from the flute, and is followed immediately (again) by closing material, this time leading to the dominant at the hinge to the recapitulation.

The recapitulation eventually incorporates a return to the beginning of the Adagio, and completely reshuffles the order of events in the exposition. Our tune appears directly after the opening theme and is accompanied (in addition to imitation in the oboe) by a prophetic foreshadowing in the horns of the first four bars of the last movement: the tune begins to embrace, rather than to undermine, the sublime (see Ex. 9.12(a) and (b)).

The diminution of the Adagio appears as a suffix to the Adagio's return, like a demonic parody of *its* claims to an aura of mystery: high and low have begun to trade places.

The flowering of the new tune of the first movement of Symphony No. 99 and the decay of the 'main theme' create a musical narrative which is much more compelling than resolution through rhyming symmetries alone could ever be. The bracing beginning of the Allegro provides the material both for the transition (bars 34–47) and for the first four bars of the second group (48–51). It continues to influence the vigorous passage leading to the beginning of the new tune at bar 71. This humble petitioner, introduced about two-thirds of the way through the exposition, gets ten bars to plead its case before being shouted down by the closing material of bars 81–9.

The development begins with two questioning and diffident statements of the Allegro's opening motif, followed by eleven bars of the petitioner's theme, emboldened enough now to expand its harmonic range (in the exposition it never strayed from close relatives of its local tonic). The shouting-down material which follows (bars 104–19) includes the voice of the petitioners (low strings, *forte*); their return at bars 120–37 (getting longer each time) marginalizes the shouters-down of bars 104–19, now understood as an unstable middle section.

The recapitulation shortens the main theme's appearance from fifteen bars to eight and already gets to the petitioners in its twentieth bar. The next twenty-four bars (leading to the climax and structural cadence of the movement) give them even more life and depth (including the shadow of the minor mode in bars 162–5) and transform them into agents of heroic action at bars 185–91. The coda seems to give the opening theme its due, but actually reduces it to the role of confirming what others have accomplished; for a long time the new theme, originally appearing with hat in hand, has called the shots.[25]

If we were to interpret the first movement of Symphony No. 99 in political terms, we would see it as endorsing a shift of power from the aristocratic to the bourgeois by peaceful means; bars 162–5 seem to suggest the new problems a new political order would have to confront. While the

[25] Webster, *Haydn's 'Farewell' Symphony*, pp. 326–7.

social and political implications of Haydn's narratives of liberation are often obvious, they are seldom mentioned: Haydn must be kept in his place. We usually prefer to consider Haydn as playing with form for purely musical purposes, or to read his recapitulations, if anything, as metaphors for social order. We recognize Haydn as a musical revolutionary, but cling to the stereotyped view of him as a servant of the *ancien régime*. Instead, we should emphasize Haydn's crucial role in freeing music from the constraints of continuo-based textures, in incorporating popular materials into high art and in replacing an essentially static, architectural conception of form with one which can accommodate narrative, progress and radical change. The 'hijacking' of the first movement of Symphony No. 80 is by no means an isolated case. See, for example, the first movement of Symphony No. 100, whose main theme is of such sublimely rustic simplicity that our first encounter with the brazenly pushy operator introduced in bar 93 is enough to suggest what the outcome will be. Or consider the last movement of the String Quartet Op. 76 No. 1, which begins with minor-mode gruffness and ends with a major-mode polka!

But the first movement of the String Quartet in G major, Op. 76 No. 1, is a much more complicated case, and the popular tune which appears late in the exposition plays a relatively small role in this movement's multiple plots. These plots can accommodate literal recapitulation of long passages of intense and unstable material dominated by relatives of the minor tonic (bars 54–68 are transposed as bars 177–91), which finally lead to major-mode release; but they require the drastic recasting of those parts of the exposition which might threaten the recapitulation with too much stability. Bars 3–18, for example, are completely recast as bars 140–51; the full cadence of bar 32 is replaced by a half-cadence in the recapitulation's twenty-sixth bar; and the unstable material beginning at bar 51 returns as early as the recapitulation's thirty-fifth bar.

One of this movement's plots takes off from the confrontation between the tonic and the supertonic in bars 3–10. This garden-variety progression is eccentric here because the material mimics the relationship between an absurd fugue subject and its even more absurd answer, all in an inappropriate monophonic texture, and using a tune of modest origins which has no place in the learned (and antiquated) world of (bogus) counterpoint. All this is made more absurd by the mock-pompous introduction.

Example 9.13 Quartet in G major, Op. 76 No. 1, first movement, bars 144–9; the triumph of the ascending scale

Relationships of roots a second apart are pervasive both locally (bar 23 – over a tonic pedal – bars 35–6, bars 52–5) and over longer spans: tonic pedal, bars 19–25, supertonic pedal, bars 42–7; dominant (72–92), submediant (93–111); and from the subdominant (118–21) to the (minor) dominant (122–3), to the submediant (124–9), and back to the dominant (from bar 130 to the hinge at bar 139). This stepwise plot climaxes (just after the recapitulation) in the ascending 5–6 sequence in canon (bars 144–51 – compare with bars 109–22 of the fourth movement of Symphony No. 88). The highest strand of this sequence manages to move up an octave by step; this is striking in a movement in which even a portion of an ascending scale has been a rarity (see Ex. 9.13).

Another plot is the growth of real counterpoint from the crypto-imitative beginning. This plot's climax encompasses both the false (bar 119) and the real recapitulation (bar 140); its resolution is achieved by the 'child's-play' counterpoint[26] of bars 144–51 and by its more retiring descending counterpart at bars 165–71.

The incongruity of popular and mock-learned aspects of the opening theme is only the first indication of this movement's wide-ranging mixture and collage of topics. When, for example, is an (aristocratic) pedal point merely a (poverty-stricken) drone? Why are monophonic passages in octaves so prominent and why do they always involve relatives of the minor tonic (bars 56–63, for example)? Why are strong references to the Baroque concerto inserted between polyphonic passages in the development (bars 96–118)? Why does the popular tune's return in the recapitulation begin to transform it into something more assertive – a hybrid of the pushy tune of the first movement of Symphony No. 100 and the opening of Mozart's

---

[26] Rosen, *The Classical Style*, p. 408.

Symphony No. 40, K. 550 (in bars 202–7) – only to retreat first to its original form (bars 208–11), then to its most plebeian personification (bars 212–15)? Popular materials, it seems, can temporarily put on aristocratic masks, but end up back in the street. The movement's ending rhymes with that of the exposition, but also recalls the open-ended two-bar introduction and the first two notes of the cello tune, as if to suggest that we could start the whole comedy over again.[27]

*

The progressive, plot-like features of Haydn's music of the 1790s both incorporate and seem to reverse some of his earlier preoccupations and eccentricities. The Haydn of the 1790s is perhaps less eccentric in detail than the Haydn of the early 1770s; but if the details of the later Haydn are easier for listeners to process, his sense of form is increasingly and powerfully eccentric.

Even the movements in which a progressive or narrative sense of form is most decisive have features which point to something like temporal dyslexia, as though before and after, cause and effect, could be reversed at will (as in the first movement of Symphony No. 103). Here I am not considering dyslexia as the serious problem it unquestionably can be, but as something whose most benign symptoms might include mild problems with spelling, love of palindromes and proficiency with anagrams. I take these to be the verbal analogues of ellipsis or interpolation, mirror recapitulations and reorderings or reinterpretations of function of the exposition's main events when they return in the recapitulation (in which parents and children are often wilfully kept apart and are forced to consort with strangers).

Haydn's music of the late 1760s and early 1770s frequently confronts us with weird harmonic progressions which would be perfectly normal if the order of events were reversed: see how far you can go backward from the beginning of the second bar of the recapitulation of the first movement of Symphony No. 49 before finding an incongruity as strange as the actual hinge. Equally strange is the transition from the trio to the main section of the Menuetto (second movement) of String Quartet Op. 20 No. 1, where a

---

[27] For narrative accounts of other movements of Op. 76 No. 1 see George Edwards, 'The Nonsense of an Ending: Closure in Haydn's String Quartets', *Musical Quarterly* 75/3 (1991), 247–9.

Example 9.14 String Quartet in E flat major, Op. 20 No. 1, second movement: bars 62–6 and the return to bars 1–4

weak backwards-looking half-cadence on a dominant $^6_5$ of the supertonic precedes the tonic of the return. Is the return to the tonic, and to the Menuetto, merely part of a weird path from the supertonic to the dominant $^6_5$ which ends the Menuetto's first phrase (see Ex. 9.14)?

Similarly, the tonic $^5_3$ often precedes, but does not usually follow, a dominant $^4_2$, as it does in bars 55–6 of the first movement of String Quartet Op. 20 No. 5. A tonal phrase usually makes no sense backwards; yet Haydn was interested enough in exploring the possibilities of retrogression to write a minuet and trio *al rovescio* in Symphony No. 47, one of his finest works of the early 1770s.

Haydn's backward-looking half-cadences are part of the normal language of the late eighteenth century; doubly backward-looking half-cadences are not. Like many features in Haydn, the doubly backwards-looking half-cadence has a backwards counterpart: it is to double lead-in (first movement of Op. 20 No. 3) as false recapitulation is to false end-of-development. The 'off-stage effect . . . as if it didn't belong' of the treatment of a cadential tag (first introduced in bars 25–6) of the first movement of Op. 20 No. 3's development (see bars 108–10, 146–7 and 152) is the kind of dramatic discontinuity performers often try to 'play through', as if they hadn't noticed it.[28] Sometimes, as in the second movement of Symphony No. 64, Haydn seems to be writing in code, as surface groupings utterly refuse to listen to the harmonic structure ($^6_4$s resolving to $^5_3$s from the 'end' of one phrase to the 'beginning' of the next).

Finally, I have long been puzzled by the beginning of the recapitulation of the first movement of String Quartet Op. 20 No. 4 – why, after so many premature, false (or just plain bogus) recapitulations should it be so

[28] Keller, *Haydn Quartets*, p. 47.

Example 9.15 String Quartet in D major, Op. 20 No. 4, first movement. The recapitulation's beginning as (a) a continuation of the false recapitulation and (b) as forming a palindrome with the end of the lead-in

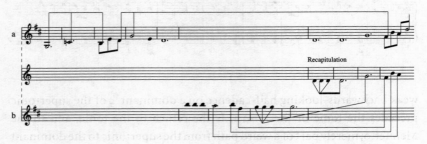

disjunctly approached? My best answer to date has been to notice Haydn's obsession with 'up a fourth, down a second' (bars 1–6, 51–4 and so forth) climaxes here: the false recapitulation (bars 207–12) could lead straight into the real recapitulation (bars 217ff.). This is prevented by the disjunct insertion of a lead-in which leads in rather poorly *except* that it begins a palindrome whose centre is the beginning of the recapitulation (see Ex. 9.15). This recap caper is not one of Haydn's slacker recalls.

10 Haydn: the musicians' musician

ROBIN HOLLOWAY

> One is rather embarrassed at having to call him original; it is like
> saying that a Cheshire cat smiles.
> > Randall Jarrell on William Carlos Williams

> Natural utterance did not come naturally: it was a quiet triumph of
> sustained artifice. > > Clive James on Kenneth Slessor

The current picture of Haydn is something like this: a great inventor, intelligence, humanist, wit, who works with juvenile diligence to master every available old technique while simultaneously eager to embrace and advance every new, forced by the isolation of his employment 'to be original', quivering for a time to strains of emotional turbulence which immeasurably deepened his art, then learning to wear it lightly with tropes and timing from *opera buffa*, before broadening with maturity and age into the expression of social, ethical, religious values with genuinely popular appeal – all held together in a balanced synthesis that embodies to its fullest in music and perhaps in all the arts the concept of Enlightenment. The musical character is perceived as sunny, energetic, impersonal, normative, unbowed with *Angst*, cheerfully pious, a life-enhancer: *Laus Deo*.

Such a 'Haydn the Accessible' is certainly not wrong. It is the basis of the affection in which he is held, especially in the country which took so immediately to him and his music in the 1790s. Yet he is not, and probably never will be, a wholly popular composer like Mozart, Beethoven, Tchaikovsky, and now Mahler and Shostakovich. Not even an ampler grasp of his true size and scope will bring this about. There is something inherently unembraceable. Even in minuets his good humour can frequently not be quite what it seems; the *innocentemente* of variation themes and finales is definitely not to be trusted; the unmistakable *affettuoso* of slow movements can also be austere, even chilling; and the cerebration of sonata-allegros is

321

sometimes so urgent as to drive out immediate musical pleasure. 'Haydn the Repellent'? There is also, alongside the up-front straightforwardness, an emotional reserve or veiling which invites another sobriquet: 'Haydn the Withdrawn'.

Such qualities have never alarmed professional musicians – performers, connoisseurs, academics, analysts and perhaps composers most of all. From the discriminating appreciation of his middle life and the wide dissemination of his old age, Haydn has enjoyed the praise of fellow practitioners. Testimony from the greatest of his immediate successors is more in works than words: Mozart and Schubert, very different kinds of composer from him and from each other, are audibly saturated in Haydn as source and example; Beethoven, audibly the same kind of composer, owes enormous and quantifiable debts (which are fully repaid). The early Romantic generation had little regard, as they had no use, for Haydn's particular mastery. But even as the Romantic century advanced and his repertory was contracted and his style patronized, his stature for the chosen few remained unimpugned. To the avid creativity as well as the nostalgic historicism of Brahms, Haydn stood in parity with the other three Viennese masters. 'I want my ninth symphony to be like this!' he exclaimed, playing the Andante of Symphony No. 88 'with wallowing enthusiasm'.[1] More surprising is the cordiality recorded by Cosima in Wagner's conversation: a few favourite symphonies and quartets were often piano-duetted or played live, eliciting joy and reflection (sometimes profound). What must surely be the same Andante ('of Haydn's G major symphony') 'is one of the loveliest things ever written; and how wonderful it sounds!'[2] On 19 October 1873 R. takes 'infinite delight' in the 'masterly art' of the 'London' Symphony: 'Haydn, spurred on after Mozart's death by Mozart's genius, became the true precursor of Beethoven; varied instrumentation, and yet so artistic; everything speaks, everything is inspiration.'[3] On 3 February 1874 R. 'plays the Andante (G minor) from another [H.] symphony, explaining its beauties, above all its concision – everything expresses something, no arabesques,

[1] See Donald Francis Tovey, *Essays in Musical Analysis*, I (London: Oxford University Press, 1931), p. 142.

[2] Cosima Wagner, *Diaries*, II (New York: Harcourt, Brace, Jovanovich, 1980), 26 February 1878, p. 31.   [3] *Diaries*, I, p. 689.

the two themes circle around each other like sun and moon.'[4] (I think Cosima might mean the C minor/major Andante of No. 103; there is no G minor slow movement in the Paris, Oxford or London sets likely to have been available at the time.) 'How wonderful it sounds': another master of the large up-to-date orchestra, Rimsky-Korsakov, actually placed the 'primitive' Haydn at the summit of this branch of the art.

The last Romantics, like the first, felt least rapport. For a Delius, a Debussy or a Rakhmaninov, such music has nothing beyond dead formulae. Mahler, notoriously contemptuous of eighteenth-century development sections, invoked Haydn for association in the principal subject of the Fourth Symphony's first movement and, still more, its accompaniment. Strauss's feeling for the epoch was confined to a periwigged and chocolaoded Mozart – Haydn's lack equally of sensuality and dinkiness had no appeal. And for Schoenberg the evolutionist, Haydn is merely the first in a Viennese Classical package that awards him no distinguishing features. But his progress with moderns and post-moderns has been triumphal. In his old age Stravinsky's listening included the quartets and symphonies in its very select company;[5] Britten used to curl up in bed with pocket scores of the quartets. Their attitude can characterize at the highest level the prevailing view. As appreciation has widened, from Tovey (who as usual implied it all) into Rosen and Webster, with Robbins Landon for vociferous documentation, and the advocacy of performers like Brendel and Schiff, rather than sloggers like Dorati and the Aeolian (though some old-stagers – the feline Beecham, the granitic Klemperer, the sinewy yet singing Rosbaud – remain unforgotten, and Britten's *Creation* from the 1966 Aldeburgh Festival is the single most inspired Haydn performance I've ever encountered), his standing in general has never been higher. And in particular among composers, there is scarcely a dissenting voice.

Yet even here, amidst his loyal subjects, Haydn remains oddly shadowy and elusive. Acknowledged by all, he is still without influence. Of the Viennese package, Beethoven hung like a thundercloud over his progeny from Schubert to Schoenberg, emphatically including Brahms, Bruckner and Wagner. Mozart's influence has been a complementary

[4] *Diaries*, I, p. 730.
[5] *Conversations with Igor Stravinsky* (London: Faber, 1959), p. 127.

rebound all the way from *Mozartiana* to *The Rake's Progress* and beyond; but more often he has been made to embody an attitude rather than a style, as in the ideal posited by Busoni's 'Young Classicism' or the very different versions invoked by Ravel in his two-hand concerto, Strauss in his wind sonatinas, Messiaen in his *Sourire*. Whereas, apart from Robert Simpson, possibly Elliott Carter and a facetious tootle from Vaughan Williams ('Haydn to the rescue' from a temporary impasse in composing *his* ninth symphony), Haydn has had no progeny and has received only a few rather cursory *hommages* – from a distinguished French handful (including Ravel and Debussy) for the centenary of his death in 1909, from six British composers (including George Benjamin) for his 250th birthday in 1982. He appears to be insusceptible to 'recomposition' à la Stravinsky (except, appropriately, for certain Haydnesque features of Stravinsky's *Symphony in C*): no doubt because he has already done it all himself.

For no composer before, and none again till modern times, has been so self-conscious. The former image was one of innocence, unaffected simplicity, cheeriness, whether of a 'Papa' or childlike ('Haydn is like a child, for there is no knowing what he will do next' was Keats's reaction when his friend Severn played him symphonies on the piano in Rome in 1820). It accompanies a sonorous stereotype of C major openness, music of clear outline and definite goal, unsullied by self-expression, stilted heroics, lachrymose pathos: music in a pristine state. This picture has now been enormously amplified, and partially reversed. Haydn is now seen as a sort of scientist or doctor of music: knowledge is explored and exploited, experiments are undertaken, both these things sometimes without the alleviation of aesthetic charm. There is little reliance upon moulds or self-evident formulae ('for heaven's sake, a new minuet!'): despite the fertility there is great care not to do the same thing twice, which can produce dryness but never routine like Mozart on an off-day or sleepwalking like Schubert, let alone the trickle or gush of a Vivaldi, Raff, Martinů, Henze. Rather than childlike and spontaneous, Haydn is 'artificial' – deliberate, quizzical, critical; even (dread word) 'ironic', inasmuch as he can achieve his complex ends with hackneyed material of no intrinsic worth.

This expanded view of him fulfils a modernist dream of the composer as craftsman, an impersonal maker of functioning objects. So conspicuous a devotion to the craft of composition is valued both for itself and as a stick with which to knock expressionist splurge and impressionistic haze, equally with avant-garde pseuderie and the blackmail of 'commitment'. Further aspects yet are so alien to previously received notions of him that they are still coming into focus: Haydn the mannerist, the whimsical, the Shandyan; Haydn who teases – not always in fun, less cat-and-mouse, more tigerish – his material, his forms, his players, his listeners. Just as he leavens his learning with 'obsequious' acknowledgement of licentious infringe-ments on the local scale, so, on the large, whole movements, whole works even, can be sarcastically subversive – not with the tedious doctrinaire 'absurdity' of Dada and surrealism but, rather, within the synthesis and integration that remain so paramount that he has always to be called one of their greatest exemplars.

All this could make him into a somewhat forbidding icon of 'the right attitude' to the materials of music and their proper deployment – the master of small points in a comprehensively cogent musical speech so well understood that allusions, jokes, surprises, ambiguities, subversions, ironies become normative too, and confounded expectations as expected as straightforward fulfilment of the rules of the game. Which suggests not so much an icon as a sacred cow ruminating the cud of every correct notion in cultural studies at large; the composers' composer or musicians' musician yielding to the analyst's, the academic's, the historian's. Which is as boring as Dada without the fun. If there is an angle from which this complex figure can be seen steadily and whole, it must surely be in the idea of music's intrinsicality; whatever else might or might not be present, music as music, unsullied or compromised by extraneous matter, autonomous. Haydn leads more directly than any other composer to this easily uttered but end-lessly slippery idea.

He is the purest of all composers; his art has the fewest external refer-ents, is more completely about itself than any other. Bach is rightly regarded as the supreme celestial mechanic; but possibly the most characteristic, cer-tainly the deepest, aspect of Bach is his weaving a tissue of messages and meanings soaked in *Affekt* way beyond the norms of his epoch, evincing a personality of morbid inwardness wholly compatible with his robust func-tionality, vigorous physicality and learned 'science'. Mozart is always opera *manqué*, his articulation and phrasing vocal, his setting theatrical, his forms and processes not organic but, rather, whisked on and off like prefabricated flats. His great instrumental genres are concertos or chamber works with eloquent protagonists – the soloist in the clarinet quintet, the amorous duetting of first violin and first viola in the Andante of the C major String Quintet, K. 515, the two right hands in that of the F major piano-duet sonata, K. 497, the trio of first oboe, clarinet and basset horn in the Adagio of the twelve-wind Serenade, K. 361, all four winds in the Larghetto of their quartet with piano in E flat major, K. 452. He doesn't argue, or build, or grow; he sets out the sections in finely judged symmetry/asymmetry and sends them through a constellation of closely related keys. Interest derives from the fine draughtsmanship which distinguishes high calibre from routine; sensuous pleasure, from his perpetually fertile melodiousness.

Beethoven is music made from music for sure, supreme in the processes of development as argument and journey, and also in extracting the ultimate potential from his thematic material. As Wagner remarks, he is, in this, the fulfilment of Haydn. He raises the temperature and the voice, enlarges the durations and the difficulties; the strain waxes heroic–pathetic, with a rhetoric of struggle and victory aimed at more people, in bigger rooms, aimed at Humanity *en masse*. He has something important to tell them. Put in words this message tends towards inert abstractions like 'brotherhood', the 'ideal feminine', 'freedom', etc.; but what he really has to show that is so important to him as to compel audiences ever since into feeling that it is also important to them, is of course his *notes*. And sonata's greatest victor has imbued his actual notes with a new tone – ethical, moralistic, idealistic, 'improving'. Music, as it were, returns to church (secular, non-denominational: First Church of God Pantheist) after a few generations at court, at the theatre, in the market place.

Schubert, by contrast, is all voluptuous hedonism and 'amorous propensity', driven by a libido which is wholly compatible with such complements as great stillness, great radiance, or temper-tantrums of extraordinary violence, and severity pushed towards unsurpassed extremes, as in the *Winterreise* songs which so signally disconcerted his circle of friends. And so to the first Romantics, to Wagner, late Romantics, expressionists, degenerates: a tale of degradation – the wholesale invasion of music as a medium of sociability and intellectual exchange by subject-matter, story-telling, atmosphere-painting, message-bearing, capable of gushing over into autobiography both lubricious and spiritually ostentatious, the confessional quadruple *forte* and sextuple *piano* (both are to be found in the first movement of Tchaikovsky's *Symphonie Pathétique*) which have become for its average lovers what music is expected to be. And so to the modernist reaction which gleefully topples the rotten tree.

Haydn alone gives no handle: there is nothing to latch on to, biographically or in subject-matter. *Sturm und Drang* of course; 'Farewell', *La Passione*, the *Lamentatione*. But what are they beside a Bruckner Ninth, a Mahler Tenth, an Elgar Second or Sibelius Fourth? Nor do any quartets reveal the secrets of sickroom and convalescence, let alone an *Aus mein Leben*, an *Intimate Letters*, a *Lyric Suite*. His operas, for all the musical value, do not apparently live as drama, nor is he, like Mozart, an instrumental dramatist via the concerto. When he does produce an instrumental *scena* the result is stilted or parodic, or both. The primal archetype for his melody is often neither vocal (like Mozart again) nor instrumental, but rather a sort of fabrication which can cope equally well with values from a semibreve to a demisemiquaver in one long line, throwing in plentiful turns and graces, with triplets and other divisions *en route*. Haydn the Artificial.

Onomatopoeia *does* figure of course, both early – *matin, midi, soir* – and in the two late oratorios: whether juvenile or mellow the result is so one-dimensional and pantomimic as to seem naïve even when manifestly sublime – a classic instance of naïve as opposed to sentimental art. Unlike the, in some ways, comparable Brahms there is no body of secular vocal music to suggest by analogy any interpretation of his favourite turns-of-phrase (but who could find Brahms abstract or impersonal anyway? The character is almost palpable in his textures, harmonies, contours, procedures). Neither affects, nor onomatopoeia, nor a clear projection of personality (though they are not exactly lacking) provide the clue to his core, as they can with every other composer, even when, as with Stravinsky, such things are deliberately eschewed. Even while practising with consummate perfection the art of music as amical intercourse, the doors are closed. Haydn the Impenetrable.

This music is pure because it cannot be translated. Despite one's ready recognition of a ragbag of tropes and types – snippets of nonsense from *opera buffa* and pathos or elevation from *opera seria*, tags from textbooks, snatches of folksong 'from Croatia's woods and fields' or urban serenade from Vienna's back-alleys, opening and closing gambits from contemporary cliché – it owes less than any other to metaphor, simile, association. Haydn doesn't seem to invest his artistic capital in such stock; he does not fully ally himself with it. Other composers inhabit; Haydn is aloof. Then to proceed to build entirely from such material, and entirely upon points of grammar and proportion, would seem a flagrant courtship of dryness. 'Music as music', upon which he is so single-mindedly fixed, is, artistically, a dead letter – mere grids, blueprints, engineers' working-drawings.

He is music's supreme intellectual. Yet every lover of Haydn recognizes within the cerebral power many characteristics difficult to name without absurdity, so wholly are they musicalized. But the risk is worth taking. The range is enormous. High spirits, all the way from physical brio and athletic bravura (Tovey makes the connection with the cerebral power: 'his forms become the more subtle as his animal spirits rise')[6] to jokes, puns, games of sometimes surprising intellectual and even expressive weight, profound in their ambiguity, exploratory in their paradoxes, witty like the metaphors in metaphysical poetry, touching on rarified places which no other means could reach. (When unambiguously farcical as in *Il distratto* and other mid-period symphonies the effect is quite different – *simply* silly; it's a pity that this side of Haydn receives disproportionate emphasis.) There is serenity and hymn-like calm; Enlightenment openness, sage and humane; radiance without shadow like tempera, pure colours on a white base. Their opposite – twisting strangeness, contortion, mannerist extremity – is almost as frequent, and this too is shadowless in that it is never morbid. Compare Bach with his worm-gnawed chromatics of sin, guilt, corruption; the hectic consumptive flush of Mozart in G minor; the driven *Tod*-tarantellas of Schubert (to go no further than composers who overlap Haydn's life at both ends). Rather it is part of his unceasing exploration of yet another aspect of music's extent that fascinates him for a moment or a movement, something he can *use*, as he *uses* stale old contrapuntal routines both for earnest and for effervescent purposes. Then there is deep still contemplation, simultaneously remote and glowing, giving utterance to an extreme of inner solitude paralleled only in Bartók and possibly Kurtág: a bare space wherein something exceedingly quiet, intense and private is apprehended with a nudity beyond sensuous beauty, making music an

---

[6] Tovey, *Essays in Musical Analysis*, I, p. 147.

object both of meditation and solace, worked out in a dream-realm of punning harmonic labyrinths. Into this, cheerfulness is always breaking, for these pools of loneliness are always adjacent to the body-rhythm of a minuet or appear within the tearing energy of a finale.

The tone of voice ranges similarly from such confessional impersonality to the late development of a successfully common-touch *lingua franca* in the oratorios and last Masses, whether raptly devotional or ceremonially jubilant, with a repertory of moods between the two that satisfactorily renders whatever it sets out to and wisely evades characterization (those three Archangels! that Hanne, Lukas and Simon!!) – though the birds, beasts and insects are vivid, and the injunction to the whales to multiply touches the depths. But a further secret side of him gives tongue with extraordinary passion – such places as the wild improvisatory gypsy flourishes of the first violin above the chorale on the other three strings in the second movement of the String Quartet Op. 54 No. 2; or, in the misleadingly-titled Allegretto of the Piano Trio No. 44 in E major, the uncurling of the melody above and then below the gaunt stealthy bass, in octaves then thirds and tenths, till the tension is so great that the movement literally breaks apart before snapping shut like a slap in the face. Utterance of such unsullied-by-*espressivo* intensity makes the Romantics seem extrovert, showy and babyish, whatever the higher pitch of their anguish or the urgent pressure of their engagement. Just as startling is Haydn's mastery of the primeval, not so much in *The Creation* itself as in the powerfully pregnant slow introductions to eleven out of twelve London symphonies, and most particularly the 'London' itself, No. 104. When the *fortissimo* tutti falling fourth of bar 2, answering the rising fifth of the opening, is replaced in bar 15 by a *pianissimo* falling fifth on strings alone, the space and mystery evoked are as vast as such effects in Bruckner, though the actual duration is tiny.

Mendelssohn's famous declaration that music sets up resonances more definite than words receives a supreme testing in Haydn's instrumental works. A couple of further concrete instances might extend the sense of a language in use, of which both arts partake. The first is comparatively early – the *Affettuoso e sostenuto* movement from the String Quartet Op. 20 No. 1. What is it? Certainly not a melody: rather, a theme-less continuum, momentum, texture, not quite homophony; not quite polyphony either, making a dense serious sound, sometimes close-spaced, sometimes wide, often peculiar, with perverse interlocking and crossing of parts, arbitrary doublings, passing chords that if lingered on would be solecisms or even Stravinskyisms. Everyone plays all the time almost without exception, in even quavers almost without exception; the only rests come with the first-violin solos which also produce the only decoration, at the double-bars and for the three bars in the second 'half' which leads to the 'return'. For 'half' it is not: despite the impression of unbroken tranquillity, the larger structure and the smaller phrasing are asymmetrical and unpredictable (except for the movement's one weak link: the sequential repeat, in the second 'half', of bars 52–3 as 54–5, though the compensating descent in bars 58–9 seems to rectify by retrospect). From start to close the listener glides on an imperturbable loop of endless melody, renewing itself out of its own motion – a gentle, modest ancestor of the *Tristan* Prelude and the *obbligato recitative* from Schoenberg's Op. 16. In *mood*, however, this movement achieves an encapsulation of Largo religioso feeling without any hint of 'religioso' sanctimony: everything inheres within the notes.

Next, a middle movement from the end of Haydn's quartet-writing life: the Andante from the String Quartet in F major, Op. 77 No. 2. Again it is a matter of an ongoing momentum: but here textures, spacing and density are perpetually changing and the whole movement is melody-led and propelled by a walking bass, whose combined impulse is so strong that both continue to be felt even when either surprisingly ceases. The melody (essentially 'three blind mice' with twiddles) is a sort of *faux-naif* Lego, whose every link can be used to make a different thing. It is at once genuine-simple and true-complex in its tone – how serious? how light? – as in the apparently artless, actually ultra-experienced, twists and turns of its perpetually reinterpreted harmonizations. The crunch comes from bar 74 on, where it makes its most elaborate reappearance. The spacing is marvellous – low viola on the march-bass, high cello on the melody, first violin delivering a decorative descent of arpeggios and scales in staccato demisemiquavers (with second violin confined to occasional help filling out cadences). Instead of rounding off, it opens out. Taking up the bars of bare minims earlier in the movement, all three lower strings hold broad chords, but violin I continues its brilliant *essercizi* as the accompanying trio become explicitly military, even peremptory ♩♪ ♩♪, then urgent ♪♪♪♪, then *pesante* ♪ ♪ in crescendo to *fortissimo*, as the solo violin flourishes cadenza-like on D major triads then scales, the last being joined by the second violin and viola in an upward rush of parallel first-inversion chords. It ought to be commonplace; in fact it is tense and electric, creating an effect of extraordinary liberation – a tethered eagle unleashed. Yet the great bird is left in mid-air, and the movement's only silences follow (still perceived in measure), with one slashing dominant, brutally banal; then the resumption of the opening melody, richly harmonized à 4 in sonorous low-position *pianissimo*, winding down via its internal self-recycling in ever-new textural subtleties and harmonic/rhythmic inflections, to close in a brief coda-ish extra. The feel of the movement altogether is haunting yet ordinary, obsessive yet open, short-circuiting yet free: persistent in dogged stoical trudge, genial but not wholly amiable, as much defiant as cheerful.

How are we to take music that seems to evoke such ambiguities and contrarieties as these, but that certainly supersedes their merely verbal expression – that offers, in its own intrinsic terms, a play of mood, as of material, simultaneously so straightforward and so ungraspable?

Things as remarkable, and extremely various, could easily be multiplied from the quartets between Op. 20 No. 1 and Op. 77 No. 2, as well, of course, as from his other greatest genres – mid-early and very late piano sonatas and symphonies, and the fascinating treasure-house of piano trios. But how would such adjective-laden prose-poems as they might well elicit square with the claim that Haydn is concerned more purely than any other composer with music's intrinsicality? Painting can more obviously than music be at once abstract and concrete. In the landscapes and still lifes of William Nicholson

> [h]orizons fall at endlessly surprising intervals and angles across the canvases; objects are unexpectedly aligned or misaligned with each other, placed with odd centrality, or half-dropped off a canvas's edge. Viewpoints are often unusually high, or low; boldly frontal or oddly oblique. As purely formal arrangements of tone and colour, the works have great individuality and sonorous beauty. These very formal and perceptual paintings are also, of course, highly metaphoric.[7]

---

[7] He might actually be writing about Haydn! Merlin Ingli James reviewing the landscapes of William Nicholson, *Times Literary Supplement* 17 May 1996, pp. 18–19.

It would be idle to ask further: metaphors of *what*? This is the area at the heart of all the arts where structure and process fuse inseparably into expression; the total result is an emanation, however direct or oblique, from the life of the unique individual who is doing the making and summoning into being.

Music is about notes, whether the upshot is Tristan's delirium, Tchaikovsky's floods of passion, cardiac convulsions in Mahler and Berg, or any sonata, trio, quartet, symphony by Haydn. If it's not good composing, neither is it good expression of an emotion, or depiction of a character, or evocation of sunlight playing on the waves and all the rest. If 'words, not ideas, make a poem', how much more true for the relatively unconnotational art of music. Not passions, neuroses, concepts, pictures or any other extraneous intentions make a piece of music, but pitches, rhythms, durations, timbres, in all their infinite potential for organized combination.[8]

Yet music does render all these extraneous things. If it were indeed just 'pure music', something – the main thing – would be missing (as in Mondrian, or Nicholson fils, when the viewer hankers to see apples, boughs, faces). So what is abstraction, and how can unmitigated concentration upon the process of composition be at the same time a quest for what Debussy called 'the naked flesh of emotion'? It must be that the materials of music themselves not only convey passions, pictures and so forth, but that they actually *are* passionate and pictorial – intrinsically, of their nature. The 'extras' inhere; they are of the essence too. The problem is to reconcile music's natural tendency towards extra-musical content with the impulse to make pattern, argument and structure that are equally intrinsic to the art. And Haydn is poised right at its centre: because of the exceptionally nice balance he strikes, he compels one more than any other composer to ask what music actually *is*.

If there is, fortunately, no answer, further parallels from painting can again shift the ground. 'Significant form' was the once-familiar phrase coined to indicate the composition of a picture to be its own subject in the teeth of its ostensible replication of a nude, a landscape, a still life.[9] Music as

---

[8] Compare Hayden White's 'challenge to theorists', cited by Michael Spitzer in 'Haydn's Reversals' in this volume; see p. 183.

[9] That this stiff idea can be made supple, sensitive, attractive is beautifully borne out by James's review in full.

its own subject produces for Haydn a representation of itself – the disinterested exploration of compositional possibilities, the posing of difficulties, the pleasure and astonishment of their resolution – with 'sonata', 'double-variation' and all the rest of his composing-kit for playground or chessboard. Its material is the mass of sonorous actualities available to him – clarinets here, no trumpets in Lent (etc. etc. *ad nauseam*) – together with, of course, shapes and gestures that have been used over and over again and are dense with associations. The rest is all specific and particular: invention, resource, experience and experiment, intelligence focusing hard and fantasy flying free, the dispassion and involvement, amusement and interest, the piety and warmth of heart, the essential strangeness and solitude, and all the other traits of personality and character with which this individual human being will perforce infuse almost every one in the succession of musical objects he makes.

Confronted by this oeuvre, discrepancies between abstract and concrete seem factitious. One could even sophistically claim that Haydn's very concreteness makes him so abstract, and vice versa. Moreover, his awareness of such sophistries is a part of his genius. He is as consummately in control of such questions about how music is doing what it is doing as he is of the materials and processes of a particular piece. There is an omniscience to his art that surpasses even Bach's, who knew everything about the science of music but was, one senses, unconscious of what his music was saying through its extraordinary transcendence of its stylistic norms and ostensible aims. Bach is the profounder artist; Haydn is the greater realist. None of which renders him any more graspable. To the last, Haydn the Ambiguous.

And how appropriate for Haydn the Ambiguous that his most inspired movement, *The Representation of Chaos*, should be simultaneously the representation of Order in a perfectly formed introduction-sonata, the weird contradiction expressed in sounds that sometimes come from some chuckling Biedermeier serenade (bars 28–31), sometimes grope into Bruckner at his creepiest (bars 32ff.), sometimes heave and pant with the sheer physical strain of giving birth (bars 26–7, 48–9), touch upon the metaphysical without strain throughout, and for the final ten bars (till the cadence) stray into the 'music of the future' fifty years before time. But Haydn is the music of the future still. The true extent of his greatness is for the connoisseur a well-kept secret, for the larger public a ticking time-bomb that has yet to go off. When its hour comes the explosion, rather than a Big Bang, will be a still small voice telling of the strange within the normal, the vast within the modest, the dark within the bright and vice versa: the essence of human experience in essentially musical terms.

Index